MW01054942

Dancing with Fireflies

By
Clemens Carl Schoenebeck

— clem Schoenebeck

Copyright © 2013 Clemens Carl Schoenebeck

All rights reserved.

ISBN: 1490423710

ISBN 13: 9781490423715

For my granddaughters, Alexa and Angela

Lamentation

Yesterday,
the incessant creak
of my mother's rocking chair
echoed in my memory's ear.
Her swaying beat synchronized
with shadowed songs of fear
from voices only she could hear.

Yesterday,
my brothers and I marched
with exquisite softness, like spiders
traversing wispy webs in unlit corridors.
Our cadence dutifully mimicked
the thin drumming which accompanied
my mother's entrances and exits,
her unpredictable attendance to our boyhood.

Yesterday,
we walked with feathery steps
as if on crusted snow, waiting
for the surface to let go.
We well knew the packed cold
in our shoe, the clammy wetness
which would be a long time drying.

Yesterday,
my mother rocked, Book of Prayers
clutched to her breast. She stared
through her bedroom window, searching
for God, and she could not see
her three sons standing in the doorway
        as awaited our instructions
                about following the Shepherd,
                        about the gathering of sheep...

PART ONE

Chapter 1

October, 1997

My favorite sandwich is a BLT, with toasted pumpernickel and well-done bacon, almost charred. I like it crispy and crunchy with a slice of juicy tomato, locally grown, if possible. That's what I'd just ordered at the Buckhorn Truck Plaza on Interstate 80, in central Pennsylvania. Bonnie and I had stopped for lunch on our way to visit my ninety-four year old father. He still lived in State College, the town where I grew up.

But my perfect sandwich sat untouched on the plate. Thanks to a picture hanging on a nearby wall, I'd lost my appetite. I had been studying a local photographer's exhibit, displayed in the main dining room. I was hoping to see an image or a scene that would give me an idea for a new poem, since I'd been in a creative dry spell. But the last thing I expected was to be upset.

The black and white print was darker than the rest, showing a Gothic building, a spare and severe image from my childhood. Looming over its roof was a steeple-like tower, its harsh outline tapered to a point high above the imposing structure, seven floors above ground level. Perched on top was a stone angel, wings rigidly unfurled, more for blocking out sunlight than for flight.

Each brick of the building was defined by varying densities of gray. The steep roof was rinsed in the day's pale illumination, the sky's available light eclipsed by the heavy fortress. Windows were like tall slits in the dark brick façade, as if their narrow dimensions were designed to prevent the sun from illuminating the interior. A thin flicker of light glinted off the windows, subdivided by steel bars.

This had been my mother's residence fifty-two years earlier, when I was eight years old. She'd been taken from Dad and my brothers and me for six months; for her own good, we were told. And ours. This was the State Mental Hospital at Danville, PA.

Lately I'd been thinking about this place. Some of my recent dreams flashed with images of dark hallways and the deflected sun coming through those bar-crossed windows, illuminating long passageways with no open door to the outside. Sometimes the to and fro sway of my mother's rocking chair lifted my head right off the pillow. My shout in the night woke up Bonnie. We would talk for a few minutes, then go back to sleep. Then a similar nightmare would awaken us a few weeks later.

My poetry had started to shift from joyful stanzas about my two little granddaughters to darker reflections about my youth. My latest writing was metered by my mother's unpredictable presence in our childhood. I remembered how she could fill my whole field of vision, then become invisible. We never knew when she was with us, if she really was with us.

Why was I thinking about all this now, when my mother had been dead for eleven years?

Bonnie and I finished our lunch. I left half my sandwich on the plate. Over coffee, I told my wife how that photograph pulled me back into that time when my mother's *voices* ruled her life, and ours. It was a time when my two brothers and I had learned to dance with her shadows, in the hide-and-seek choreography of being seen and unseen; a time when we learned what to say, and when to say it. We had become experts at knowing what my mother had to hear in order to keep those voices from screaming at her. And us. If we spoke the right words, it meant safety and peace, at least for that moment. The wrong words were dangerous for all of us. My brothers and I had become fluent in the language of schizophrenia.

The Danville interchange was a few miles west on interstate 80. On our previous visits to State College, I purposefully ignored the hospital sign as we drove by. But recently I'd begun to comment to Bonnie about my childhood trip to that hospital, when I visited my mother. Then I would quickly drop the subject and put it out of my mind. I had happier things to think about. My mother had been dead for all those years. So what if we had unfinished business between us? That chapter of my history was finished.

Not this time, though. I was staring through the window when Bonnie set her coffee cup on the table and touched my hand. "I think it's time for a visit." I contemplated my half-eaten BLT.

She was right. It *was* time for a visit.

Minutes later we were in our car, continuing our journey on Interstate 80. The sign announcing the Danville exit came at us so quickly that I never had time to reconsider our decision. We drove south on Route 54 to the middle of town, where we found the signs pointing to Danville State Hospital. The road meandered through the tired farmlands, summer's green already surrendered to the approaching season. Sculpting the distant border between land and sky, the Blue Mountain Range shimmered with the off and on light of broken clouds.

And there it was. The far-off tower loomed on the horizon, a dark imposition against the mellow afternoon. I eased the car into the driveway and parked on the far side of the lot. That unsettling image of the photograph was now in front of me, unchanged from my childhood. I got out of our car and stood in the shade of a lofty oak tree. I scanned the building's dark brick walls, tinted by the pastel light of October. Across the vacant yard stood the heavy wooden door through which I bravely marched with my father, when I was that eight-year-old boy. The curtain in my memory was lifting. I closed my eyes.

I am standing in the thin November gray of a day 52 years ago. I see my mother and her companions seated around the perimeter of the big room, each person in his own rocking chair. I feel the uncomfortable presence of the visitors, my father and me among them. Those restless patients focus in my mind, like a print in a photographer's darkroom. Their images emerge from the solution, sharpening and rising to the surface, as if gasping for breath. And now I hear those sounds, long forgotten: the muffled flutter of wings; creaking rocking chairs; voices swirling above my mother's hummed drone; pleadings of her troubled congregation. The discordant murmuring, after 52 years; I heard it then and I hear it now.

I felt Bonnie's easy touch on my arm. The sun warmed my face as it filtered through the autumn leaves. I returned from wherever my memory had carried me. Standing under the tree, I had revisited that time of my childhood fear; I'd gone back to join my eight-year old self in that denied history. The echoes diminished like forgotten words to an old song. I climbed into the car and sat down behind the steering wheel. Numb. I could not speak and I could not look into my wife's eyes. Without a word, I twisted the ignition key and we drove away.

We silently retraced our route through the acres of stubbled cornstalks, fallen in their rusty wait for winter. This was one of those days when the farmlands rippled with the bronze warmth of late autumn. Maybe this was my poem: about the annual shedding of T-shirts and shorts, and the gathering of coats and gloves. No need to talk if I'm savoring the day. No need to talk if I'm thinking about a new poem. Bonnie was looking at me, but I stared at the road ahead. Soon we were back on the highway, heading for my father's home.

She broke the silence with one word. "Well?"

At first I denied what had just happened. It didn't seem real. But avoiding that memory wasn't working. My wife knew there was more to come. So did I.

I struggled with the description of what I had just experienced. It was the turmoil that I'd heard, the sounds of that long-ago visit that unsettled me. I tried to dismiss the encounter with my past: "Just my imagination; a fragment of a dream; a scary movie, with a frightening sound track." I looked at Bonnie.

My wife looked me in the eye. "You're not finished with this."

I said nothing. We continued west on Interstate 80.

*   *   *

That evening my father and I lingered at the dinner table. We'd brought lobsters from New England, a treat my dad always enjoyed. We sipped wine and carried an easy conversation about my brothers and their families, my work, my dad's health. Then, silence. I took a deep breath.

"Dad." He reached for his wine glass and slid it toward him. My voice must have warned him that our talk was about to shift gears. "We stopped at Danville on the way here."

My father lifted the glass as if studying the wine's changed illumination in the overhead light. He took a sip, with his eyes fixed on mine. He lowered the glass. His eyes, back to the ceiling. *Perhaps a new coat of paint?* Dad could exercise durable patience when it was time for a difficult discussion.

"Okay. Danville. What about it?"

Over the next hour, my father gave me one of the most meaningful gifts I have ever received from him. At the age of ninety-four, he methodically reviewed the details of my mother's tormented journey. Remembering the most painful time of his life was uncomfortable for him. But he answered my questions.

"Dad, what about that trip when you and I went to see her?" My father was quiet. "How come it was just you and me?" I persisted.

"I could not go alone." My father's words were barely audible. His attention went to his gifted hands, now worn and weary, surrendered flat on the table. "You were the oldest. That's why I took you with me." Now he was looking me in the eye. "Your brothers were too young for a visit like that."

"Why did Mom have to go, Dad?"

"She was becoming dangerous."

"What do you mean, Dad. How was she dangerous?"

"Voices. She was listening to the voices. They told her what to do. Bad things, sometimes. I told her not to pay attention, just make up her mind to ignore them." He stared at me for a few seconds. Then he lowered his gaze back to his hands. "I wish she could have listened to me, half as much as she listened to those damnable voices."

He took another sip of wine. "She never got enough exercise. A little fresh air and exercise would have done wonders for her. Clears your mind." *Fresh air and exercise*: my father's cure for everything.

"What do you mean about dangerous, Dad. Who was in danger?"

"She was." My father pushed his chair back, stretched out his arms before wrapping himself in his own rigid hug. He did not look me in the eye. "And you boys. My three boys."

*   *   *

It was early morning when we approached the Danville exit on our return to Boston. A parade of signs announced the Holiday Inn, MacDonald's, the Dutch Pantry. Just before the turnoff, a small blue rectangle with white lettering: *State Hospital.* It was impossible to ignore.

As we drove past that intersection, my silence spoke for me. I'd been thinking all weekend about my father's conversation and the flashback in front of the hospital, remembering that visit so many years ago. Something else was elbowing me for attention, as if I had been trying to outrun my shadow and it was now on my shoulder. I was racing against my own denial. I was a long distance runner who had labored through many miles and marathons, but I could no longer outrun my own guilt for how I felt about my mother. For too much of my childhood, I had been weighed down by anger and unkindness toward her. Now I was sorry about those feelings.

By the time I understood that it was her disease that I hated and not her, she'd become senile. But it didn't matter whether or not she would have understood my apology. I had to tell her I was sorry and that I loved her. My amend was as much for me as for her. But what was the point in asking her forgiveness when she would simply look at me in confusion, perhaps not even sure the words were being spoken by her first-born son? Besides, she had been dead for eleven years. "Too late," I told myself. "At least I meant well."

End of story.

But it was not the end of the story. As that Danville exit receded in my rear view mirror, my wife looked at me with an expression that I knew very well after thirty-six years of marriage. The face that says *give me your eyes, look at me, you must hear this.* Finally, I did look at her. And I heard what she had to say.

"Honey. I think you have work to do."

My eyes were still on the road heading east, back to Boston. Going home, to where the questions that flickered in my dreams and poems had to be asked and answered. It was time to study the family pictures and written words that protected my mother's story. And mine.

Bonnie was right. I did have work to do. Here it is.

Chapter 2

'm studying a faded photograph of my family, probably taken by a neighbor or a relative. The penciled date on the back is smudged, but it looks like 1943. We're gathered on the front yard of our house on Beaver Avenue. This was our first home in State College, near the flat edge of town, where the green stretch of farmlands reached for the distant Tussey Mountains.

My parents are standing together behind Bill and me. Dad is holding my youngest brother, Alfie, who is dressed in white, a small knit cap tilted on his head. His hand is at his mouth, maybe sucking his thumb. I'd guess him to be only a year old, which would make me six, and Bill four.

My father looks tall in this picture, lean and trim. He walked to work or rode his bike whenever possible. He only drove the car when the weather was bad. Dad has a full head of wavy dark hair, brushed straight back. Studying him from this side of our history, I realize that he was a handsome man, athletic in his frame. He was capable of laughter, but here his expression is worried. There is a soft pinch between his eyebrows, his mouth fixed in a rigid line. He's pressing his lips against the upward curl of a smile, as if it's hard to be happy for this picture. Alfie is loosely braced against my father's chest, with just enough freedom to wiggle around. My little brother is twisted toward the camera, inspecting the photographer.

Bill and I are in the front. My eyes are closed, either from reacting to the glare of sunlight, or from poor timing with the camera's shutter. I'm wearing knickers and a light coat over my buttoned sweater. My cap has almost slid off the back of my head. I remember how I hated wearing those knickers and how the fabric bunched up at my knees and chafed the inside of my legs when I ran, which was nearly all the time. When I look at this picture of my brothers and me I feel sadness, remembering how hard we tried to please Mom and Dad. So much depended on it.

On my left is Bill. He's about a head shorter than me. His hair is so light that it almost shines its blondness, even though we are posed in a black and white snapshot. He's lucky. No knickers, just straight dark pants. His jacket is stretched over his shoulders, buttoned up to the top. He's squinting at the camera. A toy lamb is in the grass at my brother's feet, glowing white as sun on new snow.

My mother stands behind Bill. Her light coat hangs straight and loose off her small shoulders. Under it, she's wearing a dress with a floral print. Her face takes the camera straight on, her eyes slightly narrowed through her round, wire-rimmed glasses. She looks thin and tired, but not so tired that she isn't with us. She's not smiling, but seems to be considering it. Her hands are in her pockets, instead of resting on Bill's shoulders, which are immediately in front of her. There is also open space between my mother and my father, who is standing next to her. She is not touching any of us, but her eyes tell the camera she is connected with us, in her own way. At least for now.

My mom's hair is full and neat, parted on the right side. A pine tree looms in the background, directly behind her. Because of the lack of contrast between the tree and Mom's hair, I can't tell where one begins and the other ends. Either something white is hanging on the tree, or my mother has placed a white butterfly ribbon in her hair. It seems such a whimsical thing for my mother to do. I hope it was a ribbon.

The sun appears mild and forgiving in this picture. It is providing warmth enough that we are not thickly insulated from each other as we would be in our winter coats. It could be spring. But I think it's early autumn, and I'll tell you why. The cold is coming. I can feel it in this picture. I see it in our faces.

Soon my mother would go away from us. I see the slight inquisitive lift in her eyes. Perhaps she is beginning to pay attention to something she alone can hear: *the voices*. Are they becoming too strident to ignore? Is she listening to their instructions? Maybe Mom's eyes are adjusting in their accommodation to darkness, and what was patiently waiting for her in the shadows. My mother's eyes never closed in their vigilance on her family's behalf. But I wonder: is this when her vision of Jesus begins to blur in the deepening shadow of Satan's presence in her life?

Yes, I think. This picture was taken in autumn and the light is beginning to thin into pale illumination. I could not see it then as a child. But now it is magnified through the looking glass of our history. My mother is getting ready to be a host to her visitors. She'll grip her fear with white-knuckled prayers, but it won't be enough. It will drag us into my mother's dark night until we loosen our own hold on it. Her voices will speak to us, through her. My mother's fear will be our teacher.

Before I close the album, I come back to the toy lamb nestled at my brother's foot. It is brilliant white, pure and unblemished, like a soul without sin. No dog or teddy bear for us; our toy was a lamb. My mother bought it for her boys. She'd already named it in the store, before she brought it home: *Agnus Dei*.

As in, *agnus dei, qui tollis peccata mundi:* lamb of God, who takest away the sins of the world.

Alfie, Bill, and I could never hear the instructions that controlled my mother. She told me that as long as she listened to those commands, we wouldn't have to. My mother would figure out how to keep us at safe distance from Satan. It was her duty to keep us in the healing light of Jesus.

Sometimes when Dad was at work, Mom tried to describe the voices to me. I was usually the one who listened to her, not my younger brothers. I didn't want them to be scared. She said sometimes they were mean and bossy, and other times they could be soft as a lullaby, singing "jump, jump" when she was near a window. I even thought I understood what my mother was listening to. It was scary when that happened. Mom said she trusted me the most because I was serious and wouldn't laugh about it. It was important to her that I believed her. *I believed her.*

Dad would get upset and tell her the voices didn't exist. "It's just your imagination, Sophie. They're all in your mind." Then he would tell her to exercise. Fresh air would be good for her, too. We could tell by the glaze in Mom's eyes that she wasn't paying any attention. She'd heard that advice too many times.

Usually the voices just whispered to her. If she kept busy, she wouldn't hear them. They liked being in shadows, but lately they had started moving to different parts of the house. Mom told me that something else was beginning to happen; the voices got angry if she didn't pay attention. They'd flow along the neighbor's electrical wires and start buzzing. If that didn't work, they came in through our radio. It didn't matter if the radio was switched on or off; my mother could still hear it, as if she had a special receiver in her mind. Mom was afraid of what they would do to Bill and Alfie and me. Maybe the voices would get inside us and make us sin in the eyes of Jesus. That's why Mom prayed her rosary so much just trying to keep us safe. She needed our help too. We had to pray the rosary so often that I thought our fingers would become dented from the beads.

The voices started whistling, high and shrill, when Mom tried to pray them away. When she covered her ears, I knew they were really bad. Her eyes got scary, with a weepy glow in them, like they were hot with tears that wouldn't come out. When she got like that I knew she was halfway between angry and frightened. Mom would look at me and I had to look away; her eyes burned right through me, freezing me. How could her eyes be so hot and cold at the same time? That's when my brothers and I learned to be invisible.

My mother always knew where to find me when she wanted to tell me what her voices were saying. She knew not to tell Bill and Alfie the real scary stuff, but I was brave enough to listen. No way she would tell Dad because he'd get mad at her and tell her to make up her mind to stop listening. The only words she'd say to him were like rules from Jesus or the Holy Mother about how to live free of sin. Sometimes that would make him explode the air with bad words. We'd never hear my father swear like that, unless he accidentally hit his finger with a hammer.

Mom's voices were busier than ever. She thought one of our neighbors murdered a woman in her bedroom. Then she heard the victim say "Why did you do this to me?" after she was dead. Mom's voices kept repeating that question. She put her hands over her ears to block them out. Then strangers began to appear, darting in and out of shadows, especially after sunset. Mom said they smiled at her, but she knew they were trying to tempt her into committing mortal sins. She knew that my brothers and I were not safe around them. She'd protect us with the help of our lord and savior, Jesus Christ.

If my father went outside to work in the yard, my mother locked the door. She saw people waiting to come in. They'd lean their faces into the sunlight, long enough to make eye contact and smile at her. Then they'd duck back into shadows, so nobody else would see them. They made themselves invisible so we wouldn't believe Mom. She locked all of us out so often that Dad hid an extra key outside.

Aunt Frieda sent food when my mother could no longer cook for us. She couldn't do much of anything because most of her time was spent in her rocking chair. If her hands weren't worrying her rosary beads, she was paging through The Bible. She fluttered and folded the pages as if she were searching for a map to guide us home, but Mom never did find the page she was looking for.

The first time Dad asked for help, he phoned Father Gallagher on a Sunday afternoon during the Christmas season. Mom always got agitated during the holy days. But it was absolutely the worst as we approached the birthday of Jesus. The arguments between my parents were getting really bad and loud. Dad closed windows as quickly as Mom opened them. My mother was convinced that someone was trying to poison our air. She was trying to air the dope fumes out of our house. But she was letting winter into our home and we were shivering from more than the cold.

Our priest came within an hour of Dad's call. That was fast because we lived at the edge of town and Father Gallagher had to siphon some gasoline from a neighbor's car. With gas being rationed because of the war, he never had enough fuel to keep up with his house calls or his visits to the hospital.

My brothers and I met him at the door. Bill took his coat and tried to hang it up in the hallway leading to the living room. He couldn't reach high enough, even jumping with his arms stretched up as far as they'd go. So I hung up the coat. Father thanked my brother for trying. Then he reached in the outer pocket of his hanging coat and removed a purple stole, which he draped around his neck. From the other pocket, he slid out his black prayer book and thumbed through it, until he found the page he was look-ing for. He tugged a red ribbon into the book, marking the exact location of his prayers. His hand brushed Bill's hair while he nodded toward me.

"Boys, let's go see Mother."

My mom was swaying in her rocking chair when the priest walked in. Her eyes darted side to side, before locking on Father Gallagher when he appeared in front of her. She puzzled over him, squinting, until her eyes loosened their grip, softening and remembering. The priest placed his hand on Mom's forehead. He wanted to be sure she knew who was standing in front of her.

"Sophie?" Father reached down for Mom's hands, which were tangled and looped within her rosary beads. "Cast you out, unclean spirits. Be gone from Sophie, this child of God." My mother tilted her smile upward toward the priest's face. Then she lowered her gaze to the three of us, lined up in single file, tallest to shortest, peering at her from alternating sides behind the priest.

Dad shuffled us into the kitchen so Father Gallagher could be alone with my mother. Through the door I heard his voice. *Confiteor, deo omnipotenti...* he was hearing Mom's confession. I was learning to be an altar boy, so I knew the Latin. But why confession? What was there for her to confess? Were the voices punishment for something bad my mother had done?

In a few minutes, we were called into the room so we could be with Mom. Bill and Alfie stood on each side of her. Father Gallagher wanted to know how it was for my mother. Was there any part of the house that was worse for her? Did the voices visit her all day long? He wanted to know where to do his work.

"Everywhere." Dad pointed to the kitchen, to the dining room, all around the living room. "Upstairs, too. Day and night. There's no rest in this house. Not one little corner of peace. *Gott in Himmel.* Please, a little peace." Now my father was hugging himself.

When the priest pointed to the closets and looked at Mom, she shook her head, Yes. *That's where they go at night*. That's what my mother said to me, too. They said something else to my mom. *Come and be with us, Sophie. It's nice in the dark.*

We followed Father Gallagher through the house, while Dad stood by Mom's chair, looking out the window. The priest waved the sprinkling wand like a sword slicing the air, back and forth, raining holy water side to side, where it dribbled down the walls. *Kyrie Eleison, Christe Eleison*, he chanted, chasing something we couldn't see. *Kyrie Eleison, Christe Eleison*, trying to scare away something that had never been invited into our home.

I tried to follow him upstairs, but Dad waved me back. Bill and Alfie and I stood on the floor below, listening to our priest's prayers as they swirled above us, like storm clouds, thundering his entrance into our bedrooms and hallways.

Vade retro Satan... Dominus vobiscum... Pax vobiscum, the Latin echoes heavy in the air, singing into each other, trying to choke the breath out of my mother's tormenting voices.

Our priest's prayers and magic worked for a while. My mother smiled, as if her scary visitors had gone on vacation. During those restful periods, it seemed as if we had more oxygen to breathe. But Father Gallagher's visits became more frequent as his incantations lost their power. The voices were getting used to the holy intrusions. Mom said they were starting to move to other parts of the house, playing a game of hide and seek with Father, getting darker, blending more easily into the shadows. She said the voices were making faces, taunting our priest. They were lining up against him and they had an unfair advantage. There were more of them than there was of him.

My vision was never so acute as when I trembled in the company of my mother's shadows. Today when I look back on my childhood, I remember thinking my role as guardian of my brothers depended on shielding myself. How could I protect them if I was not safe? I became the watchman who remained vigilant, day and night.

My mother's eyes told us everything. When they narrowed into sharp focus, we veiled ourselves in the dim periphery of her vision. We learned to trust our hearing for warning sounds that could not be ignored. We listened for the creak of her rocking chair: incessant and metronomic meant danger, as if she were keeping time with her companions; sporadic and lazy was safe, the coast is clear. We went to sleep with a light on in the hallway.

We moved in dark silence, spiders on wispy webs. Walking with held breath made us less heavy afoot. We kept watch of her in her chair, rocking, book of prayers clutched to her breast. My mother stared out the window, searching for God, and she could not see her three sons standing in her doorway, as we awaited instructions about following The Shepherd, and the gathering of sheep.

Chapter 3

There are two family albums in my bookcase. The oldest is dusty, untouched for too many years. Its leather cover dried out, it seems a cracked and wrinkled metaphor for our distant family history. The newer album is a homemade book, consisting of pictures and papers collected at a recent reunion of my cousins. We all brought photographs, letters, and memories, to be shared at our gathering. At the time of our reunion, only three of our twenty-two parents were still alive. Someone suggested putting together a book, in order to preserve our family story. I raised my hand: I'd do it. Little did I realize that I was beginning my research for this memoir.

I titled my homemade book, *A Family named Droege.* The cover is scanned from a page found within Grandmother Droege's family bible. On it she had listed the name, date and birthplace of each of her fourteen children, my mother among them. Also included are the dates on which three of my grandmother's children died, two of them in infancy. After we had been apart for so many years, my cousins shared their stories about our parents' history. The Droege's story is one of courage, faith, and connection with each other. Facing significant adversity and hardship, they survived with dignity and pride.

I hoped the mystery of my mother would be revealed by my search of those collected words and images. I was about to begin a formidable journey on returning from that visit to my father, when Bonnie suggested that I had work to do.

I opened the albums. The writing followed, I had no choice.

I found a framed picture with the oldest album. It is bordered by antique brown wood, gilded by a trace of stippled gold. A shield of glass protects the image. The portrait is a rainbow of gray, a subtle shading of black and white. My mother is obediently seated on a plain wooden chair, her left foot gracefully tucked behind the right. Her head is festooned with a crown of flowers so delicate they seem to flutter their whiteness for the camera. A veil flows down like a gauzy waterfall, caressing her shoulders, softly brushing her neck. She is wrapped in such vibrant whiteness that she glows like a silhouette against the dark background. Ruffles adorn the front of her dress, framing a cross which hangs on the chain draped around her neck.

My mother's small hands are gloved in white, left hand resting in her lap, while she grasps her prayer book with the right. A white-beaded rosary creases the opened page.

It is the day of Sophie Henrietta Droege's First Holy Communion.

My mother's face is softened by the available light, which comes from over her right shoulder, leaving her left side dimly shadowed. Her sweet face reflects her love of Jesus in that luminosity, the glow not harsh, but fluidly radiant on her dress. Her right cheek looks as if it would feel warm against my own cheek, if I held my face up to hers, on the other side of the glass. My mother's smile is subtle, hopeful, and watchful. *Looking for Jesus?* Her smile says *I believe.*

Her eyes are shaped like almonds, each eyebrow traced like the thin outline of a floating gull's wing. Can a nose be perfect? Not too big or small, not too sharp or blunt? My mother's nose is perfect, with a straight line running down its ridge, between the sunlit right side and the shaded left half of her face. Her lips are straight, not the slightest upward curl at the ends, and yet her smile takes hold of me, blurs my eyes and my heart. The outline of her face is soft and symmetrical, tapered to a delicately rounded chin. A faint shadow brushed beneath her lower lip, a hint of a dimple; something saved for a future smile?

She confidently looks out from her portrait, the unshadowed eye focused on me. She is speaking to me. *I am here,* she seems to say. *Everything about me is in this picture.* It's as if that image, with its black and white contrast, is a metaphor for the light and shadows my mother would come to know: one crucifix darkly blurred behind her, another glinting in hopeful clarity beside her.

Something else about this portrait; I look at her left eye, on the cloudy side of her face. If I study it carefully, hold it in just the right slant of sun, I see her searching for Jesus, in the unlit places. Already, Sophie Henrietta Droege can see in darkness.

In the old family album is a portrait of Joseph Droege and Regina Wenzel. My mother's parents are young in this picture. Perhaps it was taken shortly before their marriage, which would be approximately 1898. I am not in a hurry to turn this page.

Joseph sits on a heavy wooden chair. His pose is formal, as if he is holding his breath until he hears the click of the camera. He is on the left side of the picture, with his body angled slightly toward Regina. She faces straight on to the photographer, staring out with great confidence at anyone who pages through her family's history. Joseph's face is also square with the camera. His eyebrows are proudly arched, as if inviting the viewer into conversation. I can imagine him saying, "Who are you, and what is it that you are so curious about?" My grandfather's expression is wide-eyed, as if he doesn't want to miss anything. His face is clean-shaven. I think it is a friendly face trying to look serious. He will catch his breath and laugh as soon as the picture is taken.

His hair is parted in the middle. He is wearing a three-quarter length coat, neatly cinched with a shiny buckle in the middle. Six buttons glare like an orderly constellation on his dark garment. His arms are relaxed, slightly bent. Hands rest in his lap, mirror images of each other. They appear to be strong hands, ready for the fierce grip of hard work. His posture suggests that he is confident and comfortable with himself. I think the man in this picture would have been fun to know. His sober dedication to his family's welfare was matched by his love of laughter. For my mother, he was a perfect father.

Regina Wenzel stands partially behind her seated husband. She could be nineteen or twenty, already in America for six years. Her presence suggests that she is not posing, but has been interrupted from some task. She's not the least bit pretentious. I can imagine the photographer has been given notice that she has other things to do. Her dress is dark and plain, unembellished with glittering jewelry. Her smile is plain, minimal, more from her eyes than from her face, but the set of her chin implies strength and determination. I barely knew Grandmother Droege; she was a gray wisp of my memory, having died when I was four years old. But I learned that she was the one who kept everyone in line; the parent who kept everything in order when times were difficult.

My grandmother's eyes sparkle life into the picture. She's staring right back at me. The subtle lift of her eyebrows suggests her gentle interrogation of me. *Wie heissen sie? What is your name? What is it that you want to know?*

I want to ask her how it was in those early days.

She would tell me she was barely fourteen years old, when she came to America from Germany. She stayed with her uncle in New York City, who had immigrated a few years earlier. She worked as a housecleaner, rising at five in the morning and working until ten o'clock at night.

Joseph Droege arrived in New York City, several years before Regina Wenzel. He was only nineteen years old. Each came in search of a better life, and they were willing to work hard for it. They met in that city, where they married in 1898.

My mother was the seventh of Joseph and Regina's fourteen children, born over a period of nineteen years. Two of the children lived for less than two years. Their first daughter died at the age of eighteen, a victim of the Great Flu Epidemic of 1918.

My aunts and uncles often spoke of their childhood and the daily challenges they faced. But through it all, I heard in their stories the unchanging theme of their family history: *they were loved.* Each day the children waited for their father to come home from work so they could spend time together. Both parents found energy for singing and laughter before supper. There was daily check-in about school. For all the hard-muscled determination and energy my grandparents brought to their American journey, their children were treated with tenderness and patience. They were told that as difficult as things were in America, their lives were better than if they had grown up in Germany. Joseph and Regina Droege were blessed by the gift of their children. *Blessed is our family,* was the brief prayer shared with the children at bedtime.

My mother heard time and time again that she was a blessing, and that she was loved.

Chapter 4

When my mother smiled and laughed, our home lit up with shafts of sunlight. My brothers and I skipped to wherever the warmth flickered, but the brightness was occasional and severely defined. As time went on, it visited less frequently, as if we were rude hosts.

My father couldn't really talk about Mom's illness. He couldn't explain what he didn't understand, so he tried to distract us instead. He tried his best to keep us busy with a work project, a car ride, a game. Dad took us outside to play whenever he could find the time. Sometimes we pushed each other on the swing set he erected in the back yard. We played kick the can, or hide and seek.

"Fresh air, boys. Keeps a rosy color on your cheeks." Hard work would be good for us. We raked leaves, helped dig and turn the garden. We already knew how to take care of the yard. The summer before Mom went away, Dad taught us to cut the grass. Because Bill and Alfie were still little kids, they worked as a team, marching in step like a pair of soldiers, as they pushed the lawnmower. Dad said he was proud of us because he didn't have to remind us of our responsibilities.

Toward the end of that summer, Dad had repaired some second-hand baseball mitts for us. They were hand-me-downs from our older cousins. The leather was dried out and split between some of the fingers. The pocket of each glove was pounded paper-thin from catching more base-balls than we could dream of. There wasn't much padding left to protect our hands from the sting if the ball was coming in hard. We compensated for that by slipping a thin sponge inside each mitt, to cushion our hands against the impact. The webbing was frayed, but Dad weaved in pieces of narrow rope. "Good as new" he claimed. We played catch together, throwing underhand to my youngest brother. Bill and I aimed for his mitt, which he held up like a target. Alfie was getting better at catching, but he was still learning to keep his eye on the ball. Dad promised us that someday we'd each have new baseball gloves. It was a promise we wouldn't let him forget.

There was someone else who played catch with my brothers and me. Indoors, that is, when Mom wasn't looking. His name was Sweet Jesus. Shortly before she went to Danville, Mom had rescued the plaster statue from a church bazaar. She said he cost 75 cents. Sweet Jesus looked as if he had stepped right out of a pastel-colored bible picture, except he didn't have a pale blue sky behind him. Not in our house, where he was posi-tioned at the end of the bedroom hallway, backed up against the wooden door of the towel closet. The holy statue was draped in the usual white robe, a red shawl over his shoulders, and dark sandals on his feet. His long brown hair and beard were neatly trimmed.

The eyes captured us. Always lifted upward, as if looking for a signal from his heavenly father, those eyes followed us down the hall, into our bedrooms, even to the bathroom. When we stood next to Sweet Jesus, his eyes seemed to angle sideways, always on us. As far as the three of us were concerned, his peripheral vision was so sharp that we could never quite escape observation. It didn't help one bit that those sacred eyes were at the same level as mine.

From the far end of the hall, the statue appeared to be casting a friendly wave. But close up, one could see that he was just raising his right hand in the upstroke of the sign of the cross, ready to dispense a blessing. Bill placed his baseball mitt on that right hand, making Sweet Jesus a lefty. That's when we invented our game of catch. We stood about four or five feet away and gently lofted a tennis ball into the open mitt. We couldn't use a real baseball because it might break his plaster hand. If the ball landed too softly, it bounced out onto the floor where we'd field it like a grounder. But with just the right amount of impact from the toss, the thumb and little finger of the mitt collapsed inward, folding the ball in the glove's pocket, resulting in a real grab. When Mom wasn't around, we'd have contests: best out of five successful catches won. More throws than that took too long, and she might find us in the middle of our sacrilegious act.

About two weeks after Mom planted the statue in the hallway, Bill put a Pittsburgh Pirates baseball hat on our new playmate. The afternoon sun slanted through the open door of my bedroom, glowing the left side of his face in radiant splendor. Alfie could barely reach the hat, but he managed to twist it sideways in order to keep the light out of Sweet Jesus' eyes.

We must have been laughing too loudly. We got real quiet when we heard my mother's footsteps coming through the kitchen, getting louder and dangerously close. The door to our hallway slowly squeaked open. We held our breath. Mom looked straight past us as she marched to the statue. I thought we were really going to be in limbo, with the *just you boys wait 'til your father gets home* routine. Instead, she reached up and straightened Sweet Jesus' baseball hat. When she turned to face us, she was almost laughing. We didn't mind one bit when she suggested that a quick Hail Mary might keep my father in the dark. That was one time we were happy to pray.

My dad wouldn't have cared that much. After all, he was the one who named the statue. Mom strategically positioned the plaster savior so my brothers and I would constantly be under its vigilant gaze, given the proximity to our bathroom and bedrooms. The problem for Dad was that he was also under surveillance. "If I wanted Jesus to be staring at me all day long, I would have been a damn priest." My dad didn't know I was listening to him. He had to lift the statue up and plant him a few feet away so he could get to the towels. "I could have joined a goddamn monastery. Gott in Himmel."

When my father realized my bedroom door was partially open, he leaned his head in and lowered his voice. "Carl. Forget what I just said. I lost my temper." Dad came in and sat on the edge of my bed. "I lose patience sometimes. I didn't mean what I said. I shouldn't swear. Let's think about how kind Jesus was? How about a name that reminds us of that?"

"Sweet Jesus" seemed to work, we both agreed. As I got older, I understood something else about that name. Depending on the tone and velocity with which it is uttered, Sweet Jesus could be a prayer or a curse. Although I heard both from Dad, sometimes it was hard to tell the difference.

The statue was a companion in another way. He joined us in our secret game, Playing Priest. This was a routine that Mom started before she went to Danville. She said Jesus would be our playmate. I was already learning how to serve Mass. Along with the ritual, I'd memorized much of the Latin. Before long, I would be old enough to really be an altar boy.

We played priest only when Dad was at work.

Mom always bragged about her oldest brother, Aloysius, who had studied to be a priest. He dropped out of the seminary to take care of the family when they were in difficult times. Mom's eyes were always on me when informing us that a good Catholic family was extra special in the eyes of God, if that family contributed a priest to carry out His will and His good works.

My bedroom became our church. We draped a clean white sheet over my desk, making it an altar. There was enough room to wedge Sweet Jesus between the desk and the wall on which a crucifix hung. Mom always juggled the statue so the cross looked like it was balanced on Jesus' haloed head. Standing before my altar, Jesus was eye to eye with me. I wondered if He thought I was making fun of him. *I* wondered if I was making fun of Him.

We used one of my dad's sturdy wine glasses for a chalice. Mom gave us two candles, which we placed on the altar, one on each side. For special occasions or holy days of obligation, I could even light the candles. We just had to be sure that we returned the matchbox to Dad's shelf, where he displayed his pipes and tobacco. We understood that it had to be exactly in the same place as before we borrowed it.

Then there was the matter of vestments. A colorful window drape served as my chasuble. Underneath I wore one of Dad's large white T shirts, in place of the alb. My stole was a dark blue necktie from my father's closet, draped around my neck like a sacred scarf. For a final touch, Mom looped her chain of wooden rosary beads around my neck.

Bill was my altar boy, since Alfie was still too small for such an important assignment. He and Mom sat together on the bed, a congregation of two, as I bowed and genuflected and elbowed Bill, reminding him it was time to move left or right, up or down, or just plain try to look pious. "Just keep your hands folded in prayer, Bill. Keep your head bowed, but aim your eyes up just a bit. Like you're lifting your sight to God, looking for Jesus to inspire you. No, I did not say Jesus would perspire you. And don't laugh." Bill was not easy.

Part of the altar boy's duty is to help the priest put on his vestments, but Bill wasted too much time tying knots in Dad's T shirt, so I couldn't put my arms through my alb. If that wasn't bad enough, he hung Christmas ornaments on the back of my chasuble when he knelt behind me. I heard them clinking into each other, every time I genuflected my knee to the floor. My brother had a ways to go with his church manners.

Mom was always in a good mood when we held mass in my bedroom. She was very happy about the way I played priest. I never laughed the way Bill did. Even if it was a game, she said we were including Jesus in our fun time together. But every once in a while she got real serious; she stared at Sweet Jesus a long time without looking at us. That was a good time for silent prayers. When she had that look in her eyes, she really was in church.

We used pieces of saltine crackers for communion wafers. Mom and Bill and Alfie lined up on their knees while I held the broken cracker above them, asking Jesus' blessing on all of us. "Corpus Christie," I chanted. "Amen," they responded, as they consumed the body of Christ. Sometimes Bill sneaked in a broken cookie to substitute for the holy bread, and Mom would be pleased with Bill's increased hunger for the nourishment of Jesus. It's good we didn't have some of Dad's wine instead of grape juice in the chalice.

An altar boy is supposed to respond to the priest's prayers and supplications for God's love and mercy. Bill thought it was just hilarious when my perfectly pronounced Latin was answered with his drawn-out belch, or worse, an abrupt fart. I'd about had it when Alfie laughed so hard that he wiped his eyes on my blanket. When I saw my mom's eyes glowing at me, her hand hiding the upward curl of her mouth, I figured my priestly duty had run its course. The priest wasn't supposed to joke around. But sometimes I couldn't help it.

We weren't allowed to laugh in church. But it was a good feeling when Mom laughed at our secret church service. If she was happy, we were happy. When we were in real church, the adults looked deadly serious when they thumped their mea culpas against their chests. Between all the prayers and statues on the walls, there were too many reminders of hell. Why did my mother seem so full of joy when we played our game? She never smiled like that in church.

We didn't know of any other kids who played Priest. Mom wanted us to be quiet about it. She said our offerings at our special Mass would be better heard by Jesus if we didn't tell anyone else about it. Especially Dad.

Chapter 5

Paging through the newer family album, I found a color print of an old church. Shortly after the reunion with my cousins, I felt inspired to visit the nearby places where my mother's family lived. Tattered letters and washed out photographs guided me to this location, where I framed the Droege family's place of worship within the lens of my Nikon camera. This snapshot is of Holy Trinity Church, Shawmut Avenue, in Boston's South End. A sign proclaims the founding of the church by German Catholics in 1823. A bronze plaque on the stone wall is engraved with the following:

Holy Trinity German
Catholic Church
Die Katholische Deutsche
Dreifaltigkeits Kirche.

My father, Clemens Wilhelm Schoenebeck, emigrated from Germany in 1923. This was a time of great economic uncertainty in his country. Only twenty years old, he had the blessing of his parents as he sought a better life in America. Separating from his loving family was the most difficult thing he'd ever done. He encountered stormy seas, emotionally and weather-wise, in his Atlantic crossing before his ship entered the United States at the Port of Baltimore. He then took the train to Boston and found his way to Holy Trinity Church.

A priest from my father's hometown was assigned to Holy Trinity. Father Giesler gave young Clemens a place to stay in exchange for his labor as a janitor and handyman. My father attended night school in order to learn the language of his new country. Within two years, he was able to speak and write English with flawless grammar and vocabulary. During his daytime hours he attended Boston Trade School, where he studied to be a machinist. After my father's death, I found a collection of certificates from the school proclaiming his excellence and mastery of his craft. He never bragged to his sons about his academic record. His work spoke for him: handmade bowls and dishes, wrought-metal candle holders, the home that he eventually built for his family. All of these gifts from his hands brought him deserved and hard-earned praise.

Soon my father became friendly with a generous and happy German family who lived in the nearby suburb of Roslindale. They worshipped at Holy Trinity, where they met my father. They loved my dad, and he loved them. Within a year of his arrival in Boston, the Gundals invited him to be part of their family. His new mother asked, "What's one more mouth to feed when we already have six children?" It was a happy time in my father's life. While he was adapting to his new life in America, he was secure and safe in the familiar German traditions of his new home and family.

My mother's family lived in Roxbury, part of the inner city of Boston. In the early 1900s this section was home to one of the largest German settlements on the East Coast. Holy Trinity Church was also the congregational center of the family's Catholic faith. It was here that the paths of Sophie Henrietta Droege and Clemens Wilhelm Schoenebeck crossed.

My mother's father went wherever his work called him, so the family moved frequently. Within twelve years, they had traveled from New York City to Connecticut, Virginia, Massachusetts, Brooklyn, and finally to Boston. Joseph Droege was employed by a company that manufactured wire and metal products. The work was dangerous and exhausting. He was always in the perilous company of molten metal and the fire needed to heat it. Noxious fumes and flammable chemicals were part of his daily life. His work environment demanded vigilance for his safety and for that of his men. He was the shop foreman, directly responsible to his boss. While carelessness was a guarantee of disaster, extreme caution promised no insurance against it.

It was said of my grandfather that he never brought his problems home from work. He was loving and kind with his children. He had a beautiful voice and sang in the choir at Holy Trinity Church. Joseph Droege was a baritone who could rumble stern commands to his boys when they were negligent in their family duties. Then with ease, he'd slide upward into his falsetto voice, singing light-hearted soprano for the applause of his girls. Each day young Sophie waited for her father to come home from work. After he cleaned up from his dirty and strenuous labor, he'd sit down at the piano with his adoring daughter and they sang together. He always had time for music with his *liebchen:* his little girl, who was *so very good.*

That's what my aunts and uncles said about my mother: "Sophie was so good; she was the sweetest child; she always wanted to please her parents." Another thing my relatives told me was that Mom lived by the teaching of her catechism. Her purpose was to love and serve Jesus in this life, so that she could be with Him in the next.

There was another reason for my mother's perfect behavior. Something frightened her, and sometimes flickered in her dreams: the eternal fire of hell. Young Sophie prayed that Jesus would spare her and her loved ones from that fate, that the final judgment would lift her family to heavenly escape from earthly sins. The searing words of the gospels were not meta-phorical for my mother; they were real. I believe that for Sophie Henrietta Droege, the fear of hell was more real than the promise of heaven.

Some pages of the Droege album are filled with pictures of family gath-erings, such as church celebrations or birthday parties. In an old photograph of a picnic scene, all of Joseph Droege's children are clustered around him. My grandmother is not in the group. She may have been behind the camera. My mother looks about 8 or 9 years old. Because I know the birthdays of her siblings, I can estimate their ages. This picture was taken about 1916.

Once the good weather arrived, my grandparents' favorite routine was to spend Sunday afternoons at a local park. Everyone went to mass, dressed in their Sunday clothes. They would return to their home on Mission Hill and pack a festive lunch. They exchanged their shiny shoes for comfortable walking shoes, then hiked to their destination, still in their best clothes.

In this photograph, they are at The Arnold Arboretum, located near their home in Roxbury. The family is posed in a garden littered with bloom-ing flowers. The children are wearing light-weight coats and dresses, except for my grandfather. He's shed his jacket. His black tie is perfectly knotted, tight against the buttoned, starched collar. His white shirt reflects a soft glare from the muted sunlight. This must have been on Lilac Sunday, in the month of May, the only time when picnics were allowed in the Arboretum. The whole scene looks like it's brushed with springtime.

My mother's sisters are lined up behind their father, trapping him with laughter and playfulness. Frieda and Margaret are 13 and 11. They are try-ing to balance a small basket of flowers on their father's balding head, easy to reach since he is sitting on a blanket, hugging his knees. Frieda has one hand on the floral arrangement, the other on her hip. Her eyes are frown-ing at my mother, as if she is about to scold her. Perhaps she's beginning to earn her reputation with my mother: *Bossy*.

Next to Frieda and Margaret is the oldest girl, Wilhelmina, nicknamed *Minnie.* Minnie is about 16 years old. She's much taller than her sisters. Sturdy in posture, she projects a commanding presence among her siblings. From beneath her broad-brimmed hat, she beams a jolly smile. Mom said her big sister was like a second mother. Minnie's right arm cradles Emil. At the time this picture was taken, he was the youngest child, barely a year old.

The youngest sister, Regina, stands almost behind Wilhelmina. She is named for her mother. She's thoughtful and considerate of everyone. She'll let others be the center of attention, until she's needed. Then her generosity brings her forward.

Three of the brothers stand behind young Sophie. Aloysius, Joseph, and William seem a bit impatient. Perhaps they've got more important things to do. My uncles are dressed in suits and crisp white dress shirts. Their shoes are glowing, probably buffed up on the previous Saturday afternoon. Even the boys are shining.

Aloysius wears a bowtie. He's the oldest, 17 or 18. During the next year Uncle Al would enter the seminary. It was expected that such a large Catholic family would contribute a priest to help carry out God's work. He made sure everyone kept up with their schoolwork and their chores. Just as Minnie was like a second mother, Aloysius was a second father.

Now I look at my mother. She's the focal point of this picture. She's about 8 years old. Because her father is seated on the blanket, she is almost cheek to cheek with him. Young Sophie wraps her embrace around him, her right arm circling his neck. Her left hand pats in place the tulip she's wedged over her father's left ear. Sophie ignores the camera. She's beaming at Joseph Droege. Everything about young Sophie's attentive presence, at least for this click of the camera, shows that her father is her universe.

If this picture had been taken two years later, three more children would have been included. Theresa and Tony were twins, born in June of 1917.

Mary was born a year later. They are in their own photograph, sitting on a low bench, lit up in sunlight and white suits. Mary is on the left. She is the youngest of all the children, the fourteenth child of my grandparents. Her blonde hair is gathered under two white flowers, one above each ear. Her hands are folded together in her lap, and she is leaning slightly forward, insisting that the camera record her sweet face. In this old picture, I recognize something familiar in my Aunt Mary's eyes and her open smile. It is the same loving expression she brought much later, when we all lived in State College. This is the face of the compassionate nurse, who tried to lift my mother out of her dark moods. This picture reminds me of her cheerful attention to my brothers and me, when we most needed it.

Despite the collection of old photographs, there is not one single picture that shows all of the children. Only if ghosts could be imaged through the camera lens, would we see two more children: Maria Matilda, who died before her first birthday; Frank, who died when he was 4 years old. Two years after the family picnic in the Arboretum, Minnie's image would dissolve. The beloved big sister would be a victim of the Spanish Flu Epidemic of 1918.

I look with new compassion at the fading pictures of my grandmother. Regina Droege's face is textured with the terrible blessings of holding fourteen children and losing three of them. Can her gratitude for the eleven survivors overcome the durable sadness of three dead children, when the youngest victims lived long enough to be fed and clothed and lullabyed?

My grandmother was not finished with her losses.

Here's another group picture. Joseph Droege is in the middle of a gang of eighteen men, including a few young boys. Nearly everyone is dressed in black. Most of the men have coarse, scraggly beards. In this picture my grandfather wears a beard, although he's usually clean-shaven. Whether the dark shading on their faces is from the soot of their work, or from the available light leaching out of an old photograph, they are a rough looking bunch of fellows.

My grandfather stands with his arms confidently crossed over his chest. He is the only one wearing a white shirt. He stands next to his boss, his alert posture suggesting authority. His demeanor implies that he looks after his workers and that he is trusted, responsible, and reliable. But his serious expression tells me that he expects as much from his workers as he gives to them. Joseph Droege is a man in charge.

The group poses in front of the Burkeville Wire Corporation. They are in Virginia, where my mother was born. At the time of this picture she would have been an infant; her father was about forty years old. At this time, Joseph Droege had already fathered seven children, one of whom died at the age of six months.

Not one man smiles in this picture. They stare out with a collective countenanceof weary acceptance. They look like they know nothing but hard work. If they could join their voices and speak out from this old print, they would say, "hard, but what else can we do?"

Grandfather Joseph Droege is Right Center, second row, bearded man, arms folded in white shirt

Within the next year the family would be living in Massachusetts, where my grandfather would supervise a larger branch of the business. In addition to the company growing and expanding its usual work, the Burkeville Wire Corporation would be manufacturing piano wire in Boston. The owner wanted someone in charge who would be vigilant and a strict enforcer of workplace rules. With each new employee, the chance of an accident increased. At the request of his boss, Joseph Droege moved his family from Virginia to Massachusetts. He knew that no one would be more reliable than my grandfather in guarding the safety of his men.

On the next page of the album is a picture of my grandmother holding her youngest child, Mary. There is no quick thumbing past this image. Aunt Mary is seven or eight months old. She's dressed in white, perhaps for Sunday mass. The little girl's expression tells me she's been crying; her lips are puffed and pouty. My grandmother's arms protectively circle her baby, right hand gripping her left, bracing Mary against her.

My attention is drawn to those hands, the way one holds the other. Perhaps my grandmother is merely locking the circle of her embrace on Mary. But something about the graceful curve of her fingers, the way they wrap around and caress the other hand, suggests that my grandmother is also comforting herself. The sun is diminished in this picture, perhaps filtered by a passing cloud. But something else has cast shadows on Regina Droege's somber face.

My grandmother is wearing a long dress, which covers her from neck to feet. Even her arms are concealed from the day's pale light, the sleeves reaching to those expressive hands.

Regina Droege is dressed in black.

Chapter 6

My brothers and I were an audience of three, huddled on the landing at the top of the stairs. Frozen like statues, silent as could be, we were spying on the scene in our living room below.

An hour earlier my father had come upstairs and told us to get into our pajamas. It was a school day, but Dad kept us home. He didn't even go to work because of what was going on. We stayed in my bedroom most of the day since we weren't allowed to go outside. It was November, and it wasn't just the weather that was cold and gray. There was a terrible darkness in our house. We'd be going to bed before the usual time. Since Dad had already fed us an early supper, there was no need for us to go downstairs to the kitchen. No need to visit with our company. This gathering would be for grown-ups only. I kept my regular clothes on. I was the oldest and I was *not* going to bed this early.

Downstairs, my mother sat in a straight-backed chair, looking in our direction. We stretched out flat and low and kept our heads down, so she couldn't see us upstairs on the landing. Her attention was on the four people facing her: Father Gallagher, Dr. Ishler, Aunt Frieda, and Dad. Mom was still in her nightgown. Aunt Frieda made her put on a housecoat, maybe because we had company or because it felt cold in our house. The bare wooden floor made the room look really big, from where we were hiding. My mom was hugging herself. A weak smile stretched across her face as if she were trying to be polite, despite being uncomfortable with her visitors.

The drapes on the windows were open, but there wasn't much light coming in. The sun was stingy at this time of year. Winter was coming soon, but that didn't keep Mom from opening the windows to air out the dope fumes she claimed the neighbors were blowing in our house. Whenever Dad complained that she was heating the outdoors and freezing us, the arguments started again. Now the fighting was worse than ever. But today she didn't notice that the windows were shut. Mom was staring at the people facing her, as if trying to identify them from a faraway place.

My mother usually kept the drapes pulled across the windows, even in the daylight. She was more peaceful in the dark. Other times she was better in bright light. We never knew what would be best, dark or light. It all depended on whether her voices were awake or sleeping. It was best to not disturb them. My brothers and I were learning how to keep peace with whatever was hiding in Mom's shadows.

The only other light came from the dim bulb in the floor lamp. My father had built the lamp holder out of wrought metal. It extended upward from a solid base, too heavy to tip over. The upright pole must have had a thousand hand-hammered dents, each pounded in, one by one. Dad made a hammer especially for that purpose, so he could tap in each little depression with perfect size and shape.

Sometimes when Mom was in a different part of the house, we would uncover a window and shine the bright sun on the dimpled metal surface of Dad's lamp. The scattered reflections burst like tiny rainbow darts inside the room. My brothers and I would twist and wobble the base so we could dance the light on the white walls and ceiling. The part of the room still darkened with shade looked like nighttime, full of jiggling stars. Whichever one of us made the best show, won.

But now that lamp was shining behind and above my mother's head, as if her questioners were in the dark and she had a searchlight beaming at her. From where my father and his three guests were lined up, she must have looked like a lonely silhouette in front of the moon.

For the last three or four months, my mother's voices had become relentless, never giving her a moment's rest. She was paralyzed, no longer able to do housework or prepare our meals. Now I could hear Aunt Frieda's voice rising from the living room below, as she explained to our priest and our doctor how she'd been cooking for us for months, bringing meals over to our house. But now something had changed. As soon as my aunt left the house, my mother flushed the food down the toilet. My brothers and I knew all about that; the voices made her do it. The voices warned her that my aunt was trying to poison us, trying to dope us, just like our neighbors. She trusted no one but Jesus.

Mom thought her oldest sister was always trying to boss her around. She rarely took Aunt Frieda's advice, but I knew my aunt was just trying to help us. Sometimes when Mom wasn't looking, Aunt Frieda sneaked cookies or candy for us. She didn't want my mother to feel bad about not baking sweet things for us.

Now my aunt's voice was getting louder, explaining to the others how she was simply looking after us. "I just wanted to be sure the boys are being fed. You know, make things easier for Clem." Aunt Frieda stretched one hand toward Dad, the other toward Mom. "That's the truth, Sophie." She tilted her head toward the priest. "You know how she can be, Father."

My mother stared straight ahead, her eyes wide open and unblinking, still hugging herself. Her smile was unchanged until someone started speaking. Then she searched for the voice and smiled in its direction.

Father Gallagher worried out loud about his visits with the prayers and holy water. The effects of his spells were wearing off more quickly with each attempt. "I fear Sophie's soul is being torn between the loving mercy of Jesus and the evil intent of Satan. God knows I've tried." The tired priest hunched his bulky shoulders forward, shielding the open prayer book on his lap. With his eyes fixed on my mother, he folded it shut. He clamped it against his chest with both hands. "Jesus, Mary, and Joseph, I've tried to keep you in God's light, Sophie. Forgive me if I've failed." From where I was sprawled on the landing upstairs, it looked as if our priest had closed his eyes. Maybe he was praying. I could tell he was plain worn out.

Father's words and worry floated up the stairway to our hiding place. It sounded as if the priest was talking to us. I warned my brothers to stay flat on their stomachs, so we could remain out of sight. With my finger pressed against my lips, I signaled "quiet." Any noise from us and we'd be discovered and sent to our bedrooms.

I wiggled to the edge of the landing so I could look between the banister rails and see Mom. She was rigid in her plain wooden chair, blankly staring at her company. Now her smile was gone, replaced with a guarded look. It didn't matter who was speaking and it didn't matter what they were saying. Now the only movement was the twitchy scan of my mother's eyes as they swiveled side to side, trying to figure out who was speaking to her.

My father was coughing, still weak and run down from a cold that just wouldn't go away. He took a sip of water from a glass on the window sill next to him and turned to his right so he could speak to Father Gallagher. The angle of pale light from the window shaded my father's face and deepened the lines across his forehead. His eyes were lowered, as if it was hard for him to see what was in front of him. He seemed too weak to lift his head.

My father worked as a machinist at the University. The work was tiring and demanding, requiring patience and concentration. For his own safety, he couldn't risk being fatigued. But now his strength was drained by something in addition to Mom's illness. The war had ended two months earlier, in September of 1945. My father was an American citizen who was born in Germany. With his noticeable accent, Dad often worried about being perceived as one of the enemy.

Our neighbors and Dad's co-workers understood his conflicted feelings about the war. They knew he was a good American citizen. But one time when we were at the grocery store, he thought someone in line behind him used the word *Kraut* when they heard him speaking. My father was caught in the pull of loyalty between his two countries. He carried shifting uncertainty and guilt on his back, like bricks in a knapsack. He was leaning forward now, as if pushed down by that relentless weight of what his life had become.

"I can't take it anymore. I don't know what to do." His words barely drifted up the stairs. We never had to strain to hear my father's strong voice, but now we did. It seemed like Dad couldn't catch his breath.

Father Gallagher groped for Dad's shoulder and rested his hand on it. "Take your time, Clem. Easy does it. We're not going anywhere."

My dad's gifted hands could fix anything. He could bend wood into a boat, bring a dead motor back to life, and mend our broken toys. But no matter how hard he tried, he could not fix my mother.

I inched forward on my elbows, so I could lift up my head for a better look. Dad was massaging his forehead with the palms of his hands. "I get up early. I get the older boys dressed for school before I go to work. I worry about Alfred being home alone with Sophie." He looked at Mom. "I don't know if they even get breakfast. She can't seem to help with anything. All she does is pray and read The Bible." He sat straight up in his chair and shook his head. "A lot of good it's doing." Now Dad was looking at his shoes, or maybe the floor. "First we move here because Boston isn't religious enough. Now she wants to go back there because the Protestants here want to put her in a concentration camp, because she's Catholic. Sophie thinks the whole town is immoral."

My mother's expression was unchanged, her eyes curiously fixed on Dad as if trying to recognize his voice. She was sitting with her back rigidly braced against the hard chair, her feet flat on the floor. My father was always telling us to sit with good posture. No slouching, or we'd end up bent over. But my mom wasn't bent over. Not now. She was upright in her chair, a statue of perfect posture, now rigidly smiling with her lips pursed together. Hugging herself.

My father's voice was falling and soft. "And now I have a new worry." Our living room went silent. "My boys aren't even safe in this house." No one shifted in their chair, except to lean toward my father's words. My mother remained rigid and upright, not leaning toward those words.

I knew what was coming next. I slithered backwards on my belly, like a snake. I slid my brothers along with me, down the hallway, into our bedroom. I didn't want them to hear any more scary stuff. They didn't have to be reminded of what happened a few days ago, last Sunday.

"Now you guys stay here. I'll be back, OK?" I closed the door to the bedroom before I returned to the landing. I left my brothers sitting next to each other on the side of my bed. Bill had snuggled his arm around little Alfie's shoulders. His lower lip was quivering. So was mine, but I didn't let them see.

By the time I returned to my lookout spot, Dad was talking about the event that had alarmed him and Aunt Frieda. When it happened, she called my other aunts and uncles who lived in town. Then Dad called our priest. They all decided our situation was worse than ever. Father Gallagher and Dr. Ishler quickly arranged the meeting which was now going on below. "Something has to be done about Sophie," they said. *Something has to be done about my Mom.*

My mother's voices had found a new place to hide. They ended up in our Sunday clothes that Mom made for us while sitting for hours at her Singer Sewing machine. The rusty orange corduroy suits had been contaminated by evil. She had to kill Satan. My mother could not let Alfie, Bill, and me wear the devil on our bodies. So she washed our Sunday suits in kerosene, killing those evil spirits. Then she rinsed everything in water; *holy water,* she said to me, as she made the sign of the cross over the sink. I helped carry the wet load outside to the clothesline, then handed her the wooden clothespins to keep our garments from flopping and dropping in the wind. Mom was happy about the wintry breeze. *The Holy Spirit was blowing its holy breath, cleansing our newly purified clothes.* Those dead voices? *Sacred Wind would blow them all away.*

So we wore our clean suits to church. My dad couldn't understand why we were so squirmy. It started with an itch before Mass had even begun. We couldn't sit still. Dad thought we just had to go to the bathroom, but that wasn't the problem. We got warm and itchy, all at the same time. We couldn't stop scratching. When we returned home after church, we couldn't wait to rip off our clothes. That's when Dad saw how raw and pink we were: how the margins of redness followed the pattern of our suits, as if painted exactly to the length of our sleeves, and to the rim of the collar around each of our necks.

My father was spinning with anger. His words sounded like English and German and sobbing and shouting, all at the same time. He was helpless in his confusion and alarm. When he confronted my mother, she said nothing. She was perfectly still. The quieter she got, the more agitated Dad became. Her face went into a quiet smile. Mom was at peace. She was keeping her boys safe from Satan. If my father didn't understand that, *he had to get right with Jesus.* We didn't understand either. But we sure were itchy and hot.

Our aunts and uncles hurried over to our house Sunday afternoon after they got the call from Aunt Frieda. There were whispers and nodded signals between them. They were trying to share secrets about my mother, so we wouldn't hear what they were saying. But my brothers and I were already skilled interpreters in the language of *what was unspoken.* They weren't keeping anything from us. We knew something was going to happen to our mother. But we had our own question: "What would happen to us?"

Dr. Ishler also came over to the house as soon as Dad called. He treated us with cold water rinses and salve. We were much better by evening. But when would it happen again? The doctor couldn't treat my mother's whirling mind because she didn't trust him; any medicine he tried to give her would be poison. *Dope,* she called it. Father Gallagher could do no more. His holy water was dried up, his prayers too tired to work. My father was frightened and exhausted, unable to think beyond the present moment.

Aunt Frieda told Dad she would help us. She had money to send Mom to the Mental Hospital at Danville. A decision was made, but it had to be explained to my mother. And so they had called this meeting. Now the gathering below went silent. My father had finished his review of the week's turmoil. Dr. Ishler studied my mother, as if memorizing her. He leaned toward her, entering her gaze, trying to catch her eye. He was soft with the way he used his voice, as if he was inviting her to come closer to him.

"Sophie?" He sang a gentle question with my mother's name. It seemed that he wanted her to be right there, as if he didn't want to scare her away. "What do you think of this talk we've been having?"

Mom's eyes skipped back and forth from my father to the doctor. Nothing else moved. She was perfectly still, smiling and hugging herself as before.

"Sophie?" Dr. Ishler repeated and waited. Then he lifted himself up and moved toward my mother, lightly sliding his chair behind him, no scraping on the floor. Mom squinted at her doctor, as if trying to figure out who he was. I could see how hard she was trying. The muscles in her face clenched.

"Sophie. Can you hear me?" He tried once more. Finally she looked at him, as if she'd figured out where his voice was coming from. Her rigid posture softened and so did her hard smile.

Dr. Ishler leaned back with Father Gallagher, Aunt Frieda and Dad. He glanced at them, then considered my mother's gaze again. She was still focused on Dr. Ishler, as if amused by him. After stroking his chin, he leaned toward her once more. He wanted my mother to know who was speaking to her.

"Well, then. I guess that settles it. We want to take you to the hospital, Sophie. They will take very good care of you. You'll be warm and toasty. Safe and clean and all that. Most of all, get some rest, OK?" The doctor sank back in his chair. "And your boys, Sophie; don't worry about your boys. We'll all look after them until you get better." My mother was still smiling, hugging herself.

The next morning she went to Danville, but she was not hugging herself.

Chapter 7

J oseph Droege's face is right in front of me. The scanned photograph is big, almost breathing on my computer screen. It's almost midnight and I've been staring at my grandfather long enough that I've lost track of the hour. He does not blink when my curser erases the blemish on his right eyebrow, nor does he wince when I refine the faded outline of his bald head against the gray background.

I'm working on the family album. Thanks to my new software, I am able to rejuvenate this old picture as I rub out watermarks and scars. My grandfather is looking quite presentable for this book of our family's history. He wears a dark suit. A black bowtie is silhouetted against his white dress shirt. His beard has been shaved off and his moustache is neatly trimmed for his portrait. Our heads are separated by no more than two feet. I've finished adjusting the contrast and brightness. Now I am intrigued by his gaze. He has my attention, as if trying to make eye contact with me.

But Joseph Droege is staring past me, at something in the distance. His smile is held back, guarded. His taut forehead folds into a subtle wrinkle, a single line of worry. His eyebrows are lifted as if he's looking for something in the dark. The deepened horizontal line between his lower lip and the prominence of his chin accentuates his uneasy countenance. My grandfather is waiting for something.

It's his troubled eyes that pull me into this picture, which has come alive for me. His left eye glitters with the glint of a tear. I'm viewing my grandfather through a veil of mystery, until I read my grandmother's inscription, penciled on the back of this photograph: *Remember Papa in your prayers.* The picture, taken one year before my grandfather's death, was used as a memorial portrait for his funeral.

I found Joseph Droege's death certificate in the Bureau of Vital Statistics in Dorchester, Massachusetts. It lists the following: *Place of death, Boston City Hospital; Address of deceased, 33 Beach Glen Street, Roxbury; Next of kin, wife, Regina Droege; Place of birth, Germany; Occupation of deceased, Temperer, Steel manufacturing; Date of death, February 24, 1919.*

Item 17 on the Medical Examiner's Certificate of Death consists of these words; *I HEREBY CERTIFY that I have investigated the death of the person above-named and that the CAUSE AND MANNER thereof are as follows:*

Chronic and Acute Nephritis, Burns Accidental. Workplace.
Clothing ignited by spark from stationary engine. Signed, T. Leary, M.D.
Place of Burial; St. Joseph's Cemetery, West Roxbury.
Date of Burial; February 26, 1919.

Joseph Droege lingered in pain for several days after his accident. His body shut down and his kidneys failed. Fire was the cause of his untimely death at the age of fifty. The careful foreman who guarded his fellow workers against danger, was himself a victim of his dangerous work.

At the time I was searching for my grandfather's vital documents, I made another discovery. In the files of catalogued death certificates, I was surprised to find one other Droege listed; Wilhelmina, the second child born to Joseph and Regina Droege.

Her death certificate indicates that she died at the age of 18, on October 10, 1918, barely four months before her father's death. For eight days she suffered from influenza, which progressed to three days of pneumonia. Aunt Minnie was one of forty million deaths in the Spanish Influenza Epidemic of 1918.

For ten years, Minnie was a huge part of young Sophie's life. When my mother reminisced about her childhood, she would happily talk about her big sister, who was good-natured and full of laughter. Minnie was employed as a secretary for the one year of her working life. More important, she was a second mother in the family, helping her little sister with homework and catechism lessons. Every picture shows her face as confident, unguarded in its friendliness. Her loss was sudden and unexpected, a terrible blow to her parents and the entire family, and especially wrenching for my mother, who could not understand why God would take her father and her sister, in such an abrupt manner.

Minnie and her father were now together, at St. Joseph's Cemetery in West Roxbury. I decided to visit both of them, for the purpose of gathering some pictures for the family album. I found their gravesite on St. Patrick's Avenue, Section A. They share a common headstone. Under the family name of Droege, *Joseph* and *Wilhelmina* are engraved, first names only, along with their years of birth and death: for Joseph, 1869 to 1919; for his daughter, 1900 to 1918. They are in the company of endless rows of monuments and headstones with a common date, 1918. Evidence of The Great Influenza Epidemic surrounded Minnie and her father.

Young Sophie was only ten years old when she suffered the loss of her big sister and her father, with four months between their deaths. From that time on, the sight of flames reflected images of the fires of hell for my mother. Even the flickered warmth of the fireplace triggered her fearful remembrance of her father's terrible accident. My aunts and uncles told me that after she returned from school each day, she would wait at the piano for her father to come home from work. She seemed distant from her brothers and sisters, detached from the reality of her father's untimely death. After weeks of untethered floating in her isolated galaxy, Sophie was finally gathered in by the pull of her waiting family, but her siblings said she was never quite the same. It was as if she found herself in a wobbling orbit, most peaceful when she escaped into her own quiet night.

Chapter 8

There was palpable density in that month of November when my mother was sent away. On a dreary Saturday morning, my father and I drove to Danville for our first visit since she had been admitted to the hospital. Looking out the window of Dad's black Chevy, I could see a veil of clouds misting the fields, blurring the rolling hills beyond. The weighted gray of the Pennsylvania sky felt as if it were ready to be drained of rain or snow, whichever the day's temperature called for. Only then would the light filter through, and it would be pale and thin at best. Summer was gone.

Even though our trip took longer than two hours, there were few words between us. I could hardly respond when Dad tried to talk with me. I had no words to describe what I felt. It was probably the same for him. Listening to the car engine's drone was easier than conversation. My brothers remained at home with Aunt Frieda and Aunt Regina. Being the oldest, I went with Dad, whether I wanted to or not. My father made the decision for me.

The cold illumination caused me to feel restless and uneasy; I was at the mercy of something I could not understand. At the age of eight, I had memorized my own mantra about the burden of that heavy month. *There's something about November gray; November teaches me to pray.*

Dad had driven that route just a week earlier, when he delivered Mom to her new residence. Aunt Frieda and Aunt Regina had gone on that ride, to be company for my parents. Regina rode in the back of the car with Mom. She was the youngest of these three sisters, soft spoken and easy with my mother. Dad said he needed the extra passengers: one sister to calm my mother, the other to distract him with conversation.

Now my father seemed confused with the drive. I'd never seen him lost before. And this was the man who was always telling us, "One thing at a time, boys. First things first. Don't let your mind wander." So we pulled into the first gas station we found on the road between Lewisburg and Danville. From the car I could see Dad nodding his head as the attendant pointed in the direction we were already headed.

Five minutes later we stopped at a second station, this time for the gas Dad forgot to get at the first stop. We finally got back on the road with a full tank of fuel and new directions. Once again, the engine's monotone groan filled my ear.

We'd hardly pulled back on Route 45 when he swerved the car into the parking lot of the Forty-Five Diner and Grill. "How 'bout a late breakfast?" He clapped my knee. "It would be good for us. Got to be hungry by now." We'd left State College without any food because Dad was too nervous to eat, and he wanted to get an early start. By the time we had settled Bill and Alfie with our relatives, it was too late for breakfast. Now that we were almost in Danville, it seemed as if we had all the time in the world.

We had pancakes and bacon. Real maple syrup, too. It tasted better than the *Karo* syrup we had at home. Dad said the real stuff was too expensive to buy with our usual groceries. He had a refill of his coffee after he finished his first cup. Dad hardly ever had seconds on his coffee, but he did today. He took it in little sips, like our conversation, one or two words at a time. Now it seemed as if we were in no rush. Then he held up my empty glass for the waitress. "More orange juice for my boy?" He said it would be good for me, even though I wasn't thirsty.

Finally we got back in the car, but only after my father made me go to the bathroom, whether I needed to or not. Dad opened the road map before he turned on the ignition. Maybe he wanted to be sure the gas station man knew what he was talking about when he gave us directions a little while ago. He finally backed the car out of the parking space and eased it onto the road. A minute after getting back on Route 45, he pulled up on the side of the highway. With the car idling, he unfolded the map again, to be sure we were going east on Route 45 so we could get to 11 North. "I think there's some new road work since last week. Scenery's not all that familiar." My father's eyes were squinting straight ahead, as if driving through a rainy night, following headlights on a slippery road. He never really looked at the map.

Our old Chevy chugged through the countryside, finally reaching the outskirts of Danville. After winding through the farmlands of fallen corn and cut hay, we saw the Gothic tower, dark and jagged in the distance. The slate sky shivered me.

The access road was lined with trees, standing at tall attention, like rigid sentries. The building was a dark fortress getting bigger and bigger, as if it were moving toward us faster than we were approaching it. Its massive presence swallowed the dim sky. On top of the steeple, a faceless angel cast a dark shadow with its rigid wings, as if ready to crash to earth if it tried to leap into flight.

Dad slowed down, almost stalling as we approached the parking lot. He drove the car around the circular driveway twice, looking for the best place to park. Even though there were only a few cars at our side of the lot, he parked at the farthest edge. We got out and locked the car door, then trudged toward the entrance. But my father decided to go back to the car for an umbrella. Twice he stopped, opening and closing it, just to make sure it worked. Just in case it rained. I knew it was too cold for rain.

Finally, we were at the gate to my mother's world. The door was dark wood, heavy and hard to open. A nurse directed us along a dimly lit corridor to the main hall. We softly walked into a huge room where the patients were already in a circle of rocking chairs, their backs against the pale green walls. Their faces were suspicious and nervous, as they scrutinized the visitors clustered in front of them. Some of the residents seemed to shrink into the background, as if their company were too close to them. I marched in perfect time with my father, hiding my footsteps in his.

I saw my mother on the far side of the hall, swaying in her rocking chair. Her bent silhouette was softened by pale afternoon light, glaring through windows, subdivided by metal bars. Knowing we shouldn't startle her, we moved quietly. When Mom realized someone was standing in front of her, she stopped rocking and looked into my eyes. There was no melting of her frozen stare, only the upward lift of her eyebrows, confusion rippling her forehead. Was she running through a list of names? She studied my face for a moment and looked away, puzzled. She did not resume her rocking. My mother did not know me.

"Hi Mom, it's me. It's Carl."

She narrowed her eyes, squeezing her memory as she turned away. Before I could say anything, she came back with a suspicious gaze, squinting through her wire-rimmed glasses. Soon her face softened into blinking recognition. I thought of summer fireflies in our backyard, and how they flicker light into night: on, off; on, off. My mom's eyes were exactly like that, bright and dark, bright and dark, until her blinking slowed into a smile. She pulled me against her. I hugged my mother and the rocking chair.

Dad and I dragged two wooden chairs close to my mother. They screeched on the floor a little, causing Mom to stop rocking and sit up straight. I waited for my father to talk. Mom's eyes were glued on me, as if to lose sight of me would be to forget me. I broke the silence and talked about my brothers, rambling on and on about school or anything else that came into my mind. Words were no longer stuck in my throat.

"I make sure we clean our rooms, Mom. Every day. Even before I go to school." I talked fast, trying to keep something in the empty space between us. "I go to church every morning, Mom. Father Gallagher says our class of altar boys is ready to graduate. Soon I'll be serving morning mass. Alone. All by myself." Catching my breath, I talked about Boy Scouts, Bill, Alfie, and my homework assignments. I talked and talked because I was afraid that silence would break our connection.

When my father spoke, his words hung a long time in the air, as if waiting for my mother to recognize them. Sometimes we huddled together, our heads leaning in, as if all three of us were listening to a long distance call on the same phone.

At last she started to ask her questions. *The rosary?* "Yes, Mom. We've been saying the rosary. All of us. Every night before we go to sleep." *Housework?* "Yup. I won't forget my chores." She smiled at me as if I were still far away, barely recognizable in the distance. Then our conversation stopped, suspended in the air. The silence between us pushed me to say something, to speed up the slow-moving minutes of our visit. But now I remained silent.

By mid-afternoon, the low angle of November light stretched nervous shadows across the cold floor. I began to squirm in my chair. I felt a chill on my shoulders, the way it feels when dark clouds pull a curtain across the sun on a fall afternoon. The whispered conversation circling the big hall dropped into a long pause, with everyone holding their breath at the same time, as if a radio had been unplugged. Dad and I looked at each other. A spoken word would have shattered that stillness, like a glass vase dropped on the stone floor.

To my left, one rocking chair scraped and groaned. At first the rhythm was cautious, reluctantly tapping an unfamiliar solo. Then it gained its own thready pulse, nervously rocking back and forth. Like a timid chorus, the other rockers creaked in. My mother went rigid; her vigilant eyes flicked side to side, softly alarmed. Then she gripped the armrests and began her own dance, at first hesitant, then with accelerated cadence, as if she were catching up to her companions, afraid of being left behind. The noise drummed bigger and louder, spinning around the room like a whirlpool, swirling me into it. My mother rocked close to me, then away, leaning in and out of the turbulence washing around us. She was strangely present, then withdrawn with the swaying chair, somewhere between me and a faraway place that scared me.

Then a soft murmur, a hubbub, words I'd never heard before. The voices lifted, layering into a strange and primitive chanting, as if pleading to be found. Calling and answering themselves and each other. In my mother's eyes, *where am I?*

Now my mother and her congregation were swaying together, each in patient rhythm with the singing. I bent my head down and held my hands over my ears, but I could not escape that moaning which filled the heavy air. I heard a rush of flapping wings, like the ruffled air under my homing pigeons, circling and trembling the air until they found a safe place to land. In the twilight above, I imagined my mother's soul quivering, searching for a familiar place to rest. Her eyes glowed right through me. I tried to slide back in my chair, but my legs could not push against the wobbly floor beneath me.

I remember softly crying, and how, when she heard me, my mother slowed down her rocking, then stopped. She stared at me, confused, then pleasantly surprised to find me there. Mom smiled at Dad and me. Her eyes were two lights shining, no longer through us, but on us. Breathing became my part of the conversation. My mother kept smiling.

The chorus gradually diminished its persistent hum and sway. Now the music was soft, out of tune. I was getting goose bumps, either from the cold afternoon, or from the sound. I shivered. My father fidgeted with his watch and nodded toward the door. He buttoned up his sweater. My mother's eyes worried back and forth between us.

Dad slowly rose from his chair but she didn't see him. Her eyes were fixed on my face. When I lifted up from my seat, Mom leaned into me. Still seated in her rocker, she circled my waist with her arms and tearfully embraced me, would not release me. I was afraid that she would not let me go, and I was afraid she would let me go. My mother wailed while her swaying and chanting companions halted, as if signaling *amen,* abruptly suspending their afternoon prayers. Rocking chairs locked in their arc of motion. Hubbub and murmur hovered in the air, as if paying homage to my mother. The only sound was her sobbing, muffled in the folds of my heavy wool sweater.

After a few minutes, Mom was silent. She'd released me, her arms now limp, hands clasped in her lap. Her head was bowed and I leaned down into her line of sight. *Remember me, Mom?* Her eyes lifted, but they were no longer connected with me. My mother looked at me and did not see me; once again, she did not know me. My father and I hugged her and mumbled our goodbyes, more for ourselves, than for her.

Cautiously at first, then with gathering momentum, the rocking resumed. The mumbled words started up again, soft at first, then loud, like a full chorus, singing my father and me to the door. I stopped and turned to face my mother. I waved. I would have blown a kiss, but she didn't see me.

My mother had already said *Goodbye.*

Chapter 9

Joseph Droege's death brought a period of unrelenting grief for my mother's family. The heavy burden of responsibility pressed against his wife's shoulders and did not let up. Ten children lost their big sister, and less than a half year after Minnie's death, they were fatherless. Their sorrow was underlined by the loss of Joseph's salary and the financial uncertainty which followed. My grandmother's faith anchored her children against the emotional tide which swirled around them. Her resilience and determination left little time for self-pity.

She was most helped by her son Aloysius, the oldest of the children. Uncle Al was already studying to be a priest. When his father died, he came home from the seminary. There were nine younger brothers and sisters at home. Mary would be born five months after her father's death. There was never a question about Uncle Al's new place in the family; he was now the father, especially for young Sophie.

My grandfather's death certificate lists his residence as 33 Beech Glen Street, Roxbury, in the Mission Hill section of Boston. Shortly after the tragedy, the Droege family moved a few blocks away to a larger house on Thornton Street. My grandmother had the children share their bedrooms in order to free up space for rental income. One or two boarders were always in residence. Each child contributed something for the family's welfare. Those who were old enough found work after school, while the younger children took care of the laundry, cooking, and cleaning at home.

The boys made a dorm of the third floor. Since there was no heat in that part of the house, they used the fireplace to warm up bricks, which were tucked in their beds just before going to sleep. My uncles told me they sometimes forgot to remove the foot warmers before crawling into bed. Their bruised toes reminded them not to repeat this mistake.

One responsibility was clearly shared by all: no one could be casual about their education. The older brothers and sisters helped the younger children with their homework. Only their best effort was acceptable. The children attended Catholic schools, right through high school. The vigilant nuns were constantly on guard against any academic laziness, and if that wasn't enough, Regina Droege had to be answered to.

As the older brothers and sisters graduated from school, they found reliable employment. With everyone contributing, the family slowly regained its financial stability. Several years after Joseph Droege's death, the family emerged from financial hardship. But their situation remained tenuous. They needed every dollar of income they could earn.

My mother wanted to be a secretary. As a little girl, she was neat, organized, and paid careful attention to details. She was a reliable bookkeeper, working part-time at several local businesses, even as she tended to her school work. Then, at the age of 18, Sophie Droege gathered up her courage for an adventure. She went off to California to work for her Uncle Emil.

My grandfather's older brother had come to America several years before he did. Once settled, Emil Droege sent for his younger brother, Joseph. They first lived in New York City, but my Great Uncle Emil, being hard working and restless, soon departed for California to make his fortune. He ended up in San Bernadino, where he founded the Santa Fe Oil Company. Soon he owned and operated a small fleet of delivery trucks and a gasoline station. By the time any competition came along, Emil had more than his share of the market for home heating fuel. He also supplied gasoline for cars, trucks, and motorboats.

Uncle Emil was a generous man, especially after his brother's death. Whenever he and his wife Frieda came east to visit Joseph's family, they arrived with suitcases packed with shoes and clothing. My mother said the refrigerator was always well stocked when Emil visited, and the family never ate so well as when the California relatives came to town. My grandmother somehow had extra money for family bills, long after Emil had returned to California.

Seven or eight years after Joseph Droege's death, Emil sent word that he had employment available at Santa Fe Oil. The timing meshed perfectly with my mother's graduation from high school. She was encouraged to travel to California, because her siblings thought she was starting to "keep to herself." Now she could help out in her uncle's office as a secretary and bookkeeper, and possibly meet some new friends. The timing could not be better for young Sophie's confidence.

At the same time, Uncle Al was offered an important management position in Emil's business. He was recently married, having abandoned his idea of becoming a priest. He and his wife Caroline welcomed a change of scenery. With my mother's oldest brother keeping her company, she felt secure and safe. Sophie went west with Al and Caroline.

Two old photographs show Uncle Emil's oil business. In one picture, three big delivery trucks are lined up in front of the garage and gas station. Someone had penciled the year 1927 on the picture's margin. The owner's name is boldly lettered across the front of the freshly painted buildings. There can be no doubt about who is boss of The Santa Fe Oil Company. Emil poses like a bulky statue, accompanied by his poodle, Fido. He rests an elbow on the fender of one of the trucks. Although he's small in the picture, a smile is on his face. *Mine,* he seems to be saying, *and I earned it.*

The other picture is of a delivery truck that has been decorated for a parade. A huge wreath of flowers and ferns is looped around the grill. On top of the cab is an enormous pumpkin. Dressed in white and standing on the side of the tanker are seven men, each one holding a bouquet of flowers. A large sign announces The San Bernadino Night Ball Team, sponsored by Santa Fe Oil Company. All the men are grinning, as if they just won their baseball championship.

My mother is also in the picture. She stands out for two reasons; she is beautiful, and she is the only person not smiling.

She poses on the running board, by the passenger side of the cab. A white sailor hat is perfectly centered on her head, and she wears a long white dress, which flows easily from her shoulders to her ankles. A shining belt circles her waist and ties into a large bow on her right hip. If only she'd give the hat a slight tilt and align her eyes with the camera lens; if she'd curl the corners of her lips just a little, her smile would bring her own light into the picture.

But her eyes look past the photographer. Something else has her attention. She's alone. She's in the middle of ten people and she's all alone.

My mother returned from California about 1929 or early 1930, having been away from the rest of her family for over two years. She was now about 21 years old, and she was more than homesick. Something else was going on; something new and strange. Aunt Regina told me about the radio.

After a period of dependable bookkeeping for Santa Fe Oil, Sophie started having trouble concentrating on the columns of figures. The customers' accounts became a confusion of numbers, as if their manipulation by addition and subtraction was now energized by a mysterious force beyond her control. When the radio played, my mother thought she was receiving instructions about those numbers. Signals were flowing through sound waves that no one else could hear. When that happened, she could only stare at the numbers, waiting for a voice to tell her what to do. Would something bad happen if she made a mistake? But her worries were dismissed; relatives and friends assured her that she was simply tired. No doubt she was just lonely for her family back in Boston. It was time to go home.

Her brothers and sisters welcomed her home. Sophie was happy to be reunited with her mother. For a few weeks, she rested and settled in with the family. She attended daily mass. Soon she went to work in a small employment agency in Boston, answering the phone and typing letters for the owner. This was better than the job in California; no bookkeeping, no numbers, and no radio interference. No direction from a mysterious source.

Sophie joined her brothers and sisters when they attended dances or social events at Holy Trinity Church. Young Clemens came along with his new American family to these same events. He'd first met Sophie in 1924, one year after his arrival in Boston, when he was 21 and she was only 16. But she'd made an impression on him. He didn't forget her, even when she set out for California. After her return, they were older by five or six years and they renewed their friendship.

My mother's siblings encouraged her to "get out of the house" once in a while. It was time for her to socialize with people other than her own family. Clemens Schoenebeck was respectful and polite, hard-working and dependable. He didn't swear. He never drank excessively. He was Catholic. Wouldn't such a reliable gentleman make a fine husband for Sophie?

Clemens and Sophie began spending time together. My father occasionally borrowed a car, so the young couple could go for a picnic in the Blue Hills Reservation, on the southeastern border of Boston. Sometimes Sophie went with my dad's family for a day trip to Lake Massabesic, in southern New Hampshire. Most of their time together was shared with the two families on Sunday afternoons, when they gathered for dinner. Afterward, they sang and joked and performed skits and plays. *Gemütlichkeit* was the goal; fun and laughter, nourished by tasty German food and home-brewed beer. Although the young couple was always in jovial company, they were rarely alone.

Their relationship was once again interrupted when my mother's family moved to State College, Pennsylvania. Frieda, the oldest sister, had gone there shortly after being married. Her husband, George, had opened a grocery store. In his spare time, Uncle George cut hair for the Penn State students. He became so busy that he soon gave up the grocery store and opened the first big, modern barbershop in town.

Smith's Barber Shop was located on Allen Street, in prime territory for the students and the local residents, both populations growing rapidly. Aunt Frieda opened up a hair salon for women, upstairs, at the same location. She and her husband were popular and very good at their work. Soon they were the owners of a thriving business. Even with three or four additional barbers in my uncle's shop, the chairs in the waiting area were fully occupied with town residents and students, waiting their turn, paging through tattered magazines and textbooks, listening to the local news on WMAJ. Since Frieda needed help with her own schedule, she employed several women as hairdressers.

My uncle and aunt soon purchased a big home on the outskirts of the Penn State campus. Frieda missed her family in Boston and invited the Droeges to come and live with them in State College. There was enough room for my grandmother and six of her children, including my mother. They would all be together again, and she would certainly have work in her salon for some of her sisters. Sophie was about 23 years old when her family moved to Pennsylvania.

Because my father was working full-time and finishing up with Trade school in Boston, he and Sophie were forced into a long distance relationship. Over the next few years my dad did his best to keep Sophie's attention. He traveled to Pennsylvania whenever he could borrow a car, often accompanied by one of his adopted brothers. The nearly five hundred-mile trip was a journey of endurance, given the roads of that time. But it was not an obstacle for my father, who was determined to marry Sophie. In time, he had his way.

My parents' wedding picture was taken in October, 1935. My father and mother are flanked by the members of their wedding party. On my mother's left are her sisters, Regina, Theresa, and Mary. They look elegant in their full-length dresses, each of them holding a large bouquet of flowers. The three sisters are smiling, but their happy expressions seem a bit practiced.

To my dad's right are Mom's brothers, Joseph, Aloyisius, and William. At the far end is another Uncle Bill, this one married to Mom's sister Margaret. The men stand at attention, formal in posture and attire. Their shoes shine more brightly than their smiles. They look serious, perhaps self-conscious. Uncle Al's small children, Caroline and Tommy, are flower girl and ring-bearer. Dressed in white, my young cousins are glowing silhouettes against the dark tuxedos standing tall behind them. They bring needed light into this picture.

My father's face is in profile. He's turned his head to his left, smiling down at his new wife. He's slender, standing nearly six feet tall in his proud posture. His hair is dark and neatly trimmed. My mother looks up at him. At first glance her smile appears open and unguarded, her eyes dutifully attending my father's gaze. But there is a delicate lift to her eyebrows that causes me to wonder if she questions what she sees in my father's eyes. This is a smile that became familiar to me in my childhood; a forced smile, which was not what it appeared to be.

Her wedding gown, elegant in its simple pattern, was a gift of her mother's meticulous hand. Her bride's bouquet is in her left hand, and she curls the fingers of her free hand through the crook of her husband's left elbow. Something about the way my father's arm is expectantly held out for my mother suggests that they are a bit too tentative with each other. Perhaps Clemens is mildly surprised that Sophie's grip seems secure, and with good reason.

In the six weeks prior to the wedding, my mother answered none of my father's letters. She ignored his phone calls. When my father arrived in State College for the wedding, he confronted her about her failed communication. He was deeply hurt. Instead of trying to make amends, my mother flew into a rage. She tried to call the wedding off but her family intervened, convincing her that this marriage was in her best interest. And theirs.

In his old age, my father sometimes brooded over this period of his life. Had he made a mistake? His sad reflection stopped when he told my brothers and me that our presence made it all worthwhile. When I view this wedding picture through the filter of my mother's last minute uncertainty, I look again at the expressions on the faces of my uncles and aunts. Maybe the men have good reason for their guarded smiles, and perhaps my aunts are smiling too much. Had they made a mistake in second guessing my mother's decision?

After the wedding, my parents returned to Boston. My father had been working as a machinist at the Watertown Arsenal, one of the country's largest manufacturers of military weapons. With the Great Depression still clouding the economy, my father was reluctant to give up his employment. My mother wanted to stay in State College with her family, but it was not to be.

Sophie and Clemens were invited into the home of Carl and Mary Peters. They'd grown up with my dad in Germany and welcomed him upon his arrival in America. My parents could have stayed with the Peters indefinitely, but it didn't take long for Sophie to find fault with Mary. She could do nothing right, as far as my mom was concerned. Even worse, she perceived Mary as being a *Lukewarm Catholic,* who was not passionate enough about her faith. A new living arrangement was inevitable. My parents moved to a nearby apartment in West Roxbury, conveniently located for church and public transportation for Dad's work. Mom worked briefly at several secretarial jobs. But she didn't last long at any of them. She complained that too many of her co-workers were immoral. Their thoughts were unclean and my mother could read their sinful minds.

The date penciled on another black and white photo tells me it was taken after the wedding. My mother and father are sitting on a rocky ledge, on top of a hill. Lake, mountain, and sky fade into the distant background. They are dressed as if they have just come from church. It was not unusual for them to go on hikes or picnics after mass. My father wears a dark suit, white shirt, and necktie. My mother is in a simple black dress, which nearly reaches her ankles. A light-colored shawl drapes warmth over her shoulders. They are looking off to the photographer's right, their faces in profile, barely acknowledging the camera.

Clemens rests his left elbow on his knee. He is looking downward, as if he is studying the path for their return hike. His gaze is not focused on the distant scenery. Sophie's hands are clasped together in her lap. They could be folded in prayer. Her gaze is tilted upward of my father's stare. Neither one of them is smiling. My mother's expression is empty and fixed. She's looking far away, and she *seems* far away.

On my father's face is an expression I've come to know in my childhood: he looks defeated. The set of his mouth tells me his facial muscles cannot curl into a smile. He is not far away. He's right there, unable to step out of his sadness. It surrounds him.

My father's right arm circles my mother's neck, with his fingers lightly patting the shawl against her shoulder. Even though his arm holds my mother, he is angled ever so slightly away. My mother sits straight up and down, not leaning into him. They are touching, but there is space between.

Within the year, my mother became pregnant, and I was born in June of 1937, at nearby Faulkner Hospital in Jamaica Plain. I have found an old picture of my mother and me. We're aged in sepia, both of us blurry around our edges. I've just come home from the hospital, wrapped in a white blanket, eyes closed, yawning. My mother holds my tiny hand in her right hand, while her left arm cradles me against her bosom. Though she looks thin and tired, she gazes down at me with a smile of devotion and love, and possibly, a bit of amazement. These many years later, I still feel the warmth of her in the ambered light of this photograph.

Two and a half years passed before Bill was born. We still lived in Massachusetts, but my mother was increasingly unhappy being away from her family in Pennsylvania. Shortly after my brother was born, we moved to State College. Uncle George had arranged an interview for my father, who was worried about finding a new job. Dad ended up at the machine shop at Penn State University, where he would build instruments for the scientists in the School of Mineral Sciences. Aunt Frieda found a place for us to live on Beaver Avenue, where we rented our home for about five years. My youngest brother, Alfred, was born a few years after we moved to State College.

Many years after my mother died, I found a Christmas card she'd given to my wife, Bonnie. On the front of the card, the Blessed Mother is holding Baby Jesus. Her face is turned upward, her radiant smile directed toward heaven. One hand strokes her baby's head, the other snuggles him against her breast. On the inside left page is a prayer, *The Magnificat*: *My soul doth magnify the Lord: And my spirit hath rejoiced in God my Savior.* The facing page is printed with a Christmas greeting: *May you keep the joy of Christmas all year, within your heart!*

At first I thought it was an accident that I found this card. But I think not. It's a postcard mailed from the past, with a clue about the mystery of my mother.

Scrawled on the back page, in my mother's handwriting, are several notations of family information: my birthday, June 16, 1937; the date and location of my youngest brother's wedding; the church holy day celebrated on my daughter Kristen's birthday. One more notation whispers like a whiff of incense of my mother's duty to God. Along with my date of birth, she has penned the date of my conception: September 8, 1936; the Feast of the Birthday of the Blessed Mother.

How was it that my mother knew the exact day that my father fertilized my new life within her womb? Was the conjugal act between my parents such an atypical event that it could be recalled with such certainty? And what can I make of this holy day, the Blessed Mother's Birthday?

Sex was never discussed in my family. As my brothers and I grew up, it seemed that any behavior suggestive of personal intimacy was bad. That very word, *intimacy*, took on a connotation of sinfulness. Any teaching of sexuality was veiled behind the nebulous curtain of the Baltimore Catechism; the nuns and priests were equally vague and defensive. It should have been sufficient that we accept the revelation that God made us in his image and likeness. What more did we need to know? In our youthful congregation of three brothers, there was no room for a *Doubting Thomas*.

This Christmas card carried a message for me. I believe my mother came to the marriage bed in obedience to God's will: *Go forth and multiply*. It was her duty to provide sheep for The Shepherd. Above the headboard, the crucified Jesus stood watch over my parents. Mary and Joseph stared from one wall, Saint Francis of Assisi from the other. I think that's why she boldly inked that Christmas card with the date of my conception, proof that she was carrying out God's will. I believe the Father, Son, and Holy Ghost were alive and always present in my parents' bedroom.

Chapter 10

I saw little of my mother after visiting her in the hospital. For the next six months, Danville State was her home. She might have stayed longer if it hadn't been for my father's request that she come home early. Shortly after she went away, he began to question himself: was the decision to send her away unfair, and could he have tried harder to fix her? Dad's first plea for her release was turned down because Mom's doctors and nurses were worried about her safety and how it would be for the rest of us.

Everything had changed without her. Sometimes my brothers and I laughed together, but it was a sharing both tentative and uncertain. At times our home was as quiet as my return trip from Danville with Dad, when neither of us could speak. What would happen now? My brothers and I had learned our own watchful way of existing with Mom's unpredictable moods, like nervous weathermen scouting the horizon for early warning of her storms. Now that she was gone, would we have more sunshine than rain? Before Mom went away we had learned the need for shallow breathing, leaving most of the air for her. Now there was too much oxygen and we didn't know how to take it in.

My brothers and I tried to organize our own lives. We set out next day's clothes before bedtime. Bill and I were diligent about doing our schoolwork. When finished, we stacked our books and papers on the kitchen table so we wouldn't forget anything. Alfie helped make up our beds. Before he went to sleep, my father made sandwiches for our next day's lunch. He woke us up early, prepared breakfast, and got us ready for each new day.

Bill and I took the bus to school, while Alfie spent the day with Aunt Regina. Her children were too young for school, but Bobby and Carol were good company for Alfie. Sometimes Dickie Ott's mother met Bill and me at the bus stop. We spent the afternoon with our neighbor, playing or doing our homework until my father returned home with our little brother.

Bill, Alfie and I drew even closer. Even in my mother's absence, her illness was like a ghost napping in the house. We tried our best to not wake it up. But when agitated, the unpredictable presence rounded us up as if we were a herd of three sheep, always within close range of each other. As we tip toed around Mom, we kept each other away from the dark shadows surrounding her, but the needed clearance could change from day to day. Without her, we didn't know where the dangerous territory started and where it ended.

The three of us had become fluent in the language of my mother's strange country, which she entered and exited with ease and unpredictability. We'd mastered a vocabulary she wanted to hear in a dialect soothing to her, as if singing an ongoing lullaby, each of us in harmony with the other. One shrill note would startle my mother. In a heartbeat she could move from the safe distance of her trance, to being too present in our lives: she'd found all of our hiding places.

My brothers and I slept with one eye open. In my mother's absence, we were unsure of where her companions were. Dad said everything was in her mind, that her imagination allowed the voices to exist. But what about God and the saints and the Blessed Mother? If they were real, why wouldn't they protect us? Were they also something else in the imagination, like Mom's tormentors?

We continued to sleep with a light on in the hallway.

*   *   *

That winter was long and cold, meager in ways we did not understand. My father tried to save gasoline money by riding his old Schwinn bicycle to work. Because of rationing for the war, fuel was hard to get. Bill and I came home from school one afternoon to find Dad already there. His right arm was in a sling, his forearm in a cast. On his ride to work, he almost went through a stop sign. With all that was on his mind, he was probably thinking about something other than riding his bike. When he tried to put on his brakes, the tires wouldn't grab. He slid on a patch of ice and crashed against the curb.

Dad was out of work. He had been working overtime hours so he could pay some of the bills that were piling up. Now that he was home, we didn't have to stay with relatives or neighbors after school. With one good arm, he couldn't do his usual work around the house. He couldn't even drive to Danville. My father didn't like to ask people for help, but Uncle George and Uncle Joe offered to take him to visit my mother.

He took us down to the cellar and showed us how to keep the heat going. Bill and I shoveled coal and hauled out the cinders and ashes. Before his accident, Dad always went downstairs by himself to stoke the fire. Cold winter mornings, we could hear the scrape of his shovel plunging into the coal bin, and the unloading thrust clanking against the furnace door. Soon the pipes and radiators groaned and creaked with early warmth. We stayed under the covers until the air softened its bite. Now with Dad injured, my brothers and I were the early risers. Dad was counting on us to take over the responsibility of chasing away the morning cold.

We cleaned the supper dishes. Bill and I washed and rinsed while Alfie did the drying. Now he was really helping out with the chores. We used to tell him to look out for dangerous animals, just to give him something to do. Now the only creature around was our toy lamb, Agnus Dei. Thanks to Bill's irreverence, we soon had a new name for it: *Plain Old Agnes.* White as the snow outside our windows, the lamb was Mom's reminder that our souls had to be unblemished, free of sin. Maybe this was part of God's plan, because with all our chores we were too busy to even think of doing anything bad.

Dad had trouble cooking one-handed, but we didn't starve. My aunts and uncles brought prepared meals. I made sandwiches for Bill and me to take to school. I had a special lunchbox that Mom got from the church sale when she bought Sweet Jesus. It was black with a silver handle. Mom bought it because it belonged to one of the nuns, Sister Margaret Mary. On it she had stenciled three silver letters: *JMJ:* Jesus, Mary, Joseph; the holy family. Mom always placed a holy medal in the bottom of my lunchbox.

Dr. Ishler said Dad's arm was healing quickly. He placed him in a lighter cast, the sling no longer needed. Soon he would be able to go back to work. As a machinist at Penn State University, my father could build instruments for the scientists, that no one else could make. Dad could do anything with his hands. People said he was an artist with his work. Dean Steidle, in charge of the School of Mineral Science, liked my father and respected him because of his talent and hard work. Dad's boss called and told him to come back, even if he couldn't do everything he did before. He could plan his projects and help with instructions for his fellow machinists, until he was completely healed. Even though the University paid him during his disability, Dad was anxious to start earning his paycheck again. "Got to earn my keep, boys. Money doesn't just fall off the trees, you know."

Before he broke his arm, Dad had made a Christmas tree holder of solid brass. Big and heavy, it was shaped like an upside down chalice, with its flared open end resting heavily on the floor. He machined three special screws that could be adjusted against the trunk of the tree, keeping it straight within the cylinder that held the water. On that first Christmas without Mom, he decided it would be a good time for us boys to learn to polish the tree holder. At first the task was a chore; we'd rather be outside, playing in the snow. But soon it became a ritual, as important as decorating the tree.

Alfie smeared on the cream with a folded rag. It quickly dried on the brass, making the surface dull and cloudy. Bill and I took turns rubbing it with a soft towel. "Don't rush it, boys." Dad showed us how to stroke the brass up and down, then back and forth around the curved neck, leaving no smudges. "Patience, boys. The job isn't worth doing, unless you do it right." With each stroke the surface got brighter, like brushing away the fog. The more it shined, the more I wanted to shine it. My hands smoothed over its heavy form, feeling how my father made it one with the tree, *feeling my father's hands beneath my hands.* Now I took the twice-folded cloth and rubbed until it was like sunlight in my eyes, blurring my vision with a fluid glow.

I stood in my father's light.

Chapter 11

Easter Sunday came in the middle of April and Dad got us up early for church. Once we were in our Sunday clothes, he told us to stay clean and neat afterward. "No rough-housing today, boys. I want you to look presentable."

We would be going to Aunt Frieda and Uncle George's house for Sunday dinner and an Easter egg hunt. It was a day of sunshine and unexpected warmth. White and yellow tulips were in full bloom. Early buds were greening on the skeletons of maples and oaks, as if their branches had raked tiny leaves from the sky. A cardinal darted from tree to tree, like a scarlet flame trying to start a fire. Spring was boasting its arrival.

We gathered around the dining room table at noon, two families minus my mother. My cousins, George and Joe, were on the other side of the table. They were allowed to be comical at the table, making jokes and silly faces. Once we knew we were allowed to laugh, we tried to be funny, but we couldn't match my cousins. My brothers and I were so excited about sitting down at a Sunday meal, that we practically swallowed the smell of roast ham in the tasty air. Aunt Frieda decorated the table with glinty silverware and flowery cloth napkins. The table was loaded with so much food that we didn't know what to devour first. Bowls of mashed potatoes, squash, and gravy were placed between trays of green beans and carrots, everything steaming like clouds we could eat. Crinkled glasses sparkled the afternoon sunshine into our ginger ale.

*Bless us O Lord, and these thy gifts...*Uncle George started our prayers before we grabbed our knives and forks. Bill and Alfie and I kept waiting for him to do some add-ons, the way Mom glued her extra requests onto any prayers we said. But once he finished the blessing, it was done. We could eat!

Whenever Dad or one of us boys got up to help, Aunt Frieda said "Sit. You boys just relax and enjoy your meal. That's your job. My job is to take care of you boys." It was even better than the time when Dad took us to Howard Johnson's, on our way back from a visit with Uncle Bill in Philadelphia. We tried to help the waitress by clearing the table, but my father told us to just look at the menu with the pictures of 28 flavors of ice cream. Dad said we could order two different kinds if we couldn't decide on a favorite.

After Easter dinner, we sat in the playroom for a while because Aunt Frieda said we had to digest our meal. Otherwise the blood from our brain would go directly to our stomachs, because of all that food sitting there. We might get dizzy if we ran around too soon. Just like Dad telling us we couldn't go swimming for an hour after eating, because we'd get cramps and probably drown. My cousin Joe made faces when his mother explained this medical stuff to us. When she left the room, Joe looked around, and when the coast was clear, he whispered that it was "bullshit." My brothers and I checked to make sure no parent had heard Joe. We laughed only when we knew no adults could hear us. George said the real reason we had to stay in the room was to give the adults time to hide the Easter eggs.

My aunt finally turned us loose. We searched every corner of the yard, including the flowerbeds and shrubs. We discovered every hidden egg.

After we finished, Aunt Frieda seated all of us kids at the table for cake and ice cream. Uncle George and Dad were in the living room, sipping something dark from tiny glasses, while they kept their voices low, talking about grown-up stuff. My aunt leaned against the sink, watching us as we cleaned up our treats. Before we were even finished, she asked George and Joe if they would play outside for a while. And would they take my youngest brother with them, for just a few minutes? She wanted to talk to Bill and me. Alone. I put my spoon down.

"Your mother will be coming back soon. I know you boys have missed her." We didn't know what to say. We'd become used to our motherless routine. Sometimes I even forgot about her, as if she would never come back. "You know she has been terribly sick. Mostly in her mind. But she is good enough to come home, and I want you boys to do your part." Aunt Frieda leaned back and crossed her arms. She looked taller than she really was. "We don't want to upset her now, do we?" The way she said it didn't sound like a question. Her eyes stayed mostly on me: the big brother.

Bill leaned his head on his left hand and stirred his spoon into the ice cream. Neither one of us felt like finishing our treat. I was watching mine melt into different shapes, from a pointed mountain to a round bald head, and then a tiny chocolate lake...*did Aunt Frieda think we wouldn't help Mom? And why were they letting Mom come home? Would her voices stay behind in Danville? How did the doctors and nurses make my mother better, if they couldn't see what had to be fixed? Maybe her shadows would like it so much better in that dark castle, that they would stay behind. Would they flap away like angry crows in the night, or would they circle and peck at my mother, causing her to cover her head with her arms?...*and I stood my spoon up like a tree in the melting ice cream. "Carl, you can look after your brothers. Keep your rooms picked up, and make your beds. Be good boys." My aunt pulled up a chair, but she didn't sit down. She stood behind it with her hands gripping the backrest. Aunt Frieda must have thought we didn't hear her the first time. "Be good boys." She got even taller.

Bill looked at me. I looked down and worried at a scuffmark on my shoes. *Weren't we good boys?* My stomach felt like it was time to go home. Maybe there was still too much blood in it from all the food I ate. Maybe I would drown even if I didn't go swimming.

I would make sure that we were good boys. Maybe if we were better than before, my mom would be able to stay with us. Maybe if I prayed harder, God would fix my mother.

We'll be good, I promise. We'll be good.

On the way home, my father said he was not happy about my aunt's conversation with us. She had told him about her talk. Dad wanted to be the one to tell us when Mom would be returning. "I asked the hospital folks to let Mom come home earlier, maybe two months ago. They said she wasn't ready to come home. But she's almost ready now, and it's my business to tell you that."

When I told Dad that we would be good, as Aunt Frieda asked, he got really mad. "You are good boys. Don't forget that." He said something in German which I'd never heard before. Dad took out his handkerchief. Something was itching his eyes. "You *are* my good boys."

Mom's return was delayed by a month. She needed more rest and a little more time with the nurses and doctors. But by early June they let her come home. She'd been at Danville for six months. Dad told us she wasn't cured, but she was much better. We could all do our part to keep her that way. The dance with my mother would be changing, and there would be new steps to be learned by Alfie, Bill, and me.

The day Mom came home we were waiting on the back porch with Aunt Frieda. My father turned his black Chevy Sedan into our driveway and pulled right up to the back door. Aunt Regina got out of the passenger's side and opened the rear door. She reached for my mother's arm and steadied her as she climbed out. Mom wore a blue coat, even though it was sunny and warm. No hat, but her hair was brushed and shiny. Her eyes were fluttering. She lifted a hand above her eyes, and held it like a visor on a hat. She was trying to get comfortable with the bright afternoon, as if she'd just came out of a dark movie theater. She turned around and stared at my brothers and me, as we tumbled down the steps, untangling ourselves from each other as we ran toward her.

My mother pulled back like we were coming at her too fast. We stopped just in front of her, waiting for her to regain her balance. We were really waiting for her to remember who we were. We were afraid to enter the strange new space between us. Her face was pale and thin and the coat looked big on her, because of how it swallowed her shoulders. Then she locked us in her new gaze, somehow different from the familiar stare which had been absent all these months. She seemed thoughtful, and just a bit cautious. Mom leaned her elbow against the car door, as if she needed to touch something to get her bearings. Maybe she didn't know where she was?

Aunt Regina looped her arm around Mom's arm. "Say hi to your boys, Sophie. They've missed you." My mother took a wobbly step toward us and reached out her arms for us. We tiptoed as close as we could, without bumping into her. She folded us against her and we remembered that she was our mother and now she was home. She bundled us in her arms. She wasn't scared of us and we weren't afraid of her and it felt good to cry.

That summer was slow in unfolding its warmth. We needed time to thaw the thin ice between us, as if we had to be careful that we didn't step too heavily around each other. It was such a good thing, having our mother again. Why wasn't it easier?

Soon Mom wanted to make breakfast for us. She sat at the table with us as we ate our scrambled eggs and toast. My brothers and I watched her eyes as we spoke with her. Would she remember who we were going to play with, where we would be? We were learning to trust her eyes more than her words, because they often contradicted each other. Sometimes she would just sit and smile at us, until she fluttered away like a feather in the wind.

Mom seemed distracted and didn't always hear us when we talked to her. But when we repeated our words, she jerked her head toward us, as if we woke her up from a nap. I got a little scared that her daydreams would turn into the scary nightmares she had before Danville. But so far, that wasn't happening. Even though she seemed to be drifting in and out, she was with us more than she was away from us.

As the summer went on, Mom spent more time outside the house. She seemed content watching us as we played ball. My father was happy that Mom was getting her fresh air. Bill and I took turns bouncing the tennis ball off the side of the house, fielding grounders and fly balls. We shared the one repaired baseball glove that we now had, since my mitt finally wore out. We took turns flinging the ball against the white shingles, trying to trick whoever was wearing the glove. The ball thrower was also the announcer, as in "there goes a line drive by the second baseman, and a runner scores. Pirates are winning over the Cardinals, 5 to 2." Or, "Wow! The shortstop dives to his left and spears a line drive, and the game is over!" Three outs and we'd switch places.

By the end of the summer, Alfie was playing with us. He was better at throwing the ball than catching it. Mom clapped whenever my little brother did anything with the glove, like knocking down the bouncing ball or accidentally catching it. Sometimes my mother dozed off in her lawn chair until the sun lifted high and hot, chasing her into the shade. We liked it when Mom got sleepy in the sun.

I told her that we would be even better ballplayers if we had a good baseball mitt. Sometimes when Dad got home from work, he threw fly balls for us, really high and to the far end of the yard. I reminded him about the glove. We needed more padding to catch a real baseball. I showed him the mitt's thin pocket, how it barely protected my hand.

"I know, boys, I know. I would take all three of you downtown to Metzger's and get you outfitted right now, if I could. But I can't. Not now. You don't have to remind me about your baseball mitt."

I remembered not to remind him about the baseball mitt.

By now my father's arm was nicely healed, and he was getting really busy at work. The scientists in the Mineral Sciences Building were constantly praising him. They said he was clever and talented as a machinist. His perfectionism was understood and appreciated, and his work was important. Those smart teachers and scientists heard the same words my brothers and I knew so well, especially if they tried to rush him. "The job isn't worth doing unless you do it right. And that takes time! Have patience, Man!" The more credentials the professor had, the more my dad emphasized the word, *patience.* It was like they were asking Dad for a baseball glove.

*   *   *

Mom became more unhappy and restless with our location on Beaver Avenue. She wanted to live closer to the center of town, where her sisters lived. Since none of the women could drive a car, they depended on their husbands for transportation. That meant they only visited on weekends, usually after Sunday Mass. Since Mom's return from Danville, she got along much better with everyone, including Aunt Frieda. Now my aunt's offerings of dinner and groceries ended up on the table, instead of being thrown out or flushed down the toilet. My relatives agreed it was a good sign that my mother was more sociable. "Sophie's getting better, and isn't that a good thing." Sometimes the observation was spoken a bit loudly, as if we were too far away to hear those words.

Aunt Mary, my mother's youngest sister, had recently moved to State College. She had just graduated from the School of Nursing at Bellefonte Hospital. My mother was now about 38, and her younger sister seemed devoted to keeping Mom happy. Uncle Jack had recently been discharged from the army and was now enrolled as a student at the university, studying forestry and wildlife. Sometimes he took us to his laboratory to see the stuffed animals, owls, and hawks.

Our visits with Aunt Mary and Uncle Jack had a calming influence on my mother. But she felt deprived of the company of her other brothers and sisters, since we lived several miles away, at the edge of town. Even more important to my mother was their location within walking distance of our church. Dad said we couldn't afford to move right now. We had a good deal where we were. For now we'd stay on Beaver Avenue.

✳ ✳ ✳

The September after Mom came home, Bill and I would both be riding the bus to school. I was going into third grade, while my brother would be entering first grade. Since our house on Beaver Avenue was barely outside the State College Borough line, we had to take the bus to the Pine Grove Elementary School. Dad tried to enroll us in the local schools, but he was turned down. We lived about 100 feet too far to the west.

The bus picked us up in front of Musser's Grocery Store, on College Avenue. Our school was six miles away, in the middle of farm country. I never got tired of the scenery as I looked out the window on the way to Pine Grove Mills. Route 26 was bordered by dairy farms, their green pastures dotted by white and black Holsteins, brown Herefords and Jerseys, munching in the pale morning light, munching in the glare of mid-afternoon. The cows bent their heads down to the grass, as if listening to their own chomping and chewing. Bill and I looked out the window and kept score of the different breeds.

I had already been riding the bus for two years. After a week of walking with Bill and me to the bus stop, my parents decided that I was responsible enough to take care of my younger brother. Musser's was just around the corner, only two blocks from our house. I was careful about the traffic. I made a checklist for both of us: warm coats for the winter cold, boots for the unplowed snow, school books and homework. Sometimes I made sandwiches for us and other times Mom beat me to it. She always tucked a religious medal in the bottom of our lunchboxes. Once we left home, Bill had to listen to me. Dad kept reminding my brother that I was the boss.

When we returned home from school, the bus pulled up to the curb in front of Musser's store. No one could leave until the bus patrol got off and went into the road to stop traffic. When I got to sixth grade, I'd be old enough to be a bus patrol. That kid got to wear a white vest with a silver badge shining on the front. He carried a red flag, always ready to stop the oncoming traffic. The badge looked impressive and important. So was the flag.

At the end of Bill's first year on the bus, I let everyone down. Maybe the warm weather distracted me and made me careless. It was the middle of May, sunny and bright. Summer was getting a lazy start and soon school would be out. Mr. Triebold drove our bus up to the store and parked in the usual space. He cranked open the door so Jamie Kerstetter could get out and do her important bus patrol duty. With the red flag and white vest pronouncing her authority, she signaled that the street was clear. We scrambled off the bus. Five or six of us crossed the street, including Bill and me. That's when I remembered my lunch box was still in the bus, under my seat. I turned around and ran back across College Avenue, while the others waited for me on the other side of the street. I jumped up the bus steps, ran to my seat, and grabbed the lunch box.

"Take your time. Don't rush, you'll fall." The driver was always sort of bossy. *Like I didn't know not to fall.*

I guess I didn't look before crossing back over College Avenue, to catch up with Bill. I must have been in a hurry, too distracted to pay attention to Jamie's waving flag, or her voice screeching at me. I didn't see the blue flash of Dr. Ishler's father's car. But I heard the brakes screaming in perfect pitch with Jamie Kerstetter's howl.

I remember how the sound somersaulted after my first thump, loud and soft, loud and soft, dropping away when the sky and the road went spinning upside down. Even today, I could sketch the bottom of the car passing over me, as I lay flopped on my back. I can still see the big springs and shock absorbers at each wheel, the front and rear axles as they floated over me, two long bars perpendicular to my body. Then the square block of the gas tank, like a metal sky suspended above me. I still see the tires crunching into my gripped lunchbox, right through the silver initials of *JMJ,* flattening *Jesus, Mary, and Joseph* against College Avenue.

I woke up by the window, inside of Musser's Grocery Store. I was flat on my back, on a couch and covered with a blanket. My whole body felt like a thumping headache, from head to toe. Mom was hovering above me, crying and holding my hands in hers. When I opened my eyes, she pulled my bruised fingers against her lips. Something was fluffy and soft, between my shoulder and neck, braced against the side of the couch. Agnus Dei was snuggled against me. Along with her prayers, Mom brought the toy lamb.

Dr. Ishler's face interrupted my view of the ceiling. He whispered to my mother and she slid to the side so he could put his hands on me. I got it right when he asked me my name. Next he wanted to know my brothers' names and my address. I got everything right. Then he shined a tiny flashlight in my eyes. My neck hurt when I tried to turn from the light. He lifted the blanket and put his hand under my knees, checking to see that I could bend them. Someone had removed my trousers; that's when I saw that my legs and knees were scraped purple and red. Dr. Ishler pressed his fingers against my wrist, while his eyes darted between his watch and my eyes.

The door opened, groaned, and banged shut. The harsh noise slammed into my headache. My father's voice was far away, then coming closer as if winning a race against the other voices. Then he was big, looming over the doctor's shoulder, blocking my view of the peeling paint above me. Everything started to wobble and spin, until I shut my eyes. When I opened them, Bill popped up next to Dad, leaning over so far that I thought he'd drip tears on me. When I saw how scared they all looked, I started to cry. But just a little bit. I had already upset Mom, really bad. Just when she was doing so well. Maybe it would help if I wouldn't cry anymore.

"He's lucky, I can't even begin to tell you." Dr. Ishler was touching Mom's shoulder. He had to stop talking for a minute while he put his finger on his lips, as if signaling himself to be quiet, thinking of what he'd say next. "He got off with bruises and brush burns, Sophie." He stood back so my father could sit next to me. "His pulse is fine, no broken bones. But we might get a picture of those ribs, on his right side. Just to be sure." Dr. Ishler nodded toward Dad. "He responds normally as far as any bump on the head is concerned. Fingers on his right hand are slightly bent. Still had a hard grip on the handle of that lunch box." He decided my parents should take me to the hospital in Bellefonte, for a more thorough checkup and X-rays. "Lucky, lucky, lucky." He put his stethoscope in his black bag. He placed his hand on my forehead one last time. "Now I have to see how my own father is doing."

Dr. Ishler's father was 78 years old. *Old Dr. Ishler*, we called him. He was a retired physician, a beloved citizen of our town. He was driving west on College Avenue, right into the glare of afternoon sun. He didn't see the bus; he didn't see Jamie waving her red flag; and he didn't see me. But he said he heard the *thump* of me. He said he'd never forget how I sounded. He felt the bump go through his own body. Lucky for me, he was driving at an old man's speed, slow.

I had really messed things up. I couldn't be responsible about my own safety, much less my brother's. I had scared old Dr. Ishler, who later told Dad he couldn't sleep at night. Worst of all, I had taken away my mother's smile. Once again she stayed inside the house, bound to her rocking chair. No more watching us when we played ball, no more dozing off in the soft sun. Her worried hands were again knotted together by those rosary beads. The faraway gaze had returned, looking right past us. Just like before, we'd become invisible.

Thanks to me.

Chapter 12

After my accident, the summer blurred into a long stretch of dark and humid days. It didn't matter whether or not the sun was shining. Mom pulled back into her shadows, away from the painful daylight, rarely coming outside with us anymore. My brothers and I settled into our familiar routine of tiptoes and soft sliding around her, the remembered steps too easily coming back to us. Whether she was napping or not, we didn't want to wake her up.

Mom sat in her bedroom or the living room, praying her rosary and reading her bible. Since Dad was already at work, we took over the kitchen, improvising breakfast and lunch as needed. When Mom sat with us, she was distracted and quiet. If Bill or Alfie did something funny, she'd blink her eyes in amusement. Sometimes a smile or laugh followed, but it was like an illusion, born of our wish for her to be happy. All too soon we'd see the familiar lines of worry on her brow. It seemed as if we had two different mothers: one stepped out of herself to be with us for a few minutes, before retreating and merging into the other, still praying in her rocking chair.

Once again, we encountered the scary conversations. As soon as my father left for work, she began talking to herself. Mom could recite a whole litany of fervent words about God protecting us. She offered small prayers like *Saviour watch over us,* or *Jesus be our eternal guardian.* Mom always ended up with the rosary, repeating the *Our Fathers* and *Hail Marys,* insisting that we join in. If that wasn't enough, she'd throw in the joyful mysteries or the sorrowful mysteries. It never failed to be a sunny day when she wanted us to accompany her with the daily devotions. While the other kids were outside playing, we were inside praying. That sure seemed like a sorrowful mystery to me.

Mom's scariest words were coming back, and she usually saved them for those times when she was alone with me: *The darkness of Jesus' shadow carries more light than all the sunshine brought by Lucifer; The Antichrist will burn in the redeeming light of Jesus: Let us drown Satan in a flood of holy water.* It seemed as if her words were coming through a radio from a distant station. Mom's eyes were closed when she spoke like this. She opened them only long enough to see if I bowed my head when she uttered Jesus' name.

One morning when I was cleaning up after breakfast, my mother was in the living room, in her rocking chair. She was spending more and more time by the window. But on this day she'd closed off the light, pulling the drapes against the green summer outside. I thought she was calling for me; I could hear her from where I stood at the sink.

I went to the open doorway between the dining room and living room, to see what she wanted. Her voice was strong and her words were a monotone chant. She rocked back and forth, scraping the floor in cadence with her recitation. I could not move.

Beelzebub, burn in the cleansing fire of our lord and saviour. The rocking stopped and I stood still. It started again, in tempo with the words; *Serpent with forked tongue, die in the light of Jesus.* The motion stopped again, as if punctuating the silence between her chants. Then her voice rose from its steady pitch and gave an animated command: *Prince of darkness, burn in the Redeemer's purifying light.*

My mother was talking to the devil. They had found each other once again. With increasing frequency, my mother began addressing her shadows by name: *Unclean Spirit, Serpent of Forked Tongue, Antichrist, Temptress.* But she didn't do it when my father was home, and rarely with my younger brothers in sight. She seemed in touch with a living presence within that darkness, and she felt safe when I was nearby. *Why me?*

When her eyes found me standing in the doorway, she abruptly stopped. I shuddered from the cold, and from the words I'd just heard. My mother's eyes stayed on me, until she knew I could read the message she would not say with her mouth: *Say nothing.*

I said nothing.

* * *

There was a slow, good change by that summer's end. We all seemed to be healing from my car accident. Mom cautiously opened the drapes to let more light in. She began to come outside, like a kitten just past the fear of a distant thunderstorm. Dad wanted a little peace and quiet; now he had it. My brothers and I began to laugh and joke with each other without looking over our shoulders. Most of all, my mother felt that she had Jesus' attention to her request to protect and guide us. Our family had entered an uneasy truce with each other, and with something we could not see.

We returned to the gift of easy breathing. Mom began to make our breakfast, insisting that we sit at the table and talk with her while she cooked. We always checked the stove, because she sometimes forgot to turn off the red-hot burner. Although she spent more time in the same room with us and less in her rocking chair, we never abandoned our watchfulness.

As the next school year approached, my mother developed a new layer of protection for us. This time it involved Mary, Mother of Jesus. Mom had a framed picture of the Blessed Mother. She laid it flat on the kitchen table, before tearing off two scraps from a paper tablet. She wrote *yes* on one, *no* on the other. When my brothers and I wanted to go out to play, she crumbled her tiny notes into paper balls. Then she shook them in her hands and tossed them above the picture, as if rolling dice in the air. The answer that landed closest to Mary's haloed head determined our fate. The Blessed Mother would only grant permission to follow God's will, whether it was work or play. That's what Mom said. Through Mary, Jesus would be our constant shepherd.

When the answer to our request came up *no,* playtime was delayed or cancelled. My mother easily found work in the house for us to do. We fulfilled the Blessed Mother's commands by washing dishes, windows, floors, the bathroom sinks and tub. We learned how to use the stiff brush for the toilet bowl. When we finished the list of chores, Mom would again roll her blessed dice. Sometimes we got to play and sometimes the chores continued. The Mother of God didn't much care for batting practice.

We began to protest the decision-making process. Why couldn't we play like the other kids in the neighborhood? But we learned to be cautious with our objections. If Mom was in a bad mood, she was likely to add more duties to the list, always with Mary's passive approval. My father protested when he learned of my mother's actions. But she always supervised our duties when he was at work. Any complaints we uttered to Dad flew back at us like a boomerang, the next time we were alone with her.

The first time she slapped me, I think my mother was as surprised as I was. She had a strange look in her eyes, as if she didn't understand what her hand had struck. But I knew. It was my cheek, even though she had aimed for my mouth. I said my brothers and I should be able to go outside and play. "Every time we finish one job, you add more. All we do is work." My mother thought the devil was threatening to speak through me. She meant to keep Satan away from me. I had to learn to keep my mouth shut. "Don't talk back," my father warned the three of us. But I also learned to step between my mother and my brothers, and they learned to stand behind me. After all, I was their big brother.

My mother's level of agitation increased around Holy Days of Obligation and special occasions like Easter or Christmas. She said the house had to be immaculate for the arrival of the Holy Spirit. Once Bill asked Mom if the Holy Spirit used the bathroom, would we still have to clean up afterward? He whispered to Alfie and me something about the expression *holy shit!* We turned away so Mom couldn't see us trying to choke off our laughter. She didn't think my brother was very funny. Bill ended up having to clean up the bathroom again, after he had just finished.

Once Bill volunteered to write out the paper answers for the game with The Blessed Mother. "I'll even roll up the little paper balls for you, Mom." Alfie offered to toss the crumbled verdicts for Mom, but she would not give up that kind of control. Bill was always cheerful when he volunteered his act of kindness. I would have been in a good mood too, if I'd known that he wrote *yes* on both papers. The day Mom caught on to Bill's trickery, she was in a good mood. The three of us thanked God---and Mary---for that.

I wondered if we could get Dad's cooperation if we landed the Blessed Mother's approval for new baseball mitts. What did we have to lose? But for now, nearly every question we asked of our mother was answered through Mary, Mother of Jesus.

Chapter 13

Mom was most happy when my uncles and aunts visited, and my brothers and I were always glad to play with our cousins. Our home on Beaver Avenue was on the outskirts of town, bordering open farms and countryside, providing an abundance of land for exploration and adventure. A large vacant lot extended into the yard beside our house, so there was lots of room for baseball, football, or just running around. With an open front porch and upstairs bedrooms, we had places to play, away from our parents.

My cousin Joe was the adventurer among us. He organized expeditions searching the surrounding hills and woods for wildlife. His imagination convinced us that wolves, bears, and snakes were lurking in the nearby cornfields. Only one year older than me, Joe could talk us deep into a jungle in Africa; suddenly we were on the lookout for ferocious tigers and slithering pythons. The more Joe scared us, the more we wanted to be scared.

Hiking was our favorite activity. We packed our Boy Scout knapsacks with peanut butter sandwiches, pocketknives and other survival tools. Our army surplus canteens were tanked up with cold water. I always brought my compass and maps with me so I could work on assignments for my Orienteering Merit Badge. We drew our own charts, complete with directions for finding our way in and out of the nearby wilderness. Our observation camp on top of Kilamanjaro was at 45 degrees, in a northeast direction from the back of Johnny Rix's garage. It was only three blocks away from our house, a few zigs and zags and a detour through Albie Reed's back yard. To return home, we just reversed our procedure and followed the compass needle at 225 degrees, right back to our starting point. If we forgot the compass, we could simply look from atop our lookout post to Beaver Avenue. But that was too easy.

We hiked past the town limits into open country, beyond the University. There we explored The Duck Pond, east of town. This was a place for snakes and Joe knew where to find them. Sometimes he brought one home, after maneuvering it into his burlap sack with a stick and some fancy footwork. We watched and cheered him on from a carefully considered distance.

If we journeyed a mile or two south of town, we ended up in the evergreens bordering the fairways of Centre Hills Country Club. That's where the owls roosted, sometimes hooting their annoyance with us when we woke them up. Their scattered pellets provided souvenirs for our day's adventure. Joe always carried a sketchbook, which he filled with drawings of birds and animals we had sighted: hawks and owls, rabbits and fox. Five or six pages twisted with images of the snakes he captured, including one copperhead. No bears and wolves, not yet. "Just you wait," Joe warned us. "They're out there. They've got their eyes on us. Be careful in the dark shadows." We were careful in the dark shadows.

Thanks to my older cousins, we were introduced to the Boy Scouts. I joined our local troop, but Bill had to first put in some time as a Cub Scout, until he got older. Alfie was too young to join anything, so he got to stay at home and pray the rosary with Mom. I was embarrassed when I went to my first meeting because my mother had already called up the

Scoutmaster at his home. She wanted to know if Mr. Allen was Catholic. Dad was really mad about that phone call. They had a big fight, but my father told me to go. It would be good for me to get out of the house.

With the Boy Scouts, we learned about nature, spending time outdoors, camping and exploring nearby forests and lakes. Sometimes Dad had enough money that we could go to Seven Mountains Scout Camp, where we could row in canoes, swim and play with other kids besides our cousins. We slept in sleeping bags inside tents, with not a crucifix in sight.

The very best thing for me was becoming a Star Scout, when I earned my Astronomy Merit Badge. The emblem was the planet Saturn, surrounded by a white ring on a background of pale blue sky. Mom sewed the patch on my olive-green uniform, placing the gold planet on my chest. I wore it proudly.

I learned as much as possible about the night sky. It was a glorious mystery to me, those sprinkled points of light and their arrangement in the darkness above me. Even now when I look up in the night, I am lost in wondering about what it all means.

My fascination with the night sky began when I was about seven years old, before Mom had to go away. That was during the war, in 1944. The most exciting air raid drills always happened at night. I remember the siren bawling out its warning, the low drone rising and falling; then lifting and dropping again, its nagging wail loud, like a frightened child. I mastered the routine: lights out; drop the darkened shades; stay together until the all clear signal, three steady blasts, reassuring us *all is well, all is well, all is well.*

Mr. Case was the Air Raid Warden for our part of town. When he was on duty, he'd knock at the door after the siren stopped blaring. Reflected moonlight accentuated the black W on his white helmet, his insignia of authority. "Just checking in to see that you are complying with the mandatory instructions," he announced. "Just keep alert. The next time it could be the real thing!" He delayed his departure long enough that we could salute, if we chose to.

"Thank you, Andy." My father leaned out the door, smiling at the serious man. The grim protector backed up one step, before nodding an efficient farewell. Then he spun an about-face, before marching stoically into the dangerous night. As soon as my father closed the door, he told us, "The man is acting too dramatic. He's all puffed up like a balloon. Just remember, boys, the sound a balloon makes when the air rushes out of it, all at once." That always got a laugh, especially when Bill pursed his lips and trumpeted a loud fart sound.

On some of those quiet black nights, after Mr. Case departed, Dad and I tip toed outside. We moved silently into the open yard, and looked up at the ink-blue sky, the two of us connected by the moon and stars. Nights were darker then, undiluted by the wispy glare of streetlights and the glow of yet-to-be built shopping centers. Sometimes we considered the moon and the face of the man within. But I was wide-eyed when I sighted along Dad's pointing finger as he sketched The Big Dipper on the magical blackboard, stopping on the North Star, Polaris. There was bewildering comfort for me in the reliable alignment of the stars, obediently returning night after night to their assigned positions. The predictability of it all seemed impossible and wonderful. I envied it.

Mr. Allen made arrangements for our scout troop to meet with a teacher of astronomy at the University. Because the professor went to our church, he was spared my mother's questions about his devotion to the only heavenly presence that mattered, Jesus.

He came to one of our Boy Scout meetings with charts of the constellations and lists of the magical names of stars: *Alpha Centauri; Antares; Epsilon Indi and Epsilon Eridani,* the sounds singing in my ear. *Ep-si-lon-er-i-dan-i!* The music of it stuck in my head, disguising itself in the Latin words that I was learning as an altar boy. The rhyming of *Deo Gratias* with

Sirius; was it poetry? Once I knew how to find them, the stars were visible and real for me. Was *Pater noster, qui es in coeles* , a name for a constellation? Should *Our Father, who art in Heaven* be recognizable in my search of the darkness?

* * *

Our relatives tried to convince Dad that Mom was less agitated when she was with the rest of her family. Why didn't we move closer to them? Three of her sisters and two of her brothers had settled near the center of town, while we still lived at the outskirts of State College. There were good reasons for us to think about moving. My brothers and I would be closer to our cousins. We would be near our church and Dad would be closer to work. Since we could walk to school, Mom wouldn't have to worry about us traveling on the bus. I knew all too well that I'd given her reason to worry about that.

My father was still resistant. "For now, we stay where we are." My dad always told us if something was working, don't fix it. He thought we had a good deal on our rent. Our relatives talked quietly about us, when they thought my brothers and I weren't listening. But I knew what they were whispering: some things weren't working with our family. Their hushed words about my mother weren't so secret, after all. Was something going to happen to the rest of us? Dad was aware of that uncertainty and it made him more determined to keep things as they were. He'd show them that he could take care of his family.

As time went on, Dad's attitude began to change. Our landlord really started to bother him. My father never did like Mr. Stark, and I didn't either. He never smiled and he never spoke kindly. Never even said "thanks" when my father handed him the envelope stuffed with his hard-earned money. When Mr. Stark was impatient, he barked like a dog. On a good day he squawked like a chicken, and that's as good as it got. Whenever he came to collect the rent, Dad sent me to open the door. The landlord always looked off to my side, as if I were twins and he was talking to the other one of me.

Once I intercepted him by the mailbox. "Where's your father?" He cackled, so he must have been in a good mood. He stared at our mailbox so intently, that I wondered if he thought our mailman stuffed Dad in the container labeled *U. S. Postal Service*.

I retreated into the kitchen when Dad went out front to meet the landlord. I knew he didn't want any company when he and Mr. Stark discussed the rent. Although my father's voice got louder, it never became as shrill as the landlord's barrage of complaints. Soon Mr. Stark was barking. Our house usually was quiet after the man left with my dad's money.

It turned out we were going to move after all. Our monthly rent was going to be increased beyond what my father could pay. "I suppose he thinks I can just go out in the backyard and pick money off the damn bushes," Dad growled, his eyebrows furrowed. That's another thing we learned from my father. "Money doesn't grow on trees, boys. It doesn't rain out of passing clouds, and you won't trip over it coming down the steps. You have to work hard for it, boys. You have to earn it."

Aunt Frieda and Uncle George had recently built a new house on Prospect Avenue. Shortly after they moved in, they bought the house next door. They renovated it and divided it into two rental apartments. That was the house where Aunt Mary and Uncle Jack now lived, in the first floor unit.

Mom's youngest sister was gentle and sweet. My mother felt safe with Mary and loved being with her. She was now working as a nurse at Bellefonte Hospital, ten miles away. Aunt Mary knew how to soothe Mom when she was nervous. She could even make her laugh.

I remembered Uncle Jack's tall figure, the day he returned from the war. Aunt Mary met him at the bus station and they walked along Beaver Avenue toward our house, where the family was gathered for a party to welcome him home. As they approached our house, they looked like a scene from a movie: the returning soldier, tall and handsome in uniform, and his sweetheart, her blonde hair glowing from two blocks away. My brothers and I loved Uncle Jack and Aunt Mary, because everything we worried about felt better when we were with them.

When Aunt Frieda and Uncle George heard about our problem with Mr. Stark, they both came out to Beaver Avenue to talk with Mom and Dad. My brothers and I were told we could go out and play for a little while. We knew something was up, so we stayed nearby. We knew how to play catch with one ear tuned in to the open kitchen window.

When they finished talking, my brothers and I were invited back in the house. We sat together around the kitchen table. My uncle and aunt brought vanilla ice cream for us. We topped it off with walnuts and real maple syrup, instead of our usual Karo. Something was up; this had to be a special occasion.

Mom was grinning at us as we scooped into our bowls of ice cream. My father's eyes were just a bit teary, but he wasn't hunched over, looking beat up. I knew that image of exhaustion. This was different. He was sitting up tall and looking each of us in the eye, seconds away from the start of a smile. We were going to move into town, after all. Mom didn't even have to flip her crumbled papers in the air for The Blessed Mother's permission. We moved into the second floor apartment, above our relatives. Dad and Uncle Jack made the attic into bedrooms for Alfie, Bill, and me. The best part about our new location was that our cousins, George and Joe, lived next door.

Our Lady of Victory Catholic Church was two blocks away. Nittany Avenue Elementary School was three blocks distant, around the corner from church. The Community Athletic Field was across Atherton Street and down the hill; three minutes away if we walked, less than a minute, running. The field was so big that we could always find room to have our own pickup baseball game, even if the town teams were using the real baseball diamonds. With George and Joe around, there would always be something to do.

∗   ∗   ∗

As soon as we moved to Prospect Avenue, my mother's mood changed for the better. She was giddy, almost childlike with happiness. She went to church every day, and so did we. Bill and I were both altar boys by now. Mom volunteered us to serve at the 6:30 AM service whether we wanted to or not. Our attendance was mandatory, having been decided by one of her paper tosses with the Blessed Mother.

Mom had her own way of waking us up for early mass. Bill and I slept in the same bedroom so Alfie was spared, at least until he became an altar boy. She would come in the room with her bottle of holy water. There was always a jug of it in her bedroom. She bent over us and made the Sign of the Cross on our foreheads, after dipping her fingers in the sacred liquid. It was her silent way of telling us to wake up and serve the Lord. Dad told us it was a waste of holy water. He said it would go better with some ice cubes and a shot of whiskey. He mumbled something about a little spirit for the spirit.

Often the total attendance at early mass consisted of only four people: Father Gallagher; two altar boys, Bill and me; and my mother, kneeling in the first pew. That was the scene the morning Father hissed at me from above. We had just finished the prayers at the foot of the altar. I made sure to pronounce the Latin clearly so Bill wouldn't rush the words. My brother was still a nervous rookie. It might have been his first mass; I can't remember for sure. But I do know he was afraid to make any move without watching me for directions.

Father had already started with the introduction: "In nominee Patris, et Filii, et Spiritus Sancti;" *In the name of the Father, the Son, and the Holy Ghost;* "Introibo ad altare Dei," *I will go unto the altar of God.*

Bill and I responded, "Ad Deum qui laetificat juventutem meam;" *to God the joy of my youth.* We were really doing well; no mistakes so far. Father marched up to the top step, genuflected and bowed to the crucifix. He fussed with the chalice and that's when the noise began: Hissing. Like *hisssing.* I turned to my left and right, searching for a steam leak from the radiators on the walls of the church. That's when my mother caught my attention, fluttering her hand toward the altar. She was pointing at the priest.

Father Gallagher was staring down at me. It wasn't the heating system I'd been listening to. It was our priest's exaggerated whisper, almost whistling for my attention. One hand was slanted over his mouth, the other beckoning me to come up beside him. I climbed the six steps up the altar with my hands folded in prayer, as if this were part of the routine. I was practically wearing Bill on my back. He should have stayed at the foot of the altar, but he was scared to stay alone. He didn't know what was going on. Neither did I.

Once at the top step, I genuflected and bowed to Father. He bent down toward my ear, with his hands cupped around his mouth. "I shergot my teeesshh."

It was probably my puzzled expression that prompted him to open his mouth and point to the darkness within. It looked like an abandoned cave with a periphery of wrinkled lips. He placed his big hands on my shoulders, pivoting me toward the sacristy. Once I focused on the distant smile of Father's teeth perched on the sink, I knew what I had to do. He was here, and they were there.

By now my brother was lost and alarmed. This was not part of the choreography we had practiced as altar boys in training. He was my shadow as I tumbled down the altar steps, genuflected, and piously marched to the room where we had just dressed for Mass. We'd abandoned our priest, frozen like a statue on the altar, lonely and toothless at the foot of the crucified Jesus.

Father Gallagher's teeth lurked on the edge of the sink, porcelain on porcelain, incisors to molars on a pedestal of pink gums. I didn't know how to approach them; they were looking right at me. Bill peered out from behind me. Neither one of us wanted to be accidentally bit. Now I had to figure out how to catch the abandoned teeth and deliver them to their owner.

This was the worst of all the times for Mom to forget to ask if I had my holy medal and a clean handkerchief. I didn't even have a used hanky for this task. I had no choice but to fold my hand inside my white surplice, sneak up from behind and snatch the teeth within my insulated grip. I held Father's smile out in front of me, as far as my arm could extend.

On our return procession, Bill's prayer-folded hands were against my back, as I followed Father Gallagher's teeth right up the altar steps to his deflated smile. Mom's face was so deeply buried in her prayer book, I thought she was trying to inhale the day's gospel. The priest bent down, accepting our offering. He took his teeth and clucked them into place.

"Sanks, boys." He stared at us. He blinked, tugged at his upper lip and smoothed it out over his newly inserted teeth, then tried again.

"Thanks, boys." We bowed and genuflected. The Mass continued.

✳   ✳   ✳

Our summers on Prospect Avenue often echoed with happy noise. The Community Athletic Field had its own soundtrack: a mix of cheers and groans, the percussive *thwack* of bat on ball, the *thwuck* of ball into leather glove. It was welcome distraction from our daily vigilance around Mom. With the longer days, Dad had time to play catch with us after coming home from work. I was keenly aware of the sound my old glove made when I caught a hard throw from him. I heard and felt a thin *thwick*, instead of a well-padded *thwuck*.

One Saturday morning my brothers and I were playing catch. Alfie was becoming a really good catcher and Bill and I took turns pitching to him. His old glove was falling apart so badly that the tape and twine binding its wounds finally unraveled. Alfie was so disappointed that he went inside to tell Mom. She played her game with Blessed Mary, on my little brother's behalf. Mom also added a couple decades of the sorrowful mysteries of the rosary, since this was not a joyful event for Alfie. She said it was God's will that a new mitt would be in my brother's future.

Well, not quite. My dad came upstairs to see what was going on. Then he instructed us to hold out our left hands. We all threw right-handed, so we wore our gloves on the left hand. Dad measured his own hand against ours. He was quiet, solving a problem. Then he gave my mitt to Bill and Bill's to Alfie. My youngest brother's glove went into the trash bin. As for me, that afternoon I was the proud owner of a new baseball mitt.

Even though Dad repaired the hand-me-downs for Bill and Alfie, guilt weighed heavily on my eleven year old shoulders. My brothers deserved a new baseball glove as much as I did. But it was *my* left hand that was now gloved with a J.C. Higgins Outfielder's Mitt from Sears, Model 1623. It was genuine cowhide leather and it felt perfect, the way it hugged my palm and fingers. The only problem was the signature on the mitt. It was that of Enos Slaughter, the great outfielder for the St. Louis Cardinals. I had betrayed my favorite team and player: my beloved Pittsburgh Pirates, and Ralph Kiner, their All Star left fielder.

Metzger's Sporting Goods had a Kiner model, but it was a Rawlings glove and it was too expensive. Dad placed his hand in that mitt and thumped his fist into the pocket. "For that kind of money, I could outfit every kid in town." The slugger had been hitting a home run about once every fourteen times at bat. If I had his glove, it would surely bring me good luck. But I would make do with the Slaughter model. My younger brothers were a bit envious, but their newly-inherited gloves were a definite improvement over what they'd been playing with. Dad told them to be patient. "Your turn will come, Boys. It will be worth the wait."

Even though Bill and I were old enough for Little League, we had just as much fun playing in our own pickup games with the other kids. Alfie could play in our neighborhood games, but he was too young to play in the organized league. Our freedom to play still depended on Mom's mood and the variable wind currents, as the papered *yes* or *no* fluttered toward Mary's benevolent countenance, flat on the dining room table. For the most part, Mary smiled on us that summer.

Simply owning the J.C. Higgins mitt would make me a better ballplayer. At least that's what my cousin Joe told me. I'd try anything to improve my baseball skills. I tried his tip about the wad of Wrigley's Spearmint gum. "The bulge in your cheek isn't just to make you look tough. It increases muscle tension in your jaw. That's why the guys in the Majors hit so well, 'cause their muscles are already flexed and ready for action!"

The Big Leaguers used chewing tobacco instead of gum, but that was not a realistic option for us kids. Besides, it tasted like kerosene. Old Colonel Ashburn let me and my brothers try some, but I think it was for his own amusement. All three of us nearly choked to death, while he almost died laughing. We didn't know you weren't supposed to swallow the juice. Now we knew why the other kids called him Colonel *Assburn*.

When the gum trick failed, I tried another one of Joe's tips; stones in my left pocket. His explanation: a right-handed hitter shifts his weight to his left side, a power move, when swinging his bat. If I had that weight already transferred, I'd surely hit for distance. I tried a few more of Joe's tips, with no results to brag about. He just shook his head. He even pitched extra batting practice for me.

"You need a level of help that is beyond me." In desperation, he suggested praying the Hail Mary against right-handed pitching and the Our Father against lefties. I must have mixed them up, because it didn't help one bit.

It didn't take long to get over the guilt of owning new equipment. The same day I got the glove, I played catch with Dad. I had never owned a really good mitt before, always begging the use of one from a player on the other team. The most generous players seemed to have the oldest, thinnest gloves. My Enos Slaughter 1623 was not thin. The padding cushioned my hand so well that I felt no sting, even when Dad threw his hardest. The ball was never lost in the mitt. I could dig it out real fast for a speedy throw to the infield. Best of all was that familiarity of having my very own glove. It felt like it was part of my hand.

As Summer flew by, I realized another advantage of ownership. I got selected earlier when we were picking up sides for our games. Team captains wanted kids who owned their own equipment, because they practiced more. The worst feeling was not being among the chosen, waiting on the sidelines for someone to scrape a knee. Even worse was being called home for lunch or supper, before stepping into action.

My mother sometimes felt good enough to come down to the field. She said she wanted to see how well we were playing, but she really wanted to be sure we were playing with good boys; that we weren't falling under the influence of the devil, disguised in the uniform of one of our teammates. Whenever Mom interrogated us about a new player, the first question was about where he attended church. Was our friend Catholic? If she believed everything we told her, she must have assumed we were playing for the Vatican Little League.

I played right field. The older kids were nice about it. "We gotta have someone with good foot speed to cover the line. You know, prevent extra-base hits." I was a good runner, but I knew the real reason: fewer balls were hit there. But I improved, game by game. Soon I was the centerfielder. There was more action and I covered more territory than most of the other kids. I was confident that with my new mitt I would never drop anything. It was a magnet. Center field was a promotion, and I was proud.

As my confidence rose, I let the game be my teacher. By the sound of the bat, I could tell how quickly the ball was coming at me. A solid *whack* was a signal to sprint first, full speed ahead in the general direction of the hit, then look for the ball. *Thwack* was a different sound, the ball hit well, but not with full wood. I'd have more time to judge where it was going, and whether to move in or back. *Thwack* meant more time to get in position for a fast throw to the infield if a runner was already on base. I became a student of baseball's mystical geometry of lines and arcs, its angles of trajectory and descent. I paced my running to intersect the ball's obedience to gravity. Moving with confidence, I entered the magic. I felt graceful.

Whenever Dad got out of work early, he came down to the Community Field to watch us play. Sometimes Bill was picked to be on my team. Dad was happy when he could cheer for both of us at the same time. Alfie was the youngest of all of the boys who wanted to play. If there were too many older kids, he wasn't picked to be on a team. But he tagged along with Bill and me so he wouldn't be home alone. One of the older players always threw the ball with him so he wouldn't feel left out. Dad said we were all improving. "Practice makes perfect. Remember, it works for other things besides sports, boys. Don't forget that. Practice makes perfect." He continually repeated that phrase, as if we couldn't keep it in our heads for more than two minutes.

When Mom walked down the hill with my father, she quietly sat in front of him, on the next lowest row of bleachers. She would smile at us as if we were the only kids on the ball field. From my position in the outfield, I could see Dad staring straight ahead, lecturing about some new issue, probably politics or President Truman, and how he could give him some useful advice. Mom just smiled straight ahead, letting him go on and on about world affairs. She paid about as much attention to Dad as she did to our ball game. But she knew we were having fun and getting better at whatever it was we were doing. My father had to be pleased that she was in the fresh air, getting exercise with the short hike from home.

But all that confidence and earned athletic grace changed for me, when, in the space of a few days, I dropped three balls that should have been easy outs. I blamed the first error on the afternoon sun, when Bruce Walsh flared a pop-up into the four o'clock glare, shimmering over the green tumble of hills west of town. Half way into its climb, the ball plain disappeared into the blinding sunlight and I lost it. But the second miss came on the big hop off Butchy Riggs' single. The ball came right at me. It should have been an easy play, throwing out the runner on first, as he ran to second base. It jumped right out of my mitt. Maybe I just wasn't concentrating.

The final miscue was the one that really hurt. That was the day I was on Donny Stickler's team. He was one of the older kids, the best ballplayer in town. When he hit the baseball, he ran around the bases so fast that his cap flew off. His coal-black hair would trail behind like it couldn't keep up with him. All the girls liked him, and so did their parents. I always wondered what it was like to be Donny. He was nice to us younger kids. Even though I was usually last to be picked, it felt good to be on his team.

We had this really big game with the kids who lived near the University. It was like the World Series between the Townies and College Heights. There was a boundary line between us, real and imagined, which started on College Avenue, where the business district ended and the University campus began. Loyalties were fixed by whichever side we lived on. It was our biggest game so far. It was also the first time I got picked to be on Donny's team and I really wanted to play a good game.

I did play a good game, even got a hit. I was a bit surprised when I felt the *thwack* on my bat. I was admiring the way the ball skittered between the first and second basemen, when I realized I was supposed to run to first base. By the fifth inning, I had caught two easy fly balls. Next inning, I cleanly fielded a single on the second bounce. I really stepped into my throw, airmailing a strike to second base, holding the runner on first. But my good day was about to end.

Donny had hit a home run, and we were leading 7 to 5. The College Heights kids came up for their last time at bat. Their first baseman was a tall blonde kid named Paul. I knew he was a good basketball player, but I didn't think he could hit the baseball so far. I should have played him deep, because they had loaded the bases. His hit was a percussive *whack* and I took off like a rabbit. The amazing thing was that I caught up to the ball as if it were suspended in the air, just waiting for me to tuck it away in my glove. Up went my mitt and the ball just flowed into it. And right out.

The fingers of my trusted mitt suddenly acted like springs, flipping the ball onto the green pasture of center field. It rolled to a stop like a glowing snowball which would melt only after everyone in the whole world saw that I had dropped it. By the time I threw it to the infield, three runs had scored and Paul stood on third base, with a long triple. I wasn't very good at math, but I could certainly add three runs to the five they already had. And I knew how to subtract our seven runs from their eight. We lost. And it was my fault.

The College Heights kids were whistling and cheering. Most of my teammates were quiet. Never again would Donny Stickler pick me to be on his team. I had my chance and I messed up. I no longer felt graceful.

Some of the other kids gave me a pat on the back. Eddie Trembley knew I felt really bad about dropping the ball. Even at the age of ten, my best pal wanted to be a Shrink. That's what Eddie called it. He said it was a way to get paid for talking with people about things that made them sad.

I must have given him his start, because he asked me if I wanted to talk about it. But I didn't want to talk about it. "Don't worry," he whispered when we were alone. "We can always talk about it later. You might have a delayed reaction and get depressed and stuff." Eddie could see that I was close to tears. "We'll get 'em next time."

Next time? There wouldn't be a next time for me.

Bill and I gathered our equipment and began the slow trudge up Barnard Street, heading up the hill for home. My brother offered to play catch with me if there was time before supper. "Maybe you're taking your eye off the ball. You can't take your eye off the ball, you know, because…"

"I know, I know." I snapped at my brother. I didn't want to talk about anything remotely connected to baseball. Not now. Not ever. Bill offered to carry my glove and bat. He tried to distract me by talking about something else. He even said he would take my turn as altar boy for 6:30 mass next morning, so I could sleep late.

"Stop being so nice to me. I feel bad enough already, OK?"

"Carl! Bill!" A familiar voice echoed from below. "Wait up, you guys." Donny Stickler was jogging up the hill, half a block behind us. My brother and I looked at each other. Yes, he was talking to us. Nobody else was nearby. A few heartbeats later, the best ballplayer on the team was walking with us. He seemed taller than he was a few minutes ago, or maybe I just got smaller after my dropped ball.

"You know, that was a really good team we played today." Donny was between us now, trying to get my eye. I just stared at the sidewalk, memorizing how my sneakers landed on the pavement, avoiding the cracks between the sections of concrete.

"I tried to get a game with those guys next week." He stopped abruptly, right in front of us. My foot landed on a crack. "You guys show up. Next Tuesday, OK? Both of you. You're on my team." This time he got my attention.

I said nothing. I couldn't. Thank God for my brother. He did all the talking for us and said we'd be there. Donny glanced sideways at me.

"You know, Carl, this is only baseball. It's a game. You know what I mean?" Donny was now up to seven feet tall and growing. "I used to hate it when we played a game and lost." We turned uphill, and started our climb the rest of the way up Barnard Street. "My dad always told me I was too hard on myself. I mean, about losing a game." I remembered when Mr. Stickler died of a heart attack. He was Donny's biggest fan.

"Anyway. It's only a game." Donny motioned toward the stone wall by Reverend Shannon's house. We sat down to catch our breath. "That's what my dad always told me when I felt bad about losing. 'It's only a game, Donny.'"

It was more than a game for me.

He reached for my baseball mitt. Donny slid his hand into the glove, then thumped his fist into the center of it. I felt special that he was taking such an interest in my glove. He wiggled his fingers and pounded the glove as if trying to shape it to his own hand. He kept staring at the mitt.

"Carl, get that baseball. Throw me a couple pitches."

I leaped off the stone wall and scrambled to the flat driveway. Bill gave me the ball and Donny moved about forty feet away. He held up my glove as a target and I tossed the ball to him. "Come on...harder. Put some ginger on it!" I threw seven or eight pitches, as hard as I could. Donny kept the last ball in the mitt. He opened and closed his fingers again and again, holding my J.C. Higgins 1623 up in front of him. I thought he was just shading his eyes from the afternoon sun. He returned to his seat on the stone wall, and motioned for us to sit on either side of him.

When Donny held the mitt up in front of us we could see daylight between the four fingers of my glove. "There's too much slack. See what happens when I catch the ball." The fingers splayed open each time he slammed the ball into the glove. "If the ball gets stuck between two fingers, they act like springs. That pushes the ball right out of the glove." Donny handed the mitt to me and motioned for me to go back to the driveway. "Catch the ball in the fingers. You'll see what I mean."

He threw a few pitches. Sure enough, it popped right out. "That's why you always want to snag it in the pocket, but you can't always do that." He pounded his fist into the round depression between the thumb and forefinger.

"What should I do? Is it the wrong size?" Suddenly my prized mitt seemed like it belonged on someone else's hand.

"Naw. See this lace?" Donny's fingers tugged at the leather cord, which ran through the four finger tips. "This lets you adjust the tension." He untangled the knot on the outside of the little finger, and gently drew on the string. The fingers snuggled together as if they were trying to get warm. Donny retied the knot, reshaping my glove. "Now try it. See what happens when the ball hits the fingers."

He stepped back and threw a few pitches. With each impact, the fingers folded around the ball, almost caressing it into the pocket. My glove was new again, not just holding onto the baseball, but hugging it.

"It feels better. It really feels better."

"One more thing. You need a good pocket in that thing." Donny took the mitt from me and put it on his hand. He repeatedly slammed the ball into that cupped palm between the thumb and forefinger. He showed me how every part of my glove now directed the ball into the pocket. "That is the heart of your mitt, right there. Without it your glove is dead as a dishrag. You need to shape your own pocket." Donny tossed the mitt back to me. "Get a can of Neetsfoot Oil so you can treat the leather. Rub it in. That keeps the leather soft. They should've sold you some when you got the glove. And don't forget to fold the ball in your glove every night. In the pocket."

Sitting there on Reverend Shannon's wall, Donny Stickler taught me about the ritual of caring for my precious mitt; Neetsfoot Oil and the daily massage of the surface, working the magic elixir into the very skin of my glove, rejuvenating the hand upon my hand. My glove came alive, its pulse beating in time with my own pulse.

Each night I put it to bed, under my bed. At first my mother objected to its place on the floor when it should have been shelved in my closet. But I told her I would have good luck if I gave it special treatment. She didn't argue with me. She even prayed over it and blessed it with holy water the night before my next big game.

The scent of oil perfumed my bedroom air and my dreams of Forbes Field and the Pirates. And our next game with College Heights, when I bolted up from my sleep, awakened by my leaping catch of the deep fly ball, ensuring the Townie's victory and earning Donny's praise. Through those summer nights, my glove rested under my bed, its fingers and thumb folded around the baseball, forming the perfect pocket that keeps the caught ball, caught; the heart which allows no loss.

Chapter 14

My brothers and I soon discovered that one of the best things about our move into town was a nearby acre of woods. It was the unexplored and uncharted territory between the Weavers' brick ranch house and the Archers' tennis court.

We named it *The Jungle*.

It was perfect for our games of Cops and Robbers, or Cowboys and Indians. We could easily carry out our Boy Scout assignments for the Nature Merit Badge, gathering specimens of plants and bugs, abundant in our private forest. Our expeditions in search of wild animals took place here, with the screen of bushes and trees shielding our young imaginations from curious parents. But something else was going on in our secret forest. This was the home of the *Jungle Smokers*.

We operated smoothly and secretly until we let my youngest brother in our club. That's when everything went wrong. Before that, there were six of us: the Walsh brothers, Mason and Bruce; my cousins, George and Joe; my brother Bill, and me. Alfie felt left out. We finally got tired of him pestering us about joining the Jungle Smokers, so we decided we'd take him in. But only after he earned it.

We had our own secret camp, a tree house, which we built by ourselves. That is, we *sort* of built it ourselves. For a bunch of kids between eight and thirteen years old, we were pretty good carpenters. My father donated most of the wood, whether he knew it or not. When my family moved into our new apartment, Uncle George allowed my father to do some renovations. Dad fixed up the attic on the third floor, converting it into bedrooms for the three of us. Bill and Alfie shared one side and I was on the other.

We needed shelves and bookcases. Each of us had to have our own desk for doing homework. These projects required lumber and other supplies. Dad expected our help whenever he was working in our rooms. If we had school vacation or a holiday, my brothers and I knew how we would be spending the time. We'd be helping Dad. One of the benefits of working with Dad was that some of his building materials ended up in our hands. We put it to good use.

From time to time we threw in a length of something other than scrap wood, like a solid, uncut two-by-four. Bill and I justified our pilferage by reciting Dad's mantra out loud, as we were hauling away our loot: "a job isn't worth doing unless you do it right!" And to do it right, we needed proper materials. We weren't very good about thanking him for the donations. Otherwise he would have been aware of his generosity, and we didn't want my dad to abandon that good trait. My cousins sometimes took a jar of nails from Uncle George's workshop. While they were at it, they borrowed some hammers and a saw. George insisted that we'd also need a carpenter's level and a tape measure.

The Walsh boys zeroed in on a solid Maple tree, right in the middle of the Jungle. They thought a tree house ten or twelve feet above ground would keep us safe from the stampedes of wild horses we encountered in our battles as cowboys and Indians. In our more exotic African adventures, it would offer shelter from the lions and tigers lurking in the underbrush.

If that wasn't reason enough, the tree house would keep us hidden from our parents when we wanted to smoke.

Our construction project became a community endeavor. We took turns measuring and marking the wood before sawing it into proper lengths for the two open floors and supporting framework. After equally shared yelping over some hammered fingers, we'd successfully driven enough nails to anchor two platforms and the ascending steps to our big maple tree. We stood back and admired our handiwork.

But we weren't finished. My father's curiosity about his shrinking woodpile led him to the Jungle. He followed me one Saturday morning, after I'd helped myself to some of his wood scraps. We thought we were in trouble, but he must have been impressed enough by our industrious activity that he didn't get angry with us for taking his wood.

"At least you boys are getting some exercise and fresh air." Dad circled around our project, then softly kicked at the lower steps on the tree trunk. "Let's see how well you put this together." Dad reached up and gripped one of the higher rungs of our ascending ladder. Next, he lifted himself up on the first step. He stood quietly before cautiously jiggling his weight, as if standing on a diving board, testing its springy action. "I don't know boys. Feels a little wobbly to me."

Before we knew it, we were in partnership with Uncle George and my father. From bottom to top, the two men nailed over our nails and reinforced what we thought was already tight. When they finished, we had a rigid ladder which would support the biggest kid in our group. Once the platforms were made solid, they helped us build walls and a roof. Because of our careful fathers, we now had a tree house that was even better than we could imagine. We would now be safe and secure, and thanks to the walls, out of sight.

Dad found an old kitchen cabinet in the basement. He removed the hinges and anchored them onto another flat piece of plywood. We helped attach it to the open end of our shelter, providing a swinging door. We hung a bell just outside the door. It was rigged to a rope which dangled to the ground. There was even a secret code for ringing the bell, if you wanted to be admitted to the inner sanctum. The door could be locked from the inside by a hook and eye latch, protecting us from invaders.

Bruce made the most important contribution to the Jungle Smokers: he brought the butts. His grandfather was a chain smoker who tamped out his cigarette when it was only halfway smoked. We took care of the unsmoked part. The old man was very proud of the way his grandson conscientiously emptied those smelly ashtrays, helping his mother keep the house clean.

We were proud of Bruce too. We liked the way he replenished each member's butt jar, which we stowed in our own private cubicles in the tree house. Wooden orange crates made the best storage compartments. We collected the empty boxes from behind the A and P Grocery Store on Beaver Avenue. Each one of us kept a supply of chewing gum or peppermint candy to disguise our tobacco breath, before going home. We always stashed ten to fifteen half-smoked Camels or Lucky Strikes in our jars, fifteen feet above the ground.

One July evening, we were looking for something to do. The Walsh boys had just returned from grocery shopping and my cousins were finished with supper. Alfie, Bill and I were finished with our own chores. Mom had nothing left for us to do. We sneaked out of the house before she changed her mind or checked in with the Blessed Mother. A late afternoon thunderstorm had flushed out the heavy air, drying and cooling the summer evening. After a busy day of newspaper deliveries, baseball, and housework, it was a time to relax. Time for a smoke with our friends, our fellow Jungle Smokers. Except for Alfie.

Six of us gathered in our hut. I'd already moistened my cigarette after tamping the end against the back of my hand. The Walsh brothers said they'd seen cowboys do that in the movies at the Nittany Theatre. We were all in a circle, ready to light up. That's when we discovered we were out of matches.

"No fire," Mason lamented. "We got no fire. We're out of matches 'cause my mom's wondering what's with Bruce. She watches him like a hawk. Says he's like a vacuum cleaning up after my grandfather, but he can't even clean up his own room." Mason took his own cigarette out of his mouth and put in back in its jar. "Just too tricky for us to steal matches right now, at least in our house. We'd get caught for sure."

George and Joe couldn't help out either. "Uncle Bob and Aunt Regina are at our house for dinner." George shook his head. "We go in the house, we're stuck there all night. You know, being nice to everybody, showing off our good manners."

Silence. You could hear our disappointment huffing and puffing through the smokeless air. Our breathless meditation was interrupted by the sound of a tennis ball bouncing off my family's garage, three houses down the alleyway. My youngest brother, the Jungle Smoker Wannabe, was playing catch with himself.

"Alfie." My brother Bill perked up. "Let's get Alfie. He wants to join. We can make him get the matches from our house. He can earn his way in. He won't nag us about joining anymore. How 'bout that?"

My first reaction was not so positive. I wasn't sure he'd be able to keep quiet about our secret activity. "Anyway, he prob'ly can't even smoke. I bet he'd puke all over his new sneakers on the way home."

It was put to a group vote. Since everyone was one match away from lighting up, I was outvoted, five to one. I volunteered to give my little brother the news of his membership, depending on whether he carried out his assigned task of supplying matches.

I climbed down the tree ladder and strolled along the alleyway. I wasn't in a hurry. No need to act suspicious. I stopped and watched my little brother backhand a few balls with his new catcher's mitt. He was getting good. When it was obvious that I wasn't there to play catch with him, he turned back toward the garage door, ready for another throw. He pulled back his arm and lifted the ball above his head, stepped forward on his left foot, leaning into his stride, when I froze him, mid-throw. "Alfie. I got a deal for you."

He pivoted toward me, staring wide-eyed, while the ball and his right arm hovered above his head. He thoughtfully lowered his arm as I explained our offer. Alfie started thumping the ball into his mitt, as he considered his possible membership in the Jungle Smokers. He tucked the ball in the glove and folded it under his arm. He was in!

Dad kept his pipes and tobacco on a shelf at the top of the stairs. He usually had a pack of cigarettes on top of the Prince Albert can, but he would know if we so much as looked at it. There were always match boxes scattered on the shelf. He'd never notice if one pack was missing. We reviewed our plan three times. "Don't rush, just be calm. Dad will be on to you if you act different. Just act normal, kind of sleepy-like. He'll never notice."

I jogged back to the tree-house. Now I had something to be excited about, because my fellow smokers would really be pleased with me. I rang the bell, three short, three long, three short; like Morse Code for the S.O.S signal. I scrambled up the ladder as if gravity had no effect on me. Bill unlatched the door and let me in. It was a good feeling knowing that I came through for my pals by recruiting my youngest brother. We just sat back and waited for our new best buddy. We talked about the Pirates and Ralph Kiner's batting average. Someone told a dirty joke. I didn't get it, and Bill didn't either; I could tell by his blank expression, but we laughed anyway. We didn't want to make anyone feel bad by not laughing at his joke. The Jungle Smokers were very considerate of each other's feelings.

Suddenly we heard a tentative tapping sound on the door. We looked at each other, mildly startled before we remembered we were expecting our new recruit. I opened the door. With one hand, Alfie was hanging onto the ladder, the matches white-knuckled in his other fist.

"Way to go, Alfie. That was real fast. Was Dad around?"

"Nope. I think he was taking a nap. Or he might have been in the cellar." Alfie had to catch his breath. "Coast was clear."

The circle was now one kid larger. My brother was grinning, feeling like a real big-shot, about to light up with the older kids. Joe presented him with his own butt jar, like it was a trophy. Bruce parceled out a few new secondhand cigarettes to everyone. Before we started smoking, we had to go through our warm-up ritual. The closest Jungle Smoker to the door opened it, and yelled out "Phillip Morrrrisssss." I explained to Alfie about the advertisement; we had to *call for Phillip Morris*. We played no favorites. Sometimes the expression "Light up a Lucky" was hollered just as loud.

I made a big deal of lighting Alfie's cigarette for him. I struck the match ablaze, and held it up to the tip of his first butt. "Suck it in, little brother. Don't blow through it! Don't swallow it. Just pull a little in and blow it out real slow like this." I tilted my head back and propelled a smooth jet of smoke toward the roof, until the final gust sputtered into a hacking cough. When Alfie whispered out his first puff, we gave him a round of applause.

In a few minutes a veil of smoke eclipsed the ceiling, like a grayish white cloud descending on us. We looked as if we were trapped in our own weather system. I was feeling a bit feathery in the head, enjoying the rich mocha heat on my tongue. We were in rhythm with each other's breathing, inhaling, blowing smoke in unison, one for all, all for one. A band of Indians with our shared peace pipe, pals, buddies, together in tobacco, almost sleepy, just...Thud!

The floor started to quiver. Another thud. The walls echoed each thump, as if we were enclosed in a bass drum with each beat louder than the previous one. Someone was climbing up our ladder, vibration surging from each emphatic step, up the solid trunk to our rear-ends, frozen on the floor.

The noise stopped, and so did our breath. Our exhaled fumes were suspended, as if ready to reverse direction and escape back into our lungs when we resumed our breathing. The door was not latched from the inside. Whichever one of us gave the "Phillip Morris" yell forgot to lock the door. Seven hearts thumped erratically; seven foreheads misted into a glistening sweat. Silence…

The door rasped open. Lit from behind and framed in the open doorway, veiled through our turbulent clouds of guilt, was the solemn face of my father staring down all seven Jungle Smokers. He scanned our circle. His cobalt glare locked, one by one, on the eyes of my brothers and me. My father said nothing. He stared right through the three of us without even blinking. *How can he hold his eyes open so long, without shutting them?* We instinctively pulled back when he reached his arm through the open door, but he pulled his forearm up at a right angle, as he rested his upper arm and elbow on the floor. He beckoned us, his authoritative index finger pulling the trigger, curling and uncurling as if we were tethered to it by an invisible line. We were being reeled in like three hooked trout, ready for the frying pan.

Thanks to Dad's encouragement, we hit the ground running. We hurdled or trampled any small bushes and plants in our way, blazing a new trail through the Jungle. Once we emerged from our forest, we blurred our way down the alley. Dad was a step in front, hoisting Bill and me by the necks of our T-shirts, our sneakers losing none of their tread on the road. Alfie wobbled right behind, dizzied by smoke and fear. My father released his grip once we were in the yard.

"Follow me, boys." We followed.

He sat us down on the stone wall by the rear of our house. "Make yourselves comfortable, boys. Sit here and relax. You want to smoke, I'm gonna provide you with all the smokes you could ever want. I'll be right back. I know you won't run off." We didn't run off.

We were like three statues cemented to that wall. We couldn't look at each other, much less talk. Silence was our only hope. Maybe we'd blend into the dusk, camouflaged from our father's impending justice.

The door slammed behind us, jolting us into reality. Dad stomped down the steps to the ground in front of us, where he marched back and forth like a drill sergeant. He had our full attention. We didn't even turn around when the door quietly opened and closed again. Mom slid into my peripheral vision, where she remained because we didn't dare break eye contact with my father. She eased herself onto the wall on the far side from us. When I did sneak a quick look, she seemed to be smiling at us, but she was probably confused.

Dad finally stopped his parade and faced the three of us. Sitting up on that wall, we were eye to eye with him as he lifted a new pack of Chesterfields from his shirt pocket. After he peeled open a corner, he tapped the bottom of the pack against his fist. A clean white cigarette popped out. With a flick of his wrist, Dad slid the weed from the pack to my mouth. He moved right down the lineup. The scene was like rehearsed choreography, with Dad popping a new butt for Bill, then one for Alfie. We sat motionless with our eyes bulging, unlit cigarettes in our mouths. My father paraded back and forth again and finally halted in front of me. Now he pulled out the matches confiscated during our arrest, the same ones Alfie slid into his pocket as my father was painting the pantry, just beyond Alfie's vision. So much for my father taking a nap! He was wide-awake by now. One by one, he lit the cigarettes obediently projecting from our mouths. "O.K. boys, let's all start together. I'll tell you when to stop. Ready now...one, two, three, smoke! Enjoy!"

My mother smiled at us and made the sign of the cross.

Almost sixty years have gone by since my brothers and I gave up our smoking habit. If I did cheat, it was a rare event: a few celebratory cigars, perhaps for a friend's baby, or joining my buddies at the break-up dinner of a wonderful ski trip. After all those years, it only takes a few puffs to stimulate that faint flutter of nausea that immobilized me during Dad's smoking lesson. I haven't forgotten the hollow tension of my belly, how it felt like a drummer was practicing inside. None of us smoked again.

Three weeks after our punishment by smoke and fire, my father threw away the last of his cigarettes. Another month and his tobacco was gone, as if Prince Albert rode off into the sunset, hauling Dad's collection of pipes on his back. From time to time my father appeared at our tree house, which was now smoke-free. He tugged at the ladder steps and the floor boards. Sometimes he climbed up and down the tree, only to reappear minutes later with a hammer and a pocket full of nails. After pounding on a loose step, he'd quickly scan our inner sanctum. "I'm just looking after your safety, boys. Any loose nails inside?"

*　*　*

Shortly after we moved into our apartment on Prospect Avenue my father built that stone wall, where he had lined us up for our smoking lesson. In exchange for Dad's labor, Uncle George gave him a generous break on our rent. The project would not only improve the appearance of the house and yard, but it would rearrange the slope of the land, preventing the soil from washing away with each downpour of rain. It would be a good deal for both Uncle George and for Dad.

One summer morning, a truck dumped a load of stone and rocks in our parking lot. Dad told us that we would be his landscaping crew. We were going to transform our yard into a work of art. In the process, according to my father, he would teach us about the satisfaction of honest work.

We were now old enough to dig and shovel, lift and carry; we could maneuver a wheelbarrow. Alfie was bigger and stronger, no longer an errand boy. He'd sweat along with the rest of us. My father was foreman and teacher, and we were his workers and students.

Our lessons were about patience and determination. We all watched as he lifted each rock, while measuring it with it his eye. After wobbling the stone into perfect alignment and tamping it into place, Dad stepped back to inspect his own work. Final approval was signaled by a nod of his head. Each individual mass of jagged limestone or sandstone had its own purpose and destination, and it was my father's duty to figure that out. Simply watching my dad as he worked was a lesson in patience.

That was a slice of time when my mother was in a patch of serenity, as if centered in a circle of sunlight, which kept her shadows at its periphery. She often came downstairs and into the yard with a jug of lemonade when we were wet with the summer heat. Mom sat in the shade watching us mimic the sweaty, muscular construction workers paving the road on nearby Atherton Street. There was something noble about a tanned back glistening under the hot sun. It was just a matter of time and hard work until we'd have big muscles, too.

I remember how Dad sometimes took a short break, leaning his shovel against the lengthening wall. He carefully stretched his sore back until he was as tall as possible, before sitting down on the step next to Mom. She poured a glass of lemonade for him. He held it in both hands after wiping the sweat off his brow. He drank it down slow and long, and for a few moments my parents sat together, no space between them. Then Mom got up and collected the empty glasses. She smiled at us before going back up the stairs, and we went back to work.

I remember my mother reaching up with a towel to pat the sweat off my father's forehead, while he sat with his hands in his lap. He didn't like to be fussed over. But this one time, he nodded his thanks and Mom let her smile linger. They usually didn't look into each other's eyes. When Mom turned toward me, I quickly looked down at my glass of lemonade as it dripped its own cool sweat in my dirty hands. I wasn't very good about making eye contact with her, even if something nice was going on.

We always finished our labor by late afternoon. Then we'd climb upstairs for early supper. Mom told us to clean up before sitting down at the table. More than any time I could remember, my mother was cheerful and almost predictable. We were living in a time of normal breathing.

At supper time we still heard more than we wanted to about Jesus, his family, and his followers. That was because Mom ad-libbed her own prayers for extra credit, after blessing the meal: *Bless us O Lord and these thy gifts, which we are about to receive through the bounty of Christ, our lord, Amen.* This was a signal for Mom to begin her litany of prayers to the saints: *Saint Francis, give my boys wings so they may fly with the tiny birds you feed, in Jesus' name; Saint Peter, be the rock under my boys' feet so they may stand tall in the name of Jesus; Saint Thomas, let your doubt give my sons unquestioning faith in our lord and savior, Jesus Christ.* Sometimes she threw in a prayer to St. Aloysius, the patron saint of youth. By the time my mother was finished with her add-ons, we'd be a real challenge for *Big Al,* as my brother called St. Aloysius. Bill said if we didn't get through the prayers soon, we'd be old and near starvation or worse. Then Mom would have to call on Jesus to do the Lazarus act if we were to rise up and have a chance to eat supper.

It was a peaceful time for both of my parents. Mom was cooking again. My father was pleased when she asked what he'd like for supper. My mother smiled when he pushed his empty plate away at the dinner table, after finishing a second helping of pork and sauerkraut. We never saw any leftover mashed potatoes and gravy, either. Same thing for all the pies she baked. Everything tasted extra good when Mom was happy.

My father's instruction at mealtime seemed like a way to avoid washing dishes. "I want those plates sparkling clean, boys." That was followed by a confusing sermon about nutrition and geography. "Eat what you put on your plate, but don't take more than you can eat. Think of the starving

Armenians." We never knew how that worked. Besides, we didn't know any Armenians.

Sometimes my mother laughed at Dad's stern warning, but before he continued his lecture, my brothers and I helped clear the table. Otherwise we'd hear his dinner table sermons about how "you can't trust the damn politicians as far as you can throw them." Then he usually followed up with his all-purpose lamentation: "My sons, I must tell you that in this world there are more horse's asses than horses." If Sinatra was singing on the radio, we received a speech about modern music and the popular singers of the day. According to my father, there hadn't been a decent singer on the planet since Mario Lanza. Mom's timing was such that she usually brought a fresh cherry or apple pie before Dad finished his speech. That kept us from rushing away from the table.

Our source of pie fillings was Professor Meyers, who lived across the alleyway. He was a retired agriculture teacher at the University, who grew sweet and sour cherries, rhubarb, and apples. If his eyesight was better, he would have seen Bill and Alfie hanging out in the trees with his sweet cherries. I stayed on the ground supervising my brothers, keeping watch for the old man. Whenever he called on Dad to fix a broken lawn mower or dig a section of his garden, he sent my father home with a basket full of fruit. Mom would go on a pie-baking spree, returning one pie to our neighbor for every three she made for us.

My brothers and I went as often as possible to the Community field to play ball. It seemed when Mom baked pies, we got off easy with our evening chores. Sometimes Dad came along, carrying a baseball bat. When the town team wasn't playing, he'd toss batting practice with the hitter standing against the screened backstop, and two of us retrieving the hit balls. If our friends were already playing in a pickup game, we would be invited to join. My father would stay long enough to watch us take a turn at bat. Then he'd wave goodbye and head up the hill toward home.

By summer's end, our landscape project was finished. The side yard was no longer a scratchy patch of weeds. Now it was green with tender grass, with a solid walkway of flat stones running through. The new wall was divided by a set of evenly measured steps, sloping down to the back yard. The top surface of the wall was flat, a perfect bench for my brothers and me. Sometimes we'd plunk ourselves down on the wall to sit and talk, or do nothing. But that rocky bench served another purpose.

My father's talent was not limited to creating objects, or building things with his hands. That was evident on Saturday afternoons when it was haircut time. Dad lined us up on the wall, tallest to shortest, the electric hair clipper hooked up to an extension cord which looped out of the basement window, down to our shaggy lineup on the wall. Dad's routine was to start with the top of each head, moving downhill from me, to Bill, then to Alfie, as if skipping a flat stone on water, with very little airtime between landings. If Dad was in a hurry to get from one of us to the other, a few unclipped hairs would get snagged in the teeth of the dreaded instrument. There was nothing to be gained by protesting. "Ouch!" was more of a reflex than an attempt at negotiation.

After he finished the tops of our heads, he moved back to me, at the beginning of the line. Three more times he repeated his march from one end to the other, trimming each boy's right side, then the left side, finishing with the back, hopefully with our necks not too badly nicked. Once Dad got distracted and didn't complete the trim on Bill's left side. My brother walked around for a few hours looking as if a bird was starting a nest above his left ear. Alfie and I weren't going to tell him, but the mirror ruined our fun. There was no reason to complain if we were unhappy with the job. Dad always had the same answer for us. "Boys, the only difference between a good haircut and a bad one is three or four days. Just remember. Patience is a virtue."

*   *   *

When I was ten or eleven years old, that stone wall became significant in another way. That was when my father and I shared time together on Saturday afternoons, after the haircuts were finished: shoe shine time. We polished the family shoes for Sunday Mass, but we were doing more than that. Dad's finger was lightly resting on the latch, ready to unlock the heavy gate in another stone wall: the boundary between father and son.

My father was a proud man. I began to realize that he was reaching out to me for support and reassurance. He was alone in his feelings, with no one to share his fear. Now he was testing me, his oldest son. Would I be a good listener?

How could he have anticipated, in his deliberately organized life, such unpredictable unfolding of each day? The force that carried him from one day to the next was the satisfaction of a job well done. He had to believe that he was a good father and husband. My father had to believe that he was loved. He reached for that hopeful optimism through his work, the only thing he could control.

His strength and fierce determination were known to me. Some of this I already understood: his courage in leaving his native country at the age of twenty, his determination to learn a trade at which he eventually excelled, his reliable commitment to keeping his word. I never questioned my father's dependability. He was always there for my brothers and me. His stubborn commitment to duty and responsibility was a mixed blessing.

On the positive side, this fierce energy gave him strength to stay with the hard slog of his daily life. He was at his best with his three boys. He carried his patience with the endurance of a marathon runner, allowing him to stand tall long after others would have collapsed. But he had his own fears. The durable man, who walked with strength and purpose, was more complicated and uncertain than he appeared to be. He was unprepared to deal with a wife who was ruled by her own voices, and the harmful instructions they imposed on her.

That which my father could not feel and measure by hand was a mystery to him. His way of overcoming any obstacle in his path was to work harder, be stronger, and take the time needed to polish the rough edges smooth. "Just make up your mind and do it." The well of patience he tapped for his handiwork ran dry when dealing with the mystery of my mother. "All in your mind," he would lecture to my mother. But it was real for her, and it *was* all in her mind. My father did not know how to be easy with her, while trying so fiercely to fight against the demons that controlled her.

I've watched my father's hands clamp and curve a plank of wood for a friend's boat. He could polish a blemish from a brass surface, until it glowed like the sun. My brothers and I knew the sound of his softly tapping hammer as he indented the outlines of flowers into his metal trays. But he could not bend or pound my mother's will to ignore her dark voices. In this lack of control was my father's fear.

On those Saturday afternoons, my father lined up the shoes like a parade of abandoned feet, paired in black, brown, and mahogany purple---called oxblood. Now I know he was looking for love and assurance. I could not yet say "I love you." I had become so protective of my own feelings that I could not offer the words he wanted to hear. I did the only thing I could. I followed him along the wall of shoes as he daubed on the polish, camouflaging the scrapes and scuffs earned by my brothers and me. I marched behind, in perfect step. With soft-bristled brush and back and forth buffing, I lifted from the leather its glow, masking each wounded surface in reflected light. We stood in each other's shadow, in our own hidden glow.

For that efficient hour, my father shined in my presence, and I in his.

Chapter 15

Recently we'd gone through a patch of settled weather with Mom. Any storms we encountered blew through quickly, with no lightning or thunder. She smiled more than she frowned and we felt safe within our own laughter. We even joked about the holy water bottles she'd placed throughout our apartment. Bill asked Mom if Alfie would turn into a priest if we mixed holy water into his food. She smiled thoughtfully, as if my brother's idea might be worth trying.

When Dad came home from work, he happily stomped up to our attic bedrooms to make sure we were keeping up with our school work. Sometimes his visit resulted in a surprise wrestling match, with the three of us pouncing on him as he was about to leave. Dad was wiry and strong. We were no match for him, unless we acted as a team. We tried to pile on top of him, pinning him to one of our beds. When Mom heard the ruckus from the floor above her, she'd call up to us that some of our energy could be saved for an evening rosary. That got things quiet in a hurry. But we could tell from the lenient flow of her words, that she was smiling when she sent her decree upstairs. Dad's advice to us was that if reciting a few *Our Fathers* and *Hail Marys* kept the peace, just do it.

Mom usually called us from downstairs when supper was ready. But during that particular winter, she sometimes hiked up the stairs and sat on the edge of Bill or Alfie's bed, as we cooled off from our free-for-all with Dad. She just smiled at us while we caught our breath. Mom was also puffing from her climb. Dad said she was getting a little chubby. "Nothing that a bit of exercise wouldn't cure." But she was happy and her smile felt real, like we could trust it.

As that winter moved on, Aunt Mary came upstairs to visit more often than before. She was still working as a nurse at Bellefonte Hospital, while Uncle Jack was finishing his graduate work at Penn State. She worked the late shift so her husband could be home with their small children, Patty and Mike. The two sisters were together almost every day, sometimes cooking in the kitchen, while my brothers and I played with our cousins. But I noticed that the sisters often retreated in hushed conversation to our parents' bedroom, closing the door behind them.

My father had fixed up a workshop in the basement. He built his own special bench at just the right height, so he could stand up straight without hunching over his project. Dad practiced what he preached when it came to good posture. "No slouching, boys. You don't want to be bent over like an old man." He told us it was important to stand at your work like you were giving it proper respect and attention. Whether we were carrying a bag of groceries or waiting for our turn at bat, we were not allowed to be lazy, not even in the way we were standing.

Dad had built shelves on the walls, with every tool in place, every nail and screw in its proper container. "If you use something, put it back. Even a screwdriver has its home." When we could be trusted to take care of my dad's tools, he methodically taught us how to use a crosscut saw or a hammer. We learned how to stroke on a smooth coat of paint or stain, leaving no overlapping brush marks or runs in the color. "Take your time. Do it right." As if we'd never heard that commandment before.

Dad began a secret project as that winter rolled on. He'd excuse himself from the supper table and go down to the basement. Our offers of help were rejected for the time being. We would be most helpful to him if we paid attention to our own chores and homework. Keeping Mom happy was the biggest help of all. When he was ready, and only then, we could come down and help with the finishing touches on whatever he was doing. Until then we were not to disturb anything in his workshop. He kept the door locked and the key hidden.

From late winter into early spring, Aunt Mary's visits with Mom continued. They seemed giddy, as if they were having unexpected fun. My mother was unusually mellow, almost lazy. Sometimes I found her napping in her rocking chair, warm in the sunlight streaming through the living room window. Mom's rosary beads were always nearby. If not twisted around her fingers, they were coiled in beaded circles on the adjacent table. I tip toed past when she was sleeping, partly to keep from waking her up, and partly to take in how her face filled out in a dreamy smile. When I stopped and watched, I wasn't even afraid if she caught me staring at her. I wanted her to glow in that soft light for a long time.

It wasn't until early summer that Dad finally invited us into the basement. He never did ask us for help with the mysterious task. I was beginning to understand that my father prayed with his hands; the resulting work was proof of his gift. Sometimes he had to do it alone. All we could do is admire his clever workmanship and try to understand what it really meant for all of us. And keep quiet, because it was a surprise for my mother.

The crib was three feet long and two feet wide. My father built the mattress frame with adjustable latches, so Mom could slide it up or down on the supporting legs. The front railing could also be moved to different heights, allowing our new baby brother or sister to be lifted right out without bending down or straining the back. My dad's concern about posture was built right into the little bed.

The head and foot were of solid pine, softly curved at each corner. He matched and joined the rounded pieces to the square boards at each end, then sanded the joints smooth as marble. No sharp edges, no places for a baby to get bumped on the head. The final touch must have been a salute to my dad's employer. He painted the headboards white and the vertical side railings blue, the official colors of Penn State University.

My father stood tall beside it, with his arms crossed over his chest. He nodded at the three of us. We just stood there, with nothing to say. It was a piece of beautiful furniture, but it was much more than that: it came with the promise of a new member in our family. The paint needed one more day to dry, so we had to keep our hands off the crib. We wanted to slide the railings and test the adjustment of the mattress frame. We were more interested in the feel and touch of the furniture, than what it meant.

The next evening, after supper, we carried the crib upstairs. Mom had not seen it. Dad had also told her that she wasn't to go in the basement during that whole period of time when he was working on it. Mom must have sensed that it was a special surprise. Otherwise she would have sneaked a look within minutes of my father's instructions.

She stayed in the living room while my father directed us upstairs with the baby bed. Bill and Alfie backed up the stairs as they gripped the bottom edge of the headboard. I faced them, holding the slanted weight of the footboard three or four steps below, as we angled upward, one step at a time. "Take your time boys; easy does it," Dad warned as we eased the crib into the hallway. All this time, my mother obediently remained in the living room. We slid ourselves and the blue and white crib into our parents' bedroom. My father had already cleared a space between the window and dresser, against the wall at the foot of their bed. Bill and Alfie set their end down first. I settled the other end onto the hardwood floor. Dad stood back, surveying the crib's position in the room. He moved forward and carefully slid it to the right, about two inches. It had to be perfectly centered, like a picture on the wall.

"Boys, go get your mother."

My mother came through the kitchen, with Alfie tugging her hand. When Mom got to the open doorway, she stopped short. Her hand floated to her mouth. Her eyelids fluttered as if the overhead light was too bright. Then her eyes opened wide, before tearing over. She eased herself forward, as if afraid of approaching the crib too rapidly. Mom stood in front of it, then trailed her hand over the horizontal bar of the railing. After a few deep breaths she eased backward, almost staggering to the edge of their bed. Dad reached for her elbow, steadying her, as she sat down with more than her own weight. That's when I really took it in, that our family was about to change. We were about to move out of the familiar space we were now in. No matter what happened in our little uncertain lives, nothing would ever be the same.

For the past few months my mother's mood was joyful, anticipating her baby's arrival. Saturday mornings she cooked pancakes for us. When we could afford it, she would fry up a pan of crispy bacon or sausage links. Usually we had scrapple, fried brown and crunchy. We didn't rush away from the table because we didn't have to get away from Mom. It was fun being with her.

The morning sunshine brought Mom outside more often than before, especially now that Dad had a new project for us. Uncle George gave him permission to plant a garden right next to the house. Whenever my mother suggested a nourishing breakfast, *for strength and energy for my growing boys,* we knew Dad had an entire day of labor planned for the three of us, digging and raking the soil, preparing the garden for seeding.

After she cleaned up the breakfast dishes, Mom came outside to watch us working our plot of land. Aunt Mary joined her when she had a day off from the hospital. The two sisters sat on a simple bench my father built from solid oak. Dad liked to sit there in late afternoon after he got home from work, reading the news in *The Centre Daily Times.*

One morning I was raking soil between the rows of scallions, when I happened to glance up as my aunt brushed her hand over my mother's belly. Mom put her hand on her sister's hand, guiding it in gentle circles. They smiled and silently nodded at each other. When they looked up and caught me staring, I pretended I was looking past them, at the puffy clouds clinging on top of the Tussey Mountains. Mom's belly was not to be stared at.

As the Saturdays slid into early summer, green sprouts of lettuce poked through the soil. The foliage of carrots and radishes lifted upward, giving early definition to the carefully lined arrangement of Dad's garden. Bill and Alfie and I were getting taller, as if we were in competition with the vegetables. With each passing week, my mother was growing as well, although in a different direction. Her steps seemed more deliberate, her climb up the stairs more labored. We were all in the growing season.

We were out of school by early June. Our summer vacations stretched as long as possible over those warm months, so the farm kids could work when they were most needed. For those of us who lived in town, it meant more time for baseball or hiking through the surrounding countryside. Joe organized our expeditions to the Duck Pond, where we continued searching for hawks and wild birds, always adding new species to our list of discovery. By now we knew how to trap snakes. Joe had built a wire cage in his backyard, which was home to a scary assortment of reptiles. Sometimes he lifted a snake out of the pen and if we really and truly wanted to be frightened, he'd let us hold it.

On those warm days, my father went early to work so he could be with us in the late afternoon. He wanted to check on my mother, who was becoming more uncomfortable in the summer heat as her tummy enlarged. My brothers and I knew he would play ball with us as soon as he was finished with Mom, so we waited for him in our clutter of baseball mitts and bats, sometimes with a brand new ball. By now I was a two-year veteran of Little League. If I got good enough at fielding grounders, I had a chance to be moved from the outfield to second base. My coach even let me throw batting practice. I could throw with enough accuracy to get the ball over the plate. Could I ever be a pitcher?

Mom no longer sat on the steps to watch us play catch. Her visits stopped when she began having difficulty climbing back up the stairs. Aunt Mary had been lecturing her about gaining weight, but Mom said she wasn't eating that much. She was getting so tired that we sometimes skipped the evening rosary because she'd fallen asleep. Bill usually made up a prayer of gratitude when that happened.

Dad was a good pitcher. He was patient and he could throw the ball over the plate. When we had enough time before supper, we went down to the Community Field for batting practice. At first our timing was so bad that swinging our bats was like an afterthought. But he would just hold the ball up in front of us. "Keep your eye on the ball. Pay attention. See this white round thing, boys? That's the ball, in case you didn't recognize it." Dad would rub the ball in his hands before the next toss. "If you can't make your bat hit the ball, make the ball hit your bat!" In three or four days we were all making contact with the ball. Alfie was hitting straight up the middle and Bill was even playing around with hitting left-handed. He wanted to be a switch hitter. I was a pitcher. In other words, I couldn't hit very well.

As the summer went on, my father had a more urgent reason for his early return from work. By late June, my mother was confined to bed. She was gaining too much weight, even though her baby would be born in less than a month. Aunt Mary said Mom was retaining fluid. Should we be careful if we hugged her? What if we squeezed her too hard? Dad told her to listen to the doctor. Not only that, if only she'd been exercising like he told her, she wouldn't be in this predicament. Mom never liked being at the receiving end of any criticism, especially my father's relentless words about exercise and fresh air.

My brothers and I sat on the side of her bed when she wanted company. We'd bring a glass of water or a small sandwich for her lunch. But nothing with salt, since Aunt Mary said the doctor's very words were "no salt." She couldn't have bacon and eggs, so I learned how to cook her favorite hot cereal, *Cream of Wheat*. I hated it because of the way it clumped together in cold, gummy blobs, forcing me to chew it before I could get it down my throat. But I made it just right for Mom.

I took the box from its place on the shelf. When I opened the door, Aunt Jemima stared at me from the adjacent pancake box. Rastus was pictured on his own carton, stirring the Cream of Wheat, blinking from the darkness inside the kitchen cabinet. They both seemed to be giving me a message with their eyes: *Take care of your mama.* If my brothers and I could keep her happy, maybe she wouldn't go back to being the scary stranger she was before.

Mom liked the cereal cooked with milk, slowly stirred into a smooth paste. It took about ten minutes. That seemed to take care of the lumps. A little brown sugar sprinkled on top, and her breakfast was ready. If it wasn't sweet enough, she would send me back to the kitchen for more sugar. That was one more problem, according to Dr. Light; she was eating too many sweets. Even though she rested most of the time, she looked pale and tired. Mom was getting puffy.

Something else about my mother was beginning to change. She would take in a spoonful of the cereal and stop, as if she was all of a sudden confused about who was sitting with her. It only took a few seconds for her face to soften as she remembered me, and then she resumed her chewing. But I was beginning to feel that I was watching my mom in an old movie that suddenly froze on one picture, then started up as quickly as it had stopped. Once again her eyes stayed on me, puzzled and impatient. She hadn't done that for a while. I stared out the window when she looked at me like that.

Something was coming back to my mother, like a whisper hidden in a gust of wind. She seemed to be listening with curious anticipation, as if trying to remember words from a song she hadn't heard for a long time. I felt like something good was struggling to stay with her, and something bad was bullying its way back.

The arguments between my parents started up again. My father came home at lunchtime almost every day. He was worried about her, but he couldn't help bossing Mom around. She didn't like it one bit. The word of God was again finding its voice in my mother's side of their disagreements. If Dad lectured about her diet, she gave it right back, telling him to nourish his own soul *with the body and blood of Christ.* Their quarrels became more heated and more frequent. My father returned to work, more worried and upset than when he'd come home. Once again, my brothers and I had crossed the border into the familiar territory of uncertainty, as we waited for whatever came next.

Because of my mother's condition, we didn't have much time to go to the baseball field. But Dad managed to find a few minutes to play catch with us in our side yard, so he could be near Mom. One afternoon in the middle of July, the two of us were tossing the ball. I practiced throwing my knuckle ball, a pitch to mix up with my mediocre fastball and my imaginary curve. Dad held up his catcher's mitt, giving me a target knee-high. My pitch skittered off the ground and glanced off his mitt. Dad picked it up and threw it back. "Don't rush your throw." He thumped his mitt again, gave me the same target.

I was always fascinated by the knuckleball, a tricky pitch to master. A pitch with a mind of its own. You can't hold it too tight; you can't crush it. It's held like a feathery bird, between the thumb and the little finger. The other fingers barely rest on the ball, touching it only with the knuckles or even the fingernails. When the ball is released, the idea is to put no spin on it. A well-thrown knuckler just floats up to the batter. It shudders and dances, making its own wind currents as it presses against the air. The thing about the knuckleball is that the batter never knows where it is going.

The side door opened and slammed shut before I threw my next pitch. Aunt Mary came into the yard, having been upstairs with my mother. Now she stood breathlessly beside my father, who was looking up at her from his crouched catcher's stance. He slowly straightened up and took off his glasses. He leaned his ear toward Aunt Mary's soft murmuring, looking down at his catcher's glove. Dad shook the mitt off his hand and dropped it at his feet. He looked back at my aunt, who nodded her head toward the house, then followed her up the stairs. I stood alone with the baseball in my glove.

There is something else about a knuckle ball; the pitcher never knows where it is going.

A few minutes after my aunt interrupted our game of catch, my father came downstairs just long enough to tell me to stay put. "Dr. Light is on his way to see Mom. Show him in, Carl. He's never been here before."

Bill and Alfie were over in the Jungle, collecting leaves and plants for a Scout project. I could have called them over to play ball with me. But I didn't. I sat down on our stone wall. I didn't want any company. Didn't want to play, didn't want to laugh. We'd been in sunshine long enough; now it was all used up. Time to enter those familiar shadows once more.

Dr. Light was our new doctor since we moved into town. He was kind. He always talked to us kids as if we were grownups. When we went to see him for an appointment, he looked us straight in the eye. Then he asked *us* where it hurt and how it hurt. He never talked to Mom and Dad until our conversation was finished.

I jumped up from my seat on the wall when I heard a car door slam shut. I didn't expect him so soon. Dr. Light was wearing a bow tie and a white shirt, with the sleeves rolled up. His black doctor's bag was in one hand and a handkerchief in the other, dabbing his forehead. He glanced at me, smiling with his lips tight in a straight line. I ran up to the door and held it open. He was in and on his way up the stairs before I even said hello. I followed, stepping lightly. Aunt Mary and Dad were at the top of the steps.

I knew not to go into the bedroom. I sat in our living room, in Mom's rocking chair, looking out the south-facing window. I could see the farmlands unfolding like a green ocean, stretching to the Tussey Mountains, carved dark blue from the pale sky. A distant scattering of barn roofs reflected the hazy light. Like tall lighthouses, the attached silos glowed silver and red in late afternoon. Did my mother ever look outward at that mural of land and sky? Did she ever gift herself with that vision of changing light, as the sun traced its arc over the up and down hills? Or did she always have that scenery at her back, listening for her distant voices as they became louder, trying to be heard over our own hopeful noise?

Aunt Mary discovered me in the rocking chair. She heard the noise of the baseball pounding my mitt. I didn't realize I was playing catch with myself, repeatedly thumping the ball into the pocket of my glove, until someone came out to talk with me. She pulled up a chair from the dining room table. Placing it right in front of me, she sat down and leaned her face close to mine. Even with tears in her eyes, Aunt Mary was beautiful. She sat back just long enough to tug a white hanky from her pocket. She touched it to my cheeks before brushing it beneath my eyes. She leaned toward me again, curved her hand over my shoulder and whispered that we should all pray for Mom. She lifted my face and studied my eyes, even when I tried to look away.

As soon as the doctor left, Aunt Mary packed a suitcase for Mom. I followed Dad downstairs and helped him clean up the back seat of the car. He sent me upstairs for a blanket and pillow and to tell his passengers they were ready to go. I wasn't allowed to ride to the hospital in Bellefonte. Uncle Jack would look after my brothers and me until Dad and Aunt Mary returned, without my mother.

Bill and Alfie had come home from the Jungle. We were lined up along the sidewalk when Mom walked to the car, holding her big belly. Mary and Dad were on each side, patiently trying to match my mother's reluctant steps. Mom had that vacant look again, the straight-ahead stare, as if she could see everything in the distance and nothing right in front of her. But she abruptly swayed to a halt when we entered her vision, as if her body forgot to stop when her feet did. When we reached out for her, she un-tangled her arms from her guardians and pulled us toward her, all three of us at the same time. She held us in a hard hug, then kissed us. Her arms fell limp and she released us. Mom's eyes went back to that far-away look, as if we'd vanished into the distance. Dad opened the door of the car and ma-neuvered her onto the bed he'd made on the back seat. Aunt Mary got in the front with my father. They drove away as we watched. Nobody waved.

Four days later my mother returned from the hospital. Aunt Regina rode along with Dad and Aunt Mary when they brought her home. It seemed like it hurt Mom when she lifted herself out of the car. Her sisters both reached out to steady her. She was unsure of her footing, as if the path to our home was overgrown with tangled weeds. Mom lost most of her weight, but she was still puffy. She didn't see my brothers and me even though we were right in front of her. Her face looked tight, as if invisible hands were pressing against her temples, trying to squeeze away a headache. Aunt Mary guided Mom along the sidewalk to our apartment door. Mom walked right past us. My father came next. He was carrying Mom's suitcase with one hand. He carried nothing in the other.

Earlier that morning, before Mom came home, my father had dismantled his crib and carried it down the stairs to the basement.

*　*　*

Here is a portrait of my mother after she returned from the hospital, without her baby. She sits in sunlight at the dining room table. Her elbows rest on the polished surface as she hunches over a glossy brochure. Its bold print solemnly promises my mother that her baby is best remembered with a thoughtfully selected cemetery marker from *Matthew's Memorials*. She has gracefully penned my little sister's name next to one of the flat bronze markers. She's made her choice.

On the blank margin of that same page, there is another inscription by my mother's hand: *Frances; Baptized by my sister Mary; an angel for God.* On the bottom of the page is a single date. My mother's face is blank. She is numb and confused, between her pain of loss and the gift of delivering a soul for Jesus. There are no tears in this picture, only mine, shed in my viewing of it.

Though late July, she wears her blue flannel nightgown. She's just come from her bed and will return to it as soon as she finishes this task. It will be very late in summer before my brothers and I will once again sit outside with her. But for now, our home is quiet. We've learned to hear each other's whispers, even with respectful distance between us. My brothers and I wear our mother's humid grief like the summer air. My father rakes his tears into the garden.

The image described cannot be found in an album; it cannot be held in hand, or passed around a table. This picture of my mother in mourning was developed and fixed within my own imagination and memory. Shortly after my father's death, I was cleaning out his desk, taking inventory so my brothers and I could prepare our boyhood home for sale to a neighbor. In the top drawer, under a packet of cancelled checks and paid bills, I found the envelope from Koch's Funeral Home. It hid a harsh receipt for my little sister's burial and a map of Centre Hills Memorial Park. The route to her cemetery plot was inked in, as if we only had to follow the map to be with Frances. But I knew where she was: plot 9-T, between the paved access road and the tall pine tree, just to the east of Benner Pike.

It was within this envelope that Mom had placed the pamphlet from Matthew's Memorials. As I read the notations inked by my mother, I understood that her raw contemplation about her baby's grave was an act of deep love. She forced herself from the dark safety of her bedroom just long enough to enter the painful sunlight, so she could complete this task of saying goodbye to Frances.

*　*　*

The word *denial* proclaims repudiation of truth; rejection of the facts; deliberate ignorance of what happened. When I look back at this chapter of my family history, I must consider how denial shaped my acceptance of Frances' death. Until I was deeply involved in writing this memoir, I believed her stillbirth was caused by a complication of my mother's pregnancy: toxemia; excessive weight gain; some other complication of her health, resulting in her miscarriage. I learned otherwise.

On a recent visit with my brother Bill and his wife Peggy, we discussed my writing project, reviewing some of the events of our childhood. I mentioned that I'd recently requested and received our mother's medical notes from Danville Hospital. One of the entries that most intrigued me was a description of the voices that told her to "jump, jump." Peggy listened to Bill and me, nodding her head in agreement with some of the stories we remembered. She'd heard most of it before and she knew my mother. And then she stunned me with a story that gave new meaning to those words, "jump, jump."

Peggy had visited my father in the nursing home shortly before his death. He talked about his life and his great pride in his sons and their families. Having grandchildren and great-grandchildren was a huge gift, for which he was deeply thankful. Working with his hands, seeing and feeling the results of his creativity meant a great deal to him. My father believed that he would be remembered by what he'd made.

Then he turned to the sadness in his life; he couldn't fix his wife. He was sorry his sons lived with all those unhappy times. Then Peggy stunned me. "Your father told me that his deepest regret was about that one terrible argument with your mother; the one that killed her baby."

I stared at Peggy. *What was she talking about?*

"You know, the bad fight they had when she was pregnant with your little sister." Her voice was quiet. "Remember?" She waited for me to respond, but I could not respond. "When she opened the second floor window and jumped?"

I turned my attention to Bill. "She jumped? Where the hell was I?"

"You were right there with me." My brother looked at me with an expression of disbelief. "Don't you remember? A couple of weeks before she went to the hospital? We were out in the yard playing catch, when she landed on the other side of the house. We heard the *thump*. On top of the garage."

There was not one clue in my mind, not one ghost of an image to recall that sad event. If it were clear in my memory, by now I'd have written a poem about my mother soaring through that window to join the chorus of angels, beckoning her into that humid summer air. I'd have *salvaged* something of her flight. But in truth, with all the time I've had to contemplate and remember, I have nothing to connect me with my mother's weighted plunge. For these many years it was assumed that all of us remembered the details of that day, and there was no need to talk about it. *It's history; it's done.* But I did not remember.

And for me, it was not done.

*　*　*

Frances haunts me. What does it mean that a child was *stillborn?* Was she *unborn?* What would my little sister have been like, and whom would she have resembled? Would she have had even more trouble than her brothers, in dealing with our mother's voices?

Whenever I visit State College, I drive out of town to Centre Memorial Park. Frances is buried right behind my parents, under the flat marker engraved with her name. My mother selected the *Bronze Angelic Style,* sixteen inches by eight, its patina weathered thirty-seven years longer than my parents' common grave.

With every visit, I go into my meditation. What would it have been like for Alfie, Bill, and me, to be big brothers to our little sister? What would it have been like for Frances? Would we have been her protectors? Would she have softened the lines of vigilance, so indelibly worn on my mother's face?

I think I know some of the answers.

We'd have taught her how to bait a hook, how to field a grounder on the big hop. Let go of her hand? Only when she'd learned the habit of looking both ways. And what about our little sister's first prom? We'd have chaperoned, three mothers disguised as brothers.

We would have learned from her. She'd have brought some needed light, shown us how to be less heavy afoot. We were ripe to unlearn our vigilant scrambling between the hard-edged shadows of my mother's demons. Frances would have taught us to dance.

With each visit I linger over the grave. I take in the smell of sweet air from the cornfields on the other side of Route 150. Before departing, I look down and read the engraved silence on Frances' marker. Her name is embraced by an angel on each side. The space for dates is half filled, with only one inscription: July 21, 1949. There is one other notation: *You Rest With Angels.*

The haunting is in what might have been.

Chapter 16

My mother languished in her bedroom for the rest of that sad summer. Aunt Mary tried to bring her outside on those pleasant days when the breeze was moving, when humidity wasn't wrapped around us like a suffocating cloud.

Dad encouraged Mom to step out of her darkness. "Fresh air and sunshine, Sophie. And some exercise. You'll feel better." Those words we'd heard so many times before now came with a mellow edge, as if he'd lost a bit of faith in his precious advice. My father's repeated pleas resulted in nothing more than a fixed stare from Mom. Nothing worked. She pulled down the shades and withdrew into her uninvited night.

My brothers and I plunged ourselves into baseball practice, sharpening our skills for the final games of summer. Whenever we were catching grounders and fly balls and swinging the bat, we were miles away from our sadness. But trudging up the hill from the Community Field, the return trip home was always too short. We counted the dwindling days of summer with more anticipation than disappointment. School would be good for us this year.

I found another way to spend time away from our house. I got my first real job. The Centre Daily Times was looking for newspaper delivery boys. Dad thought I should be earning my own money, since I was now twelve. Sometimes Bill and Alfie walked the route with me, so they could learn who my customers were. My brothers could always substitute if I was sick or too busy with homework.

The older kids taught me about delivering the paper. Tossing the news could save steps. A special skill was required, in order to shape the paper into a smaller package that could be thrown like a missile. First day on the job, that's what I learned. Cleverly folding the newspaper resulted in a compact envelope, rigid and dense enough that it could be sailed through the air. I could fling a paper from the sidewalk to the front door of Dr. Robinson's house, thirty feet away. I could even bend its arc, curving it to the right or left. Too bad I couldn't do that with a baseball.

Being a newspaper boy meant I had a reason to be away from my house every afternoon. I could escape when Mom was angry with us for not keeping up with the work she and the Blessed Mother assigned us. Sometimes my mother didn't have the strength to play her game with Mary, but that didn't stop her from delivering instructions about how we could *get right and stay right with Jesus.*

My brothers kept me company one November evening when we lingered on Mr. Nordbloom's porch. After sticking his newspaper in the front door, we stood spellbound, staring through the living room window at his new television set. We flickered in its reflection like blue ghosts in the night, watching John Cameron Swayze on the Camel News Caravan.

Since we couldn't hear any sound, we made up our own stories to go with the images flashing from inside. When President Truman gave a speech and pounded his fist on his desk, Bill said he was telling kids all over the country that school was cancelled forever. To emphasize his declaration, the president was drumming "no more school, no more school." That was when Mr. Nordbloom came to the door because he heard us laughing at Bill's story. We thought he'd be angry at us for looking into his house. Instead, he invited us in for hot chocolate. We had to hurry on home, so we declined. But we would sure love to have our own TV.

My mother began to wander from her room as if autumn's diminished light beckoned her to the empty rocking chair by the living room window. This time of year the view from that place was austere. That was a new word I learned in Mrs. McFeater's seventh-grade English class: *austere.* The vigilant sound seemed chiseled out of cold air, warning of the deepening winter and frozen stars. The lush green farmlands were now under a rusty veil; the rolling hills were prisoners in gray. November once again dropped its heavy drag on all of us. My mother's vision seemed unable to penetrate her thin reflection in the window. Her mood was the color of the bleak landscape. She lived in a country named *Austere.*

Something else was going on. For the first time since Mom lost Frances, she was gaining energy. But it was not good energy. Once again, shortened days and extended nights carried her from the periphery into the bull's eye center of our lives. My mother was spinning back into that whirlpool. Her old shadows were stirring and coming in from the night, their vacation over. So was ours.

Mom woke us every morning for 6:30 Mass. Evening rosary was more important than school. Our complaints about heavy homework assignments were answered with the promise that the only grades that mattered were those given out by Our Lord and Savior, Jesus Christ. And we had to earn them.

Once again, my mother was flying her paper commands over Blessed Mary's picture. But something had shifted, even in that relationship. Mom got angry if Mary's answer didn't suit her. She'd roll up the papers, throw and throw again until she and the Blessed Mother were in agreement. My brothers and I were destined to live our lives in work and prayer. She was training us to be monks.

My mother was still unable to do anything resembling housework. If she started a task, she couldn't finish it. Her solution was to add the unfinished project to our litany of duties, all of which, when finished, *would be pleasing in the eyes of God.* My mother moved from the refuge of her bedroom to being so entangled in our lives, that we were unable to move without her orders.

If my father tried to intercede, it only got worse. Mom's speech took on a new and alarming tone of anger. She spoke to Dad with such mechanical coldness that I wanted to defend him. Her voice was a distant recording: a foreign language, sung from a monotone script. Her facial expression was detached from the severe words that stabbed at us, especially my father. My mother's voices had returned, playing her like an out-of-tune instrument, louder than ever.

Much of my mother's renewed energy was directed at Alfie, Bill, and me. There was no limit with our work. It was impossible to please her. Instead of thanking us for washing the windows, we were rewarded by the added assignment of cleaning and waxing the kitchen floor. It was especially bad on Holy Days of Obligation, Christmas, or the days that celebrated her favorite saints. Good Friday through Easter was a cleaning marathon. *Cleanliness is next to Godliness.* Shining and polishing was like erasing black marks from the soul.

The approaching warmth and light of the following summer did not brighten my mother's spirit. She was never at rest. At night she stalked the hallways, and our sleep. We woke up more tired than when we went to bed. Grasping for happiness was like clutching at a pile of feathers, the air stirred by the reach itself, scattering that desired joy in all directions. Sooner or later there would be an eruption of words, and sometimes we were hit with more than words. When my father tried to intervene for us, she spoke with such an edge that we got goose bumps. We were cold on the hot days of summer.

On that Fourth of July, we had our own fireworks. Holiday stress and the chaotic mix of noise, heat, and Pennsylvania humidity lit the fuse for one of my mother's worst explosions. The demons were back and my mother was dancing with them. We had lost the mother who sometimes smiled when we wrestled and elbowed each other and made our funny faces. Now we had the mother who held her hands fiercely against her ears because we tiptoed too loudly.

Out of desperation, Dad had recently called Father Gallagher to perform his ritual of holy water and prayers. It was useless to call our doctor. Mom was suspicious that any pills he prescribed were an attempt at poisoning her. Hunched under the weight of his work, our weary priest had aged before our eyes. He shared his discouragement with my dad, questioning his own effectiveness in trying to help our family. Father's sprinkled incantations merely chased Mom's tormenters to higher ground. They were nesting in the ceiling, having been chased out of the closets and hanging clothes. *Like a flock of starlings with burning red eyes,* she told us. *They ruffle the air with their flapping.* We remained frightened of whatever frightened her.

On that July holiday, some of the neighborhood kids were setting off firecrackers. Each sharp report brought Mom out of her chair and into our bedrooms, or wherever we tried to hide. She found more chores for us to do, anything to keep us busy. *Idle hands are the devil's workshop.* She was getting scarier by the day. More than ever before, I stood between Mom and my younger brothers.

All morning long we did our work. We could hear our playmates down at the Community Field, their cheering and laughter punctuated by the whack and thwack of baseballs soaring between bat and glove. That fun was a million miles away. My mother added one task too many to the list. I ignored the look on Mom's face, her lips pursed into a straight line and her eyes squeezing me into angry focus. I made a mistake, arguing for freedom from our morning obligations. I talked back.

Dad knocked on the bathroom door several times before I opened it. He had been shopping for groceries. He found my brothers in the driveway waiting for him to come home, before they would go back in the house. I'd been staring at myself in the mirror. The imprint of my mother's open right hand was still red and throbbing on my left cheek. My tears were hot and angry. I could taste my salty hatred for my mother. I knew she was striking out to drive the devil away because of my backtalk. But it didn't matter. My life would be so much better without her. It didn't do any good to pray for her to get better; God didn't pay attention to me anyway. Why should I care about God? Or my mother?

Dad told me to go out in the yard with Bill and Alfie. "Mom's in her room, in her rocking chair. She won't bother you. She's praying her rosary." He started down the hallway to check on her. He gave me a stern look. "Stay with your brothers. I'll be out in a minute. We're going to talk." I could hardly hear his footsteps as he shuffled toward the bedroom.

My brothers and I were sitting on the stone wall when my father came out of the house. The way Dad stood right in front of us, he didn't have to tell us to pay attention. "How many times have I told you boys that you can't talk to her when she's like that?" He put a tight hold on my shoulders. "Especially you, Carl. You know she's sick. And you have to be an example for your brothers." Dad put an extra squeeze on his grip. "Look at me when I talk to you. Don't talk back to her." Dad finally let go of my shoulders. "For your own good, don't talk back."

I studied my sneakers. Keds. They were black, but faded now to more of an early morning color. The string on the right shoe had a hard knot between the second and third pair of lace holes, where it had broken off.

The seam between the dark cloth and the rim of the sole on the outside of the left shoe had separated just...

"Carl. I'm talking to you. No more arguing with Mom. Is that clear?" Bill and Alfie looked back and forth, between me and Dad. I came back to my seat on the wall from wherever my mind had drifted. I was feeling sorry for myself. I could feel the hard rock pressing against my bottom. I squirmed around. I was expecting more of a lecture, but it was over.

All of a sudden, my father was softer, as if he'd unflexed his muscles after his tense words. "O.K. boys. Get some clean clothes on and wash up a bit. Let's go downtown to the Carnival. Mom's peaceful now. She's calmed down with her bible. We'll go have some fun." We let out a cheer as we jumped off the wall. Just before I went into the house, I glanced back at Dad. Now he was sitting on the wall, staring at his own shoes.

The Alpha Fire Company's Fourth of July Carnival was a big deal. There wasn't much else going on that time of year in our small town. Our walk from home to downtown took ten minutes. Stumbling along behind my father, the three of us were a gaggle of scraped elbows and bony knees, poking at each other with excitement. Dad gave us each a dollar for games and hot dogs and soda. He stuffed two extra dollars in my pocket, just in case we needed it. We could be on our own until 9 o'clock, when the fireworks would start. Dad planned to meet us then. We'd walk home when it was all over. He would be working with some of his fellow Elks at the ice-cream stand. We knew where he'd be if we needed him, or if we needed a free scoop of vanilla or butter pecan.

My cheek still felt warm.

South Allen Street was blocked off from Beaver Avenue to College Avenue, with a merry-go-round at one end and a Ferris wheel at the other. In between were the games. It cost a nickel to play Bingo. For the same money, we could throw darts at the balloons. We spent most of our time at the beanbag toss, where points were awarded for accuracy, with baseball cards and bubblegum as prizes. If we got bored with all that we could go to the shooting gallery and test our skill with BB guns, aiming at lions and tigers as they crouched in the distance, ready to pounce on us. My brothers took their turn with the rifles: first Bill, then Alfie, and finally, me.

They couldn't hit the broad side of a barn. I swaggered up to the line and picked up my gun to show them what their big brother could do. I raised the rifle and rested my head against the barrel to sight the distant tiger. My left shoulder pushed against the side of my face, as I braced my arms to stabilize the BB gun. My left cheek throbbed a little bit. I couldn't aim very well. I missed all my shots.

Did her hand hurt?

The food tent was set up at the end of Allen Street, next to the Ferris wheel. The firemen were busy waiting on customers, taking turns flipping hamburgers and hot dogs. Onions and peppers sizzled in big pans on the back of the grill. The smell thickened the air. I pointed to one of the hot dogs. I liked them slightly burnt, with the charcoal blisters oozing hot flavor. One of my teachers was a volunteer fireman, Mr. Miller. He speared the one I pointed to and wrapped it up in a toasted roll. "Don't eat that all at once, Carl. There's more where that came from." His grin was slicked up with some mustard he forgot to wipe off. He took a long sip out of a coffee cup, drinking something that left a frothy mustache under his nose. Mr. Miller wiped it off with his apron and grinned, then set the cup behind the stack of napkins, out of sight.

I slathered on a glob of spicy bronze mustard; none of the wimpy, dandelion-colored stuff for me. My brothers went for the hamburgers. They put on too much ketchup. When they chomped into their rolls, it leaked onto their chins, like bloody goatees. We washed everything down with bottles of Coca-Cola, cold, sweet, and darkly fizzy.

Was my mother thirsty?

By early evening, we heard the sound of distant sirens heralding the parade. The Benevolent Protective Order of Elks had plenty of help at the ice-cream stand, so Dad got out early, before we had a chance to sample the different flavors. We followed the mob onto crowded College Avenue. Since we couldn't squeeze in front of the spectators lining the street, we climbed on top of the wall bordering the University campus. From there we could look down on the whole scene.

Fire engines from the surrounding towns rumbled at the front of the lineup. Shiny red trucks carried firefighters on the running boards, starchy-white in their dress uniforms. The blare of the sirens went right through me, thrilling my bones. Clanging bells ricocheted off the buildings across College Avenue.

Next came the Cub Scouts, Girl Scouts, Boy Scouts, all in their pressed uniforms, blissfully out of step, searching for their cheering parents. They were followed by the baseball teams. Bill and I slid behind Dad when our Little League team marched by. We should have been in the parade with them, but my mother wouldn't let us march when she found out that Coach Benner wasn't Catholic. We didn't think she would let us play the rest of the summer, but Dad said not to worry, he'd straighten it out. He grumbled about that. "She wouldn't be happy unless the Pope was pitching and Jesus was coaching."

More fire trucks growled and blared through the crowded street. In the distance, a new sound echoed. *Thimp, thimpity-thimp, thimp*: Our local drum and bugle corps, two blocks away. Closer they came, until *thump, thumpity-thump, thump*, they were right on top of us, pounding our ears. My brothers were waving and making faces, trying to make the drummers laugh. One of the marchers saw us standing up on the wall and stuck his tongue out at us. We cheered when he lost his step and skipped his drum-beat. And then, *thimp, thimpity-thimp, thimp,* the band smartly marching away from us, the sound dropping and thinning, until it was gone.

Was my mother's heart beating loud or soft?

After the parade, we walked back to Allen Street, where we met Dad. It was time for cotton candy. For ten cents, we could make our own. Pink clouds swirled like miniature hurricanes within the big stainless steel bowls. Sugared sweetness perfumed the pepper-onion air. I wiped my paper cone against the spinning candy, which twirled around it like a feathery wrap. Each pass into the whirring mix thickened my treat, puffing it up like a balloon. Finally, Dad said I had enough. It was time to give my brothers a chance to get in line.

Eating cotton candy is an illusion. It's like sticking out your tongue to catch a snowflake, the way its whiteness quivers in its falling. The wispy lick of cold melts away as if it was your imagination, more real in the air than when you finally touch it with your tongue. Same with cotton candy. If you try to bite into it, you will clunk your teeth together, as if chomping on a feather. It's air that puffs up the sweetness. Try licking it and it smears stickiness all over your face. If you tear off little bites, your fingers spread sweet glue on everything you touch. But if you lick your fingers first, you can pinch off a small clump without it sticking to you. Then you just put it on your tongue and it dissolves into nothing. It becomes what it really is.

What would remain of my mother's puffed up fear, if its air was gone?

After the fireworks, my father said it was time to go home. Our eyes adjusted to the darkness as we walked away from the carnival lights, leaving the streaming red flares and white skybursts behind. There was something calming about the unexploded sky, where the only light came from the moon and the stars. My father pointed out some of the constellations, especially Orion and the Big Dipper. Those were his favorites. He could always put his finger on them. It reminded me of that time on Beaver Avenue, when he sketched the constellations on the darkness above us. What would it be like out there, looking back at our planet? Would we be glowing too?

Even though it was past our bedtime, we took the long way home so we could run around the community field. We were full of food and soda, sticky with the smear of cotton candy. We alternated between walking quietly and chasing fireflies, racing each other until we were falling down, worn out from laughing and running. Finally Dad herded us together and we marched up the hill toward home. Our pace slowed as we shuffled down the alley toward our house. We were reluctant to come in from the warm hug of that summer night, where everything outside our home seemed so predictable, even the erratic blinking of fireflies.

The house was dark and the back door was locked. I slipped the key from its hiding place in the pine tree and handed it to Dad. Mom locked us out so many times that we never expected the door to be open. When she was in one of her spells, she also closed the windows. She used to leave them open to let the bad stuff out. But now she tried to keep everything closed up. Along with the evil spirits, she locked us out, too.

Dad fumbled with the key in the darkness. He finally unlocked the door and quietly opened it. If Mom was asleep, it was best not to wake her up. He reached for the switch inside and flipped on the kitchen light.

My mother was sitting at the table, facing the door. Her eyes fluttered in the shock of sudden light. She'd fallen asleep, waiting for us. We came in quietly behind Dad. Sometimes the evening could be peaceful, if we didn't raise our voices, and if we walked on tip toes.

Mom's eyes adjusted and she blinked a smile at us, reminding me of the fireflies outside, with their flickering and darting light. Bill and Alfie started to tell her about the carnival. She listened for a minute, with a strained smile on her face. She kept her eyes on me, even though my brothers were doing all the talking. I had nothing to say. Then Mom got up and patted the bench by the table. We glanced at each other. What now?

Again, Mom pointed to the empty bench. *Here boys. Sit down for me.* She touched my younger brothers on their cheeks. They couldn't go to bed with all that sticky candy on their faces.

Mom went to the sink and turned on the tap, feeling the stream of water to the right temperature. She filled a bowl with a warm soapy solution and dunked a face cloth in it. Mom returned from the sink and leaned toward my brothers. She gently scrubbed one cheek, then the other, first Alfie, then Bill. After toweling their faces, she kissed them on the forehead and sent them off to bed. She saved me for last. I was still on the bench, untouched.

My mother went to the sink for a fresh bowl of water. She sat down on the bench next to me, on my left side. She washed my puffy left cheek with sudsy water. She went back to the sink to dump out the soapy water. Next she filled the bowl with clean water. Mom touched her finger into it, then added a little more warmth from the faucet. She rinsed off my cheek and dried it with a newly laundered towel, still warm. She forgot the sticky sweetness on my right cheek. My left cheek was clean. I went to bed.

Our house was quiet. For this one night, my mother was at peace. She wasn't prowling the hallway. I said my prayers. I asked for everybody in my family to be home, to be really home. It was a good kind of quiet. I went to sleep.

Late at night, I opened my eyes. I was awakened by my mother's weight sagging my mattress, at the far end of my bed. Without moving, I watched as she looked out the window, praying to something in the distance. It took my breath away how the moonlight lit her up, casting her shadow on the far wall, as if her dark silhouette was fleeing from itself in that pale illumination.

It took my breath away, how the moonlight silvered the glistening in my mother's eyes.

Chapter 17

Within the family pictures, I found an envelope with a return address of the DuMont Television Network, New York City. Above the address is the name of the letter writer, Bishop Fulton J. Sheen. The mail was addressed to my mother. Our connection with the iconic Catholic priest was made possible when my father decided it was time for us to own our own TV set.

Dad was in Hoy Brothers Department Store looking for winter boots for Bill and Alfie. Jim Hoy showed my father a brand new Admiral Television that someone returned because they wanted a bigger set. Dad took one look at it and made a deposit so it could be held on layaway. It was still in its original packing box, marked with a generous discount from the original price.

Some humorous prodding clinched the sale. "By the time a better deal comes along, Clem, your boys might be too old to even see the screen." Mr. Hoy's comment got a laugh from my father. Dad knew he'd never get a better deal.

After telling us about his purchase, he added a precautionary warning: "Listen carefully, boys. Don't even think about turning on the *television* if your homework isn't finished. I can make the set disappear as quickly as it appeared." We couldn't help smiling because of his German pronunciation of the word, *television*. Bill usually mumbled a retort, which included the same word, with *his* version of Dad's pronunciation.

Mr. Hoy knew my dad to be an honest customer, a hard-working man who always paid his bills. "Clem, you take this set home now, and pay me over the next two or three months." But not my dad. He waited until he had the money in his pocket.

Mom quickly became a watchdog for what we could view on our new TV set. Every year in church, we had to take the pledge of The Legion of Decency. We'd raise our right hand and swear to never watch any movie or television show that carried an immoral message. Same for the radio; just turn off any program that caused indecent or impure thoughts.

The Ed Sullivan Show provided our family entertainment most Sunday evenings, unless a ballerina danced across the 17-inch screen, seductively floating her bare legs in front of Sophie's three boys. When that happened Mom pounced like a cat, from the couch to the off button. Even Arthur Godfrey's Talent Scouts got the hook, if the singer's lyrics were suggestive.

One show my mother never censored was on our set every Tuesday evening at 8. *Life is Worth Living* was Bishop Sheen's weekly program. Since it was filled with inspirational messages about fully living your life with Jesus, Mom made sure we were always in attendance, and attentive. Even before we owned the new TV, we had listened to his words on the radio. Sunday evenings, *The Catholic Hour* filled our living room so we could inhale any devotional lessons we might have missed at mass. The Bishop's voice resonated with good will, beckoning us to love and serve God in this world, so we may be with him in the next; just like the words in our catechism.

But now we could actually see Bishop Sheen as we listened to him. He was so handsome and radiant with good will that we could almost feel his heat coming through the picture tube. At least Mom could. The holy man stood by a blackboard, on which he chalked the important words from his lecture: *conscience, confession, penance.* When his blackboard was filled up, two things happened. First, he stared out from the TV screen with his magnificent eyes, which seemed to channel his inspiration right into our hearts, especially Mom's. Second, an angel-shaped eraser rubbed back and forth over the writing surface, wiping it clean for the next lesson.

Before resuming his lecture, Bishop Sheen generously thanked his angel for preparing the blackboard. That's what motivated my mother's spontaneous correspondence with him. Without any knowledge or agreement on my part, my mother had planned my summer for me.

Contained within the envelope from the DuMont TV Network, was Bishop Fulton J. Sheen's courteous answer to my mom's offer.

May 7, 1951

My Dear Mrs. Schoenebeck,

You are most kind to offer the service of your son, Carl. I am sure he would be most competent in this line of work, as my angel. However, our present angel has done a good job. He also needs the work. I am sure your son does not need to be in my presence to be in a state of grace. In reading your thoughtful letter, I note that he is an altar boy, and he is quite responsible in performing his family duties. Your words also indicate that he is a good brother to his younger siblings. It sounds like he is doing fine without being in my company.

Perhaps it is God's plan that you keep your own angel with you.

Blessings to you and your family. May Almighty God love you.

Fulton J. Sheen,

Bishop of the Archdiocese of New York

* * *

It was the summer of my fourteenth birthday, when I woke up one morning after a night of thin sleep. I sat up in bed, confused by my spinning and whirling dreams. We were in a stretch of sticky summer days. I felt suffocated as I tried to catch my early morning breath. But something else was wrong. My pajamas were wet and soiled. Something had leaked onto my sheet. Had I wet my bed?

My brothers and I made up our own beds every morning, so I had a chance to rub out the evidence of my accident. I tried to make everything look normal. I felt like I'd done something bad and I wanted to keep it hidden from my mother. Lucky for me, my pajamas made it through the laundry without any consequence. Same for my bed sheet, from which I'd erased the evidence with a washcloth, towel, and my patient rubbing. I was safe for now, but my confusion had not been washed away. After a few days, I forgot the incident.

But it did not turn out to be a one-time event. Two weeks later, I woke up the same way, unsettled and agitated. Once again, I'd stained the sheets. Just as before, there had been a confusing dream. But this time I was a participant. I remembered some of it, especially the part about swimming with Esther Williams.

My mother only let us go to movies that were approved by The Legion of Decency. But I saw the preview of Esther Williams swimming and diving in *Million Dollar Mermaid*. No way I'd be allowed to see that movie, but I never heard the word *preview* mentioned in the Legion's oath, about what we'd allow our eyes to see. I thought I liked Esther Williams a lot.

In my dream, *I'm doing the backstroke underwater. The water ripples and tumbles overhead, and I look through it to the sky above. Swimming through the turbulence with impressive power and strength, I never come up for air. I can actually breathe the water. Suddenly, beautiful Esther Williams swims above me, facing down at me. I look straight up at her. Her gracefully muscled arms reach forward, first right, then left, pulling the water behind, as she gracefully propels herself above me. Her head alternates side to side in sequence with her arm movements, and between each stroke, while looking down, she smiles at me with her warm lips. I think she wants to kiss me. If I could get close enough, I might let her. I think she likes me. Now I know that I like Esther Williams a lot.*

As she passes through the water her long legs linger over me, fluttering and kicking in rhythm with my breathing and I am still holding my breath, breathing without breathing. Her bathing suit is slick against the curves and flat places of her body, which seem muscular and soft at the same time. That's how I think it would feel to the touch, If I could touch her. Suddenly I crash through the water's surface and gasp for air.

I was out of breath. Awake. I'd had another accident.

It was my cousin, who made sense of it. Anything we didn't know, we'd ask Joe. He was one year older than me, and he didn't spend much time being afraid. He was full of explanations about things our parents never talked about, like the stuff the catechism painted black, the sinful smudges we'd get on our souls by thinking about girls, or other strange feelings like I was having now.

"You had a wet dream." Joe's expression alternated between a wide-eyed smile and thoughtful contemplation, as he offered his expertise. "You're getting new hormones in your body, now that you are older. Makes hair grow on your face. That's why men have to shave." Before I could touch my face, Joe rubbed his hands under his chin. "Hear that scraping sound?" I cupped my hand around my ear to trap the sound, but Joe started to laugh before I heard any stubble being rubbed.

My cousin continued his lecture. "The extra hormones build up in your testicles, like blowing air into a balloon. That's the medical name for your balls, *testicles*. And if those hormones don't come out the way they did in your dream, you'd explode down there!"

I sat down, without squeezing my legs together too tightly. I was dizzy, like when Dad forced us smoke the cigarettes in order to make us quit. "Don't worry, Carl, there's a better way to avoid the explosion, but you're too young now. I'll tell you about that when I know more myself. But for now, you are normal. You didn't do anything bad. By the way, here's another scientific name for you." My cousin leaned his face in front of my eyes. He wanted my full attention. "What happened to you is called a *nocturnal emission!*" Joe made me repeat it a few times so I could pronounce it properly. All I could think of was that *emission* sounded a lot like *explosion.*

Joe laughed and gave me the sign of the cross, like our priest giving a blessing after confession. "I hereby save you from the fires of hell. For your penance I give you ten Hail Marys, five Our Fathers, and two more nocturnal emissions! "

Joe was laughing so hard I thought he'd cry. Not me though. I felt like we were dancing around lightning, even if there was no thunderstorm overhead. I thought of more rhymes; *emission* and *confusion.* Maybe even *confession.*

How could my parents not save me from such a fate? I knew what it felt like to take a running jump and land on my bicycle seat the wrong way. *Oooff!* The pain. Only shallow breathing for three or four minutes. But an explosion? Every time I thought of that, I got lightheaded. Just the idea of throwing up would make me hurt down there. And the sound of that hurtful explosion, what would it be like? *Sploof?*

My parents were unable to help me. This was something we just didn't talk about. I was old enough to know that my mother would lead me through a tunnel of shame. One errant step off the path of purity, and my shoes would be permanently soiled by the black stain of sin, tracking me every step of my life. My father didn't know what was going on with me. Sometimes he hinted that I was getting older now, and we'd have to talk about my becoming a man. Dad wasn't in any hurry. If I seemed puzzled, it could wait for now. "Plenty of time for that, you're just a kid."

The second accident did catch up with me. I could not erase the evidence of my swim with Esther Williams. The more forcefully I tried to blot out the stain, the more noticeable it became. I had no choice but to wait for laundry day. And pray. I expected to be found out and punished. I was.

My trial took place by the laundry hamper. My mother was both judge and jury, and she made Bill and Alfie witnesses to my crime. Mom's arms stretched out the soiled sheet in front of us, like a banner verifying my citizenship in a nation of sin. When asked for an explanation, I stood mute. Anything I'd say would be held against me. I could only bend my head in humility. My brothers stood behind me, observing my shame, perhaps taking mental notes for a future reckoning of their own.

My mother folded the sheet, keeping the stain in the center. With each new crease and fold, the background got smaller and the circular blemish magnified, staring at me like an enlarging eye of judgment. She placed the terrible bundle in a clean paper bag.

Now she had new instructions for me to follow. I washed my hands and face, brushed my teeth, combed my hair. Put on a clean shirt. I kept looking at her face, trying to make sense of it all. Her expression was unreadable; not angry, not smiling. It seemed I wasn't even there. Only when I heard her final command did I look away. But not before her image dissolved with the hot, salty blur washing over my eyes. Not until I heard my sentence. *We are going to see the priest.*

My mother and I sat at opposite ends in the rectory's sun porch. Any further apart and I would be outdoors. Mrs. Whottle, the housekeeper, told us to have a seat. Father would get to us as soon as he could. Mom didn't call ahead because she was in such a hurry to tell on me. If she got me here in time, perhaps the priest could save my soul. Maybe he could block the message of my sin before it got to God, as if canceling a telegram at the Western Union on College Avenue.

Father Kavanaugh was new. He'd replaced Father Gallagher, who just plain wore out. The old priest was starting to look like a flower in a dry spell, shriveling and bending a little more with each passing day. But at least I knew him and he knew me. More important, he knew my mother and I was sure he would not make me feel any worse than I already felt. I was scared of what the new priest might do to me.

Father Kavanaugh gave wonderful sermons. He kept my attention with the lifting and lowering of his voice, almost singing, like he was breathing air into his words and prayers. When I really paid attention to what our new priest said during Sunday mass, I felt like I could step outside of myself, and stand in a place where God could see me. But what would happen now? What would our priest think of Mom if she started talking crazy? And what about me? Would he tell me I was bad enough that he'd hear my confession right here, in front of my mother?

I felt too big, too visible. I felt undressed in front of the whole world, my body tattooed with the black marks of sin. If my cousin Joe were here, he would defend me. He'd explain about the hormones and the normal stuff that I was going through; how it wasn't my fault. Being a holy man, Father Kavanaugh was free from sin. How could he possibly understand something that never happened to him?

I was forced to squint through my own reflection, when I tried to look through the window at the flowers and trees. I couldn't escape from myself if I wanted to. All I could see was my crybaby self with puffy eyes staring back at me. I was all alone, my mother blurred and distant in that mirror. Even though Dad was at work and didn't know about this, he wouldn't want me to cry. It didn't even matter about the scene outside. I couldn't see it anyway.

I turned toward the door when I heard approaching footsteps. It wasn't Mrs. Whottle's tired scuff on the floor. I was listening to a confident march of the executioner on the other side of the door. I felt like I was in a bible story, about to be stoned for an impure act. I waited for the clunk and clatter of rocks, as he set down the sack which he was about to empty on me.

"Mrs. Schoenebeck? Carl? Please come in." Father Kavanaugh stepped tall and easy into the sunny room. He was comfortable in a short-sleeved shirt. No Roman collar today. His face lit up in a friendly smile, but I knew that wouldn't last very long. Wait 'til Mom tells him about me. He stood by the open door as he extended his muscular arm toward his desk, inside the judgment chamber.

Mom had been sitting all this time with her arms wrapped around the paper bag on her lap. She was both protecting and hiding it. She got up and followed the priest's direction into his office. Father nodded at me as I shuffled by. I'd served mass for him a few times. He knew me just a little; he was about to know a lot more about me.

Father had good enough manners to say something pleasant. He was smart enough to see that I wasn't able to look him in the eye, when he asked about my summer. So we got right to it. "You're upset about something, Sophie. Is it OK for me to call you Sophie?"

Mom gave him a big smile. It was OK for him to call her Sophie.

Then she started explaining to Father about how she made us pray the rosary almost every day, how we served early morning mass when no one else would; all the things she did to make sure her boys were clean and wholesome in the eyes of Jesus, prayers each morning, noon, and night; confession every Saturday.

I listened to my mother and thought about how many times I had to make up sins for the priest, so I wouldn't waste his time. So I wouldn't be in and out of the confessional in twenty seconds. But those days were over for me. From now on I'd have to pack supper and bring a sleeping bag.

"I know your boys, Sophie. You have done well with them."

Then it started. About the dark shadows that were always in our home, and how the brightest sun couldn't erase them. Her eyes lit up as she explained about the voices that were always telling us to sin, warning her to watch out for us. She started to rock back and forth and she wasn't even sitting in a rocking chair. Mom's voice got loud and high; then it hushed into a whisper as she told Father Kavanaugh that the *Birth Control Devil* was infecting me, her oldest son. If I knew what was best for me, I would be afraid of the flames of hell; *why didn't I have fear for the devil's flames? Why didn't I shelter myself in Jesus' shadow?* My mother was breathing fast and shallow, like she couldn't quite catch her breath. Her eyelids fluttered, as if a butterfly had landed inside her glasses. Then she closed her eyes.

My head was bowed forever. I could not lift my eyes enough to sneak a look at the priest. He was quiet, just listening. He had to be studying the bundled sheet and my wet sin staring at him, over the top of the bag. Then I felt his hand on my shoulder. I looked up.

Father lifted an eyebrow at me. It was as if he'd placed a finger against his lips and went *ssshhhh*. He shifted his eyes toward my mother and waited for her to continue. But she was finished. She seemed to have forgotten where she was and what she was saying.

"Sophie? Water? Can I have Alma get you a glass of cold water?"

Mom looked at the priest, and shook her head *no*. Then she remembered the package she'd brought. She started to lift the soiled sheet out, when Father Kavanaugh leaned toward her and put his hand on her hand. "It's not necessary for you to show me that. I understand, Sophie." Mom listened to his words, wrinkled her forehead and narrowed her eyes, like she was trying to read a message in the air between us. Then she sat back in her chair, calm and quiet, almost relaxed. With her arms folded in a cross, she caressed my sin against her breast.

Father lifted himself part way out of his chair and dragged it a bit closer to Mom and me. He folded his arms into each other and let his eyes rest on Mom. Quiet now, I settled deeper into my chair, no longer perched on the edge. The wooden back massaged the tightness between my shoulders. He leaned toward my mother. She didn't move, didn't pull away from him.

"Sophie. Father Gallagher told me about your wonderful family. Owen cared about all of you, so he filled me in before he left. It is good that you came here today. I think I can help you, if you let me." His head was a foot away from Mom, as if he had to whisper. Father never even blinked, never took his eyes away from my mother. I had to remember to breathe.

"Sophie? Listen to me now. This is a good boy. Do you understand me? Carl is a good boy. I know Bill and Alfred, too. They are all good boys." Mom turned her eyes in my direction, as if checking that Father was talking about me. "He is not sinning when this happens to him. This happens to all boys as they grow up. It means your son is becoming a man. He is maturing so that some day he will have his own children, God willing." The priest leaned back into his own chair. "Think of it this way. If Carl wasn't going through this period of his life, he wouldn't be able to give you grandchildren. That means more souls to share the kingdom of God. And isn't that a blessing, Sophie? More sheep in the flock of our Divine Shephard."

I wept.

I trailed behind my mother as we walked along Fairmount Avenue. She slowed down so I could catch up to her on the way home. I didn't catch up with her. I walked even slower. Mom looked back at me. I looked away. All I wanted was to get home and throw myself on my bed, and burn my pillow with tears. When we got to the next intersection, Mom went straight.

I went home a different way.

Chapter 18

Dad decided it was time for a family vacation. I would be going into tenth grade in the fall and Bill and Alfie would be entering their eighth and fifth grades. "If we wait too long, you boys will be too old to enjoy a vacation. A change of scenery will do us all some good." My father said the timing was right because Mom had been in one of her calm spells. We'd never gone away for longer than a weekend visit with Uncle Al, in Columbia, PA. My brothers and I were getting older and busier with summer jobs and sports. It was time for our family to have some fun.

My mother was indifferent about the vacation, which meant *yes* to the rest of us, since she didn't protest Dad's suggestion for a trip to New Hampshire. Mom now seemed accepting and at peace with the loss of Frances. We were less guarded around my mother.

Our plans depended on finding a caretaker for Dad's garden, which we'd recently enlarged. Because the property was owned by Uncle George, Dad had to get his permission for the expansion. My uncle was happy to put the additional land to use since it was little more than a weed patch. He suggested that my cousins might farm a small corner, providing some fresh vegetables for his family. George and Joe helped us with the digging and planting.

It was not a simple project, enlarging the garden at least double its original size. None of us could step on the dirt without Dad's supervision. He lined up rows of string to guide us in planting the seeds. The straight lines were separated by flat boards, which we used as walkways. When we complained about the obstacle course, Dad gave another lecture: "There is space for the seeds and space for feet. If I don't put some boundaries between the baby plants and your shoes, you boys would be like a herd of elephants squashing my seedlings." His warning was one more variation on "a place for everything and everything in its place."

My father fussed over the garden as if he were making a special piece of furniture. Every time we helped out, he inspected what we did. If a few emerging carrots wobbled out of alignment, Dad wanted to know who was guilty of the crooked planting. He spent hours weeding, cultivating, fertilizing, and watering. Once the garden grew in, it looked like a work of art. The vegetables were in straight rows, with tall plants behind short ones, arranged so nothing was cheated of its fair share of sunshine. Dad even talked to his vegetables, as if he could carry on an intelligent conversation with them. That got our attention. We were beginning to feel like they were part of the family. Bill told Alfie to wear his earmuffs when he ate a salad, so he wouldn't hear the radishes screaming for help.

Our trip was planned for the middle of August. The weather had been warm and dry, and without someone to water my father's exuberant crops, he'd return to a field of parched failure. Fortunately for Dad and the vegetables, there was an easy solution. My cousin Joe worked at the University flower gardens for his summer job; he certainly knew how to keep plants alive. Because he lived next door, it would be easy for him to take care of the garden. Joe would earn a few extra bucks and my father's thriving vegetables would have daily company.

Lake Winnisquam was the destination for our trip. Dad had spent time there when he lived with his adopted family in Roslindale. His old friends from Germany, Carl and Mary Peters, now had a summer home on the lake. They arranged for us to rent a nearby camp for two weeks.

We finally set out for New Hampshire, leaving at midnight. Dad figured we could be on the road for five or six hours before encountering any bothersome traffic. We packed our reliable Plymouth with summer clothes, groceries, and sleeping bags. Bill and Alfie were in the back, with Mom wedged between them. I was Dad's navigator in the front passenger seat, as I monitored our New England roadmap, courtesy of our local Esso gas station.

Driving at night was peaceful and focused, as the car's headlights tunneled our way through the darkness. A cool blanket of late summer air hovered over the sweep of Pennsylvania farmlands. Wisps of fog shimmered through tall cornstalks and over flat fields of wheat and hay, luminous along the roadside ahead, blurring past us into the shadows we'd left behind. Our passengers in the back seat were sound asleep. But my father and I were wide-awake, intent on our mission; pilot and co-pilot, we shared the night.

Somewhere past Harrisburg, the first glitters of morning reflected off the Susquehanna River. My brothers stirred and stretched out a yawn, as they rearranged their tangled arms and legs. They curled back to sleep, both at the same time, as if mimicking each other. Mom was now awake, staring straight ahead at the road. She smiled at me, content in her nest between Bill and Alfie. My mother seemed hypnotized by the drone of the car's engine, its hum steady and unstrained at fifty-five miles per hour. We were on our way to a real vacation. Everything was calm. Dad was right. The change of scenery was just what we needed.

We were in our own perfect world at Lake Winnisquam. The sunny weather brought us outdoors every day, fishing with Dad at a moment's notice. If we weren't swimming or rowing a boat, we could hike over the surrounding hills. Bill and I went jogging most mornings before breakfast, We had a new interest in running, since we weren't big enough to play football. Most of the distance runners seemed skinny, like us. Sometimes Alfie joined us, probably not wanting to be trapped alone with Mom, who was worried that we'd forget how to say the rosary if our vacation went on too long. We broke up our long run with hikes on the way up to Steele Hill, where we stopped to take in the panoramic view of the lake.

Mom sat on the shaded porch of our rented camp, while we splashed in and out of the water and onto the sandy beach. Her bible was often closed on the nearby table, rather than open in her lap. Even though her rosary beads were usually pinched between thumb and forefinger, the summer prayers often dangled from her resting hands as she napped. Sometimes she interrupted her meditation to walk with us, barefoot on the warm sand. Our conversations were easy as we sat together at mealtimes. Mom even joined in our careless laughter

My brothers and I slept in the screened-in porch, insulated by our sleeping bags against the cool nights. "Good sleeping, when you need a blanket in summer." That's how Dad summed it up. "A fine vacation, boys. Now you'll be well rested for school. No excuses for anything but a good report card."

Before we knew it, we were on our way home. With school starting in two weeks, we had just enough time to finish our late summer projects, one of which was to harvest the crop of ripe vegetables in our garden. Dad said we had some good eating ahead of us. We'd can the spinach, green beans, and squash so we could enjoy healthy meals in winter. "*Alles in ordnung*" intoned my dad. Everything was in order, as we slid from summer into fall, from play to study. "There's a time for everything, and now it's the serious time of year." Time to go back to school.

It was late evening when we arrived in State College. Dad slowed down as we approached the hill going up to Fairmount Avenue, before turning right onto Prospect Alley. He was guiding our trusty Plymouth into its parking place overlooking the garden when he unexpectedly slammed on the brakes, jerking the car to a convulsive stop.

"What the hell is that?" The echo of the grinding brakes edged my father's growl. We strained our eyes through the fading illumination of the setting sun. What was he looking at?

Dad launched himself from the car, keys dangling in the ignition, the motor still running. Bill reached forward from the back seat and turned off the switch. He handed the keys to my mother who sat quietly, smiling as we tumbled out of the car to catch up with Dad. My father stepped with the exaggerated efficiency of a parading general, his three sons following in single file, marching and matching his cadence. We advanced through the straight rows of lettuce, took a sharp right turn at the gap between carrots and radishes, before stomping to a halt by the onions and beets. Dad stopped so quickly that we rebounded off each other, after bouncing off his back. The plants seemed to lift themselves to attention before my father. Stirred by our breezy entrance, clusters of Kale fluttered in quiet evening.

In front of my father, two leaves of Swiss chard towered above all the other plants in the garden. One was tall enough to be at eye level, like a soldier at dress review. I thought Dad was about to salute, but his hand was just rising to grasp the bigger plant, stretching it to its full height. My brothers and I skulked behind, as if waiting for an introduction.

"What the hell is going on? These are the biggest damn vegetables I ever saw." Dad was circling, cautiously stepping between the surrounding plants. "Carl. What do you think? Maybe Joe put down too much fertilizer? Can't a man leave his garden for a few days and have a simple vacation with his…"

A door slammed behind us. Within seconds, my cousin was at my father's elbow. "Just water, Uncle Clem." He heard Dad questioning his stewardship of the garden. "Nothing but water and only when it was dry. I never saw anything grow like this, not even up at the university gardens." Joe's eyes zigzagged between the plant, Dad, and me. "They started shooting up like crazy, three or four days after you took off for New Hampshire. I asked my boss up at the flower gardens. He thought they might have some kind of hormone problem. Prob'ly not safe to eat."

We were like a flock of birds, flapping and chirping at the leafy green trophies. Dad kept his eyes on the nearly six-foot plant, as if he were about to interrogate the tallest of the green prisoners. He stepped back, careful not to flatten any of his lettuce. Every living thing in the garden seemed a bit wilted, as if intimidated by the new specimens in their midst. There was something besides amazement in my father's face. He looked at each one of us and beamed a huge smile, which was reserved for his special approval, like acknowledging a good report card or a spectacular catch at one of our baseball games. No doubt about it: Dad was proud.

A window opened above us. Curious about the noise, Mom looked down from our apartment on the second floor. Alfie held up the smaller plant, which matched his height. He waved to my mother. She smiled and said nothing.

"Well, boys. You know what we have here?" Dad took his off his glasses and huffed on them. He was really impressed with the tallest plant, stroking its length, as if reminding it not to slouch. He unfurled a handkerchief from his pocket and buffed the lenses. He lifted up his glasses and inspected them against the evening sky, then repositioned them on his face, and folded his arms across his chest. "We've got a green giant here. This is The Jolly Green Giant." The smaller plant remained nameless.

He stretched the plant up to its full height. "*Wie geht's*, Jolly. How do you do?" Then he nodded in our direction. "Say hello to my boys, Jolly.

Meet Carl, Billy, and Alf. And my nephew, Joe. And by the way, I'm the boss here, this is my garden." Dad nodded in our direction. "Boys. Say hello to Jolly."

"Hello, Jolly."

After we unpacked the car and got everyone settled, my father called our neighbor, Professor Myers. He lived across the alley from us. The old man was a plant pathologist, retired from the University. Just before we went on vacation, he complained about my brothers and me being uninvited guests in his cherry trees. He was still mad at us, so he was pleasantly surprised that my father wanted him to check Jolly and its sibling. Dr. Myers said he would come over first thing in the morning.

The old professor creaked into our garden the moment we sat down for breakfast. Dad excused himself, leaving his toast and eggs untouched. He went downstairs, two steps at a time, and glided right into the garden to intercept the old gentleman. As much as my father wanted to greet our neighbor, he wanted to prevent any trampled lettuce leaves. I followed Dad down the steps, hurried into the garden and slid in behind him. My younger brothers shadowed me. We promised to eat and wash the dishes right after our conference with our neighbor. Mom sat at the table shaking her head.

The way he shuffled through the leafy greens, Dr. Myers' eyes must have been failing. His shoes never broke contact with the soil, leaving some of the vegetables flattened in the old man's wake, despite my dad's guidance. My father appeared to ignore the damage, but I saw his eyes hopefully scanning the prostrate greens, as if praying for their resurrection. Three feet from the big plants, the professor gathered his bent posture into an abrupt halt. He slowly raised his eyes, deliberately measuring the length from Jolly's roots to the tip of the plant's fully extended foliage. The same inspection was repeated for Jolly's companion. Our neighbor scowled and wrinkled his forehead as he cautiously leaned into the larger plant. As if genuflecting, he folded his knees beneath him, one at a time, and lowered his attention to Jolly's big stem.

His fingers raked the dirt, probing the roots. He scooped a handful of soil in one hand, worrying it with the index finger of his other hand. He sniffed it. Maybe he even tasted it. After wobbling side-to-side and lifting himself up on his feet, he circled and re-circled, checking the plants from every angle. Now his attention was focused only on Jolly. With a quivering hand, Dr. Myers gently lifted the plant to its full height. He opened the leaf like an umbrella against the morning sun, illuminating the textured green with its dappled vibrancy and network of fibrous vessels. On the pale underside, a layer of wispy down gave the appearance of peach fuzz on an adolescent boy's cheek. Jolly needed a shave.

"Mutant strain. Some kind of a mutant strain." He pulled his empty pipe from his shirt pocket. Placing it in his mouth, he sucked in air as if it would energize his memory.

"These are immature plants, genetically altered from their parents, and I don't think they're done growing. I can't say I've ever seen a normal plant this big." He poked at them, as if checking for some kind of reflex. "Interesting. I'd like to document this, have someone from the university check it. Unusual enough to have the Centre Daily Times come down, too." Dr. Myers took the pipe out of his mouth and slid it into his shirt pocket. "I'll call the agriculture reporter. He was a student of mine. It's about time he put something worthwhile in his column. Wouldn't hurt to have the photographer come along either."

After Dr. Myers went home, my father called our uncles and aunts with his news about our giant Swiss Chard. The only one who was excited enough to come over and check it was Uncle Tony. He'd been trying to grow his own patch of vegetables, with mixed success. Maybe there was something to be learned by seeing what had grown in our garden. Besides, Dad thought it would be a good idea to take some practice pictures. He wanted everything to be just right when the newspaper folks showed up. So he and Uncle Tony lined up on each side of the plants and smiled at me, as I viewed and clicked them through my Kodak Brownie Box Camera.

The next day Dad stayed home from work. He invited Uncle Tony to return for the real pictures. It was his reward for responding to my father's invitation to see his miracle plants. At 9 o'clock in the morning, a reporter and a photographer showed up. My father greeted the young men before leading them into the garden. He monitored their footsteps, carefully guiding his guests along the open spaces between the vegetables. My brothers and I stood off to the side, like a reverent congregation, as my dad gave an authoritative sermon about the tall green creatures in our midst.

The pictures were unforgettable. Dad embraced Jolly, lifting it up almost to his own shoulders. He was beaming, as if posing with one of his sons at graduation. Uncle Tony held on to the smaller plant, periodically slanting an envious glance at Dad and Jolly. The photographer directed Alfie, Bill and me to line up for a photograph. It was like a family picture, with Dad, his three sons, and our new green siblings.

The men from the Centre Daily Times left in a hurry. Dr. Myers had already given them an interview about his scientific opinion. They had to make the afternoon deadline; this could be the day's big news.

That's when I spotted my cousin at the edge of the garden, under the pine trees. Joe's hands were in his pockets. He was scuffing the dirt with one shoe, bunching it into a pile, which he then bulldozed with his other shoe. "They got pictures, huh?"

Dad put his hand on my cousin's shoulder. "We'll be in the Times, maybe even this afternoon. For sure, tomorrow. Too bad you weren't here; you should have been in the picture, Joe. After all, you took care of Jolly and his little brother." Joe blushed. He repeated the earth sculpting with his feet, still looking at the ground. He mumbled something about how he would have broken the camera. The last I saw of my cousin, he was shuffling off toward our house.

A few minutes later, Mom appeared at the corner of the garden, talking to Dad. He tilted his head toward her, paying close attention. Mom smiled at Dad as she spoke, even though his eyes were aimed at the ground under his feet. I began to wonder what was up, when he started shaking his head. But when he looked up at us he was laughing. Then Mom joined in, and I couldn't remember when I'd last seen them sharing such a happy moment. Dad called us over to where he and Mom were huddled. "Boys, we've been fooled!"

I knew something was up, the way Joe kept asking questions about the newspaper folks and Dr. Myers. He was nervous about all the attention. When he heard about our news making the Times, he panicked. He was thinking *New York Times.* His little joke was getting out of hand.

Joe had a special way with my mother. When he spoke with her, she was calm and really listened to him. Now that she'd just heard Joe's confession, she was acting as the intermediary, asking my father's forgiveness for our prankster cousin.

Joe was old enough to work in the Penn State Experimental Flower Gardens for his summer job. The day we left for our vacation he was riding home on his bike when he discovered a huge pile of tropical plants, discarded from a newly renovated greenhouse. I pictured him riding through town on his bicycle, two leafy passengers named *Elephant's Ears* temporarily planted in his backpack, swaying over him like green guardian angels. But my image flashed away as quickly as it appeared, when Joe later explained that the plants were too big for his bike, so he pedaled on home. He'd just earned his driver's license, so he borrowed Uncle George's car and returned. He used a hatchet to trim each plant to fit into the trunk. Some of the sap splattered on his skin, giving him a stinging burn. He dealt with that concern by warning us that we shouldn't eat our plants.

Once Joe unloaded the plants he quickly dug a hole in the garden. He mixed in some peat moss and soil, stuck in the plants and soaked them thoroughly. Suddenly, Dad's Swiss chard had some dazzling new companions. Joe staked the plants with my father's beanpoles as a temporary crutch, while they recovered from transplant shock. He watered them daily, nurturing the plants faithfully. In a few days they'd surrendered their wilted posture. Jolly really perked up. Sparkling and teal green, erect and tall, he was the boss of the garden. Joe couldn't wait for us to get home. He figured my father had been had!

Dad was pretty good about the whole affair. When it came to practical jokes, my father could give as good as he got. He could still laugh at himself, even when the joke was on him. Joe was relieved. The people at the Centre Daily Times were disappointed. Though they briefly considered writing about the practical joke, they dropped the idea. I guess the news wasn't that slow, even in late summer in central Pennsylvania, when the most exciting event might be a murky afternoon thunderstorm.

Later in the summer, the smaller plant withered up and died, despite my father's attentive care. Dad spared no effort with Jolly. "No need to uproot him, boys, when you think about it. We'll keep him going the rest of the summer. He just needs a drink from time to time. Besides, he eats a lot less than you boys. Before you know it, fall will be here and the garden will be put to rest anyway." We were relieved. The big plant was now part of our family.

Sometimes when I worked in the garden, I noticed Dad hanging out by the Swiss chard, fussing with the soil or pulling a few extra weeds. I saw him get on his knees to pat the loose mulch by hand, covering up Jolly's feet. If he fussed over any other plant, he'd tamp it down with his shoes. The hands-on treatment was reserved for Jolly.

"How goes it?" I looked up to answer Dad; I was on my hands and knees, weeding the radish patch. But his back was turned toward me, his inquiry aimed in a different direction. Dad was at eye level with Jolly, his face tilted ever so slightly as if waiting for a response, and for the first time, I sensed that my father was not as tall as before. Maybe he was just tired.

Dad and Jolly were two lengthening shadows, fading as that summer light surrendered its warm glow.

Autumn drifted in like a cool fog, and the garden slowly went from green to gold to rust.

Chapter 19

Dad had big news for us. He was going to build us a new home. *With our help*, he announced. He'd been saving his hard-earned money so he could put a down payment on his dream. Even though Uncle George was a generous landlord, my father didn't want to rent forever.

I was about to enter my junior year of high school. It was time to start thinking about college, and Dad was keenly aware of the additional financial strain he'd be under. "Renting only gives you receipts, boys. If you own something, you have some value in your pocket." We had no idea what he meant, but there was no doubt how our free time would be spent for the next year or more. Our freedom had been confiscated; my brothers and I were now old enough to help with the labor.

There was something else behind Dad's desire to own his home. He thought a change of location would be good for my mother. "Boys, I think this is what Mom needs. Something to keep her busy." Dad had it all figured out. "Nothing like cooking in her very own kitchen and having her own home to clean. Just you wait and see. This is just what our family needs."

Bill and Alfie and I thought it was a great idea. We'd have our own bedrooms and a yard big enough for playing catch. No more climbing up a flight of stairs to get to our own home. Our first floor would be only two or three steps up from the back yard. All the other kids we knew lived in a house of their own. Now we'd be one of them.

My brothers and I understood this endeavor meant the loss of our summer evenings. As my father put it, we'd be swapping baseball for the golden opportunity looming before us. "You boys don't know how lucky you are, getting a chance to build your own home. How many of your friends received a gift like this, working and learning from their fathers?"

Dad looked up from his newly stocked toolbox when we didn't answer immediately. We were trying to think which friends of ours were so blessed. We had our hands in our pockets, shuffling our feet as if our shoes were too small. Dad was still waiting for an answer.

"I can't think of anyone," Alfie mumbled.

"Guess we're really lucky." Bill enunciated his words quite clearly, perhaps leaning on the word *lucky* with a tone that drew too much of my father's attention. My dad's eyes stayed on my brother until his feet stopped moving.

The reason we could afford to buy the lot on Atherton Street was that the location was on the main highway coming in from Harrisburg. On football weekends, an endless parade of cars and campers honked their way to Beaver Stadium for Saturday afternoon's game. Our future home would not be in a prime residential location, but it was only a half-block away from where we lived on Prospect Avenue. It was still a good location for church, school, and a short walk downtown. Most of all, it worked with our family's budget.

Dad started his project by hiring a contractor to grade the land and pour the foundation. From that time on, my father was directly involved in every step, from framing the house to nailing shingles on the roof. He took care of the plumbing, windows, floors, and cabinets, as well as bossing the three of us, as we labored under his watchful eye. The only additional help he needed was from Uncle Joe, for the electrical work.

Bill, Alfie, and I hauled and stacked the lumber for beams, siding, and hardwood flooring. When Dad was on the roof, one of us climbed the ladder, hoisting shingles by the bundle. Another brother helped unload the climber's burden. The last member of our crew had the easy job, lining up the shingles under Dad's steadily banging hammer.

We dusted off our baseball mitts only after depleting the pile of building supplies. We played with buoyant energy and gratitude, not knowing how long our brief respite would last. Restocking depended on the balance in my father's checkbook. No credit for Dad. "You can't spend what you don't have, boys. Don't forget that. And you don't eat steak when you can only afford hamburger."

Our return to the baseball diamond never lasted very long. In a few days, we'd hear the loaded truck from Houtz Lumber Company grinding and gnawing its way down the alleyway, before crunching on the brakes at our house. Before we could catch our breath from running around the bases, next week's work was looming in our driveway.

Building the house gave my father many chances to repeat his lofty proclamations about patience and hard work. But he did more than talk about it. He practiced what he preached. Nothing got by his critical eye. If any of us nailed a board out of line by one-sixteenth of an inch, it was brought to our attention in a way we clearly understood. We'd been lectured so much about "doing the job right," that the three of us could roll our eyes back and forth in perfect choreography with Dad's mantra. Bill said we were good enough with our facial gymnastics to be on the Ed Sullivan Show.

My father could do anything with his hands. When he was first married, he built a dining room set out of cherry wood. When the sun came through the window at just the right angle, the table and chairs lit up in a rosy-gold glow. I felt warm just being by that same table where my mother sat in her lament over Frances. He crafted an elegant fireplace set out of wrought metal, using the skills he'd learned as a young boy in his father's blacksmith shop in Germany. On the fire screen was a silhouette of a man warming himself by a campfire, an image welded, molded, and polished with Dad's careful touch. Next to it stood an upright holder of tools for stirring the fire or cleaning up the ashes. On those rare occasions when we had visitors, my father's fireplace and handmade tools drew attention and praise.

When Dad built the stone and brick fireplace in our new living room, we watched him fit the pieces together as if assembling a puzzle. Simply observing him at work taught us that, for my father, patience was an act of faith, a belief that each task had a beginning, a middle, and an end. His hands moved over his work as if shaping an offering. It was his way of praying. My father's hands were his gift from God.

One big task remained before moving into our new home: the installation of a hardwood floor. This project demonstrated my father's attention to detail and how he lived up to his constant preaching about perfection. Dad decided on maple, for its durability and warm color. It was more expensive than some of the other choices, but he said it was worth it. As soon as the truck from Houtz Lumber returned with that precious cargo, we had to transfer the bundles of flooring into our basement The maple wood was too valuable to leave outside.

Before he paid his final bill, Dad checked every individual slat. He sighted down its length as if target shooting with a new rifle. Then he ran his fingers back and forth along the grain and the edges of the working surface. Once my father was satisfied with the quality, my brothers and I moved the wood upstairs, out of the basement. He said the wood had to breathe for a few days and live wherever it was going to be installed. That idea got some serious eye rolling from us. Bill told my father that he was listening to the wood, and he heard a cough. "Dad, maybe the floor has a cold? Maybe we should cover it with a blanket for a few days, while we play some baseball?" When Dad didn't respond, Bill repeated his diagnosis and prescription. The only answer he got was the sound of Alfie and me coughing and wheezing, as we smothered our laughter from behind the stacked maple. I saw Dad biting his lips together as he looked away from Bill. Sometimes the boss can't afford to laugh.

We moved it one length at a time. Dad didn't want us to bang the planks against any of the newly painted walls. From the living room, through the hallway, to the bedrooms, he temporarily set each floorboard in place, just to be sure of the fit and alignment. As he nailed and completed a section five or six feet wide, he told us to start sanding the surface as smooth as possible. We did our work by hand, because Dad didn't believe in using a machine. He said it couldn't think for itself, and it was likely to gouge and ruin the wood, especially if we boys were thinking for the machine.

We methodically worked our different grits of paper: medium, fine, and extra-fine. There was no way to rush, no shortcut available. We just got down on our knees and rubbed the sandpaper back and forth, over and over again. Bill complained just loud enough for Alfie and me to hear. "I should never have to go to confession again. This is like walking all the way to Rome to see the pope. On my knees."

Dad's voice filled the hallway where we were hard at work. "If you boys do your job right, you won't need to go to confession. You'll be too damn tired to get into trouble." We lowered our voices for any future grumbling.

Once finished with our assignment, we called for my father's inspection. Sometimes we were in too much of a hurry, especially if we thought we'd have time to run down to the Community Field. We wanted to add our cheers to the summer sounds that ricocheted off the walls of our empty house.

Dad had a predictable routine for appraising our work. He got down on his knees, closed his eyes, and reached his open hand over our newly sanded wood. Back and forth he stroked his fingers, with the grain, then across, until he was satisfied. More often than not he stood up and pointed to the floor, while shaking his head. "Not yet, boys. I want it smooth as marble."

Sometimes Dad would disappear, returning fifteen or twenty minutes later with Mom. He didn't trust her to cross busy Atherton Street by herself. She could walk right into an accident if one of her voices called at the wrong time. Dad wanted Mom to see the progress we'd made. "This will be our new bedroom right here, Sophie. Plenty of cross-ventilation. Windows on two walls." Dad slid them up and down. "Real easy to work. See, you can latch it in three different positions. Try it. You'll see what I mean." My mother's face reflected confusion. She seemed disoriented, as if trying to get her bearings.

But Dad didn't give up. "Look how smooth the floor is." He lowered himself into inspection posture, his long fingers soothing the maple floor. "The boys did a good job, didn't they?" He looked up at her, anticipating a response more hopeful than my mother's bewildered stare. After a few seconds with no reaction, he dropped his gaze to the perfectly placed boards under his tired hands. Maybe they needed more sanding. Dad got back up more slowly than he'd lowered himself on his shiny new maple floor.

During the fall and winter, we slowly moved our possessions into our new home. Uncle George was gracious about our leaving. He imposed no deadline on us, giving us a chance to move one room at a time. We saved the bedrooms for last, so we'd always have a place to sleep.

It was an adventure into unknown territory for all of us. Bill, Alfie, and I were excited and enthusiastic, but my mother got increasingly agitated as we gradually moved our home from Prospect Avenue across Atherton

Street. It was a relief when she got distracted with her cleaning chores. There was plenty to do. We planned to leave our old home in spotless condition, and our new home had to be just as clean.

On the final day in our old apartment, Dad broke down the beds. We looked like a band of Gypsies as we toted the mattresses and bed frames down the alley, across Atherton Street, into our new house. A few final trips in our trusty Plymouth, and the last of our possessions was transferred from one place to the other.

We were in our new home at last, but there was no celebration. My mother was supposed to pack the kitchen dishes and silverware, so Dad could move them by car. But when my father went for the packaged plates and utensils, nothing had been done. Mom was in her rocking chair, reading the bible. She greeted my father's angry complaint with confusion. She seemed unaware that we were moving, that we were really leaving Prospect Avenue. Before we closed the door on our old home, there was one more argument. My mother's anger suddenly filled the air. She had to pray for guidance before agreeing to move. My father's frustration thickened like a dark cloud. Why was this happening at the last minute? What more could he do in order to make things better?

My brothers and I took over the chore my mother had abandoned. By late afternoon, the air was clear. We survived one more passing storm, as we'd done so many times before. Now Mom was on her feet, ready to go, as if nothing had ever happened.

Our old apartment was finally cleaned out. Dad asked me to be sure nothing was left behind. When I finished my final inspection, I closed the door really tight and locked it; I double-checked the lock. There was some stuff I wanted to leave behind.

As the winter and spring unfolded, my mother kept arranging and rearranging our furniture, as well as everything else in our new home. Nothing stayed in place for more than a few days. She couldn't make up her mind about where things belonged, including us. My father had built closets and storage shelves into the hallways and rooms. He took advantage of every square foot of unused space. Dad didn't like clutter; everything should be neatly arranged.

Mom was confused by this new routine of organization. She seemed unable to remember where things belonged, and she soon resented the routine. She lost things unless they were clearly visible. Something had to be right in front of her or it would be forgotten. On Monday we stacked the towels, blankets and sheets in the hall closet by the bedrooms. Tuesday, we moved the towels and facecloths into the bathroom, only to divide it and return half of it to the hallway, the following day. Back and forth we went, trying to keep her happy. Dad complained that his thoughtfully designed closets and cabinets were a waste of time. Mom was disoriented, as if she couldn't remember which home we now lived in. The clutter increased as my mother became less able to do anything helpful. Before that winter's snow melted, my father was beginning to feel that all his hard work had been in vain.

*　*　*

Tom and Betty O'Hara lived next door. The elderly couple knew our family from church, and they were friendly with our relatives. They were aware of my mother's illness and somehow seemed to know when we needed a kind word. They always lingered after Sunday mass, just long enough to say "Hello and how are you this fine morning?" Mrs. O'Hara cupped her hand by her ear, as if listening for a hint of alarm, when my brothers and I replied with our well-rehearsed "Fine, thank you."

Betty had an amazing sense of when to appear at our kitchen door with a pot of vegetable soup or a bowl of Tom's freshly-picked tomatoes. My mother's anger retreated whenever she heard our neighbor's gentle knock at the door. Our houses were close enough that the O'Hara's could hear Mom's harsh words when she thought we had misbehaved or messed up our chores. Our open living room windows were like loudspeakers, amplifying her warnings about what was coming if we failed to heed the teachings of Jesus, about the everlasting fires of hell.

My father returned our neighbor's kindness by marching across the yard with his toolbox, whenever Tom complained about a leaky faucet or a squeaky door. If the weather was good and my dad was too tired to work, he'd invite Tom to sit on the back porch for a beer. My brothers and I often included ourselves in the gathering, so we could listen to Tom's stories about growing up in his Irish family. He could weave humor into a tale of wretched poverty; he hypnotized us with his stories.

"You want to know how poor we were?" Tom lifted his eyebrows to see if my brothers and I were paying attention. We were paying attention. "We invented the word. *Poor* wasn't even in the dictionary, until my family came along. We were so poor that we used to make a meal out of snakes, but St. Patrick did us a bad turn when he chased all the snakes out of Ireland. There was nothing left for us to eat." Tom took a long sip of beer.

"We were so poor that my three brothers and I shared one set of clothes." Tom set his beer bottle on the stool by his chair. "That meant we only had to go to school every fourth day, while the other three stayed home." Alfie was wide-eyed. "In summer, one of us could wear the trousers and one of us could wear the shirt. Didn't bother me though. I always went to school bare-assed!" Bill and I were howling by now, while Alfie was puzzled about what was so funny. Tom winked at my dad, picked up the bottle and finished off his beer.

Mom rarely joined us on the porch. By now, she'd found her place by the window in her new bedroom. The rocking chair looked as if it had always been there, embracing her in that familiar pose, bible on her lap, the rosary in hand. Her rocking chair made a resonant sound as it began its early scarring of our new hardwood floor. My mother's swaying kept time with the choir singing in her head. Sometimes the tempo slowed, almost stopped, then accelerated, as if it caught its second wind. And always, the noise against the floor: sometimes with a harsh scraping; other times, a feathery whisper. Dad and my brothers and I were in one home, and once again, my mother was in another.

* * *

Bill's face was twisted halfway between a grin and a smirk. He'd been spying on our neighbor all week long. Mr. O'Hara had been paying an unusual amount of attention to his tomatoes. One day he was on his knees, weeding the soil. The next day he'd be raking fertilizer into the ground. Tom watered the plants continuously, especially with the dry summer we were going through. He had daily conversations with his tomatoes, which we could hear through our open window. Bill asked Dad if he had any suggestions for what Tom should tell his plants. My father was not at a loss for words. "Same thing I'd tell my vegetables. Job isn't worth doing unless you do it right. Hurry up and get ripe so I can eat you."

As the weather warmed up, Tom became more impatient. He grumbled at his tomatoes as if they were disobedient children. They were supposed to ripen on his command, as if he could embarrass them into the desired redness. Bill motioned for Alfie and me to come to the dining room window, where we had a panoramic view of Tom's garden. He'd surrounded each tomato plant with a wire cylinder to prop up the growing branches. The globes of fruit imprisoned within the cages looked as if they had been dipped in a thin wash of pink.

"Don't you think we should help Mr. O' Hara? Wouldn't it be a neighborly thing to do?" Alfie and I nodded in tentative agreement. But what could we do?

Bill stepped back from the window, spun a sharp about-face, then marched to one of the storage closets that Dad had built in the living room hall. He returned with the carton of Christmas ornaments, and plunked it down on the dining room table. He stood back with his hands in his hip pockets, while Alfie and I puzzled over the assortment of lights and hanging baubles. But it only took a few seconds to figure out Bill's plan.

Dad heard us laughing. He came up from the basement to see what was so funny. Once Bill explained our scheme, my father said he wanted to be there to see Tom's reaction. We planned to wait until Friday evening to carry out our prank. Then we would all be at breakfast early on Saturday morning, ready to watch as Tom made his daily tomato inspection.

We carried out our mission at sunset. Our neighbors were surely getting ready for bed, living by their rule of *early to bed, early to rise.* We started out with two-dozen bright red balls, some big, some medium-sized, but nothing small. In his excitement, Alfie broke one of the big ornaments. He dropped it and crunched it under his foot, just as he was about to hang it on the plant closest to the garage door. That would be the first one Tom would see when he stumbled outdoors into the morning of his magically ripened crop. We finished quickly and silently before standing back to admire our work. It was a mouth-watering vision, twenty-three scarlet globes flickering sparks of the sun, as it slid below the purple mountains in the west.

We could hardly wait for Saturday morning. Even Mom woke up in a good mood. She seemed amused over our joke, or at least distracted by it. She even made pancakes for breakfast. This was one of those rare times when laughter pushed the scary stuff out of her head.

We finished two big stacks of pancakes while we waited. Dad glanced at the kitchen clock as he stalled with a second a cup of coffee, but nothing was happening next door. Maybe Mr. O'Hara decided to sleep late since it was the beginning of the weekend. We took turns peeking through the curtain, admiring our work from the previous evening. The humid air had dropped a few degrees more than expected, glistening a veneer of dew on the entire collection of Tom's boastfully red fake tomatoes.

We were getting squirmy. We should have taken more time with our breakfast. From the kitchen sink, Mom watched us as we searched for a sign of our neighbor. Dad frowned at the clock. We had work to do. He got up from the table and nodded at us. "Boys, it just isn't sensible to sit around all day to enjoy a joke."

Just in time, the weary groan of the opening garage door brought silence to our table. The door swept out and up as it opened, releasing our neighbor from the house. Mr. O'Hara lazily shuffled along the driveway. We divided ourselves between the two dining room windows, hiding behind the curtains. After studying his driveway as if he were looking for a lost quarter, old Tom stepped onto the lawn between our houses. For a moment he lifted his face to the sun, feeling the warmth of a lazy morning. Then he tilted his face in our direction, and we ducked away from the windows. I was afraid he heard Alfie, who was trying so hard not to laugh that the air honked out of his nose, like we had a room full of geese. But Mr. O'Hara was just warming his forehead in the morning sun.

Then it happened. He turned to his left, took one step and froze. "Holy Mary, Mother of God!" His words went forth like a decree intended to get the attention of his tomatoes. He hooked his thumbs under each strap of his suspenders and stretched them forward like two big rubber bands. He'd pulled them out so far I thought if he let go, he'd snap himself backward into his lilac bushes. But he guided his hands back to his chest and released them. With his mouth wide open, he placed his hands on his knees and slowly flexed into a lower position, like a creaky football player crouched at the line of scrimmage. The space between Tom's eyes and the Christmas balls slowly diminished, got closer and closer, until the image coalesced with the realization that he'd been had. That's when Tom dropped his head. We thought he was either inspecting his shoes, or lowering his head because he felt dizzy in the warm sun. Then his whole body began to shake; first with a ripple, then a convulsive roar, until he shook his head back and forth in all-out laughter. By now we'd come out of hiding. He stood up straight and turned toward us, shaking his finger at our windows. His eyes weren't just twinkling; they were tearing.

"Just wait. Just you boys wait. By all the saints in heaven, you'll get yours!" He took a few steps toward his house, and then stopped short. He took a quick look at his decorated plants, then turned in our direction. He waved at our open windows. "Merry Christmas, boys."

"Merry Christmas to you, Tom!" Mr. O'Hara wasn't the only one in tears.

Chapter 20

It didn't take long for our practical joke to become a memory. The rest of our summer took on a somber mood. My father snapped us back to reality with a warning that we should keep our Saturdays free. Painting the house would be the next big project. He'd already purchased several gallons of paint, reams of sandpaper, and an assortment of brushes. A good stretch of dry weather was in the long-range forecast, so there was no chance of escaping our task. We were learning about responsibility; my father had too much of it, and we could handle more.

Dad had been working two jobs to keep ahead of the bills. Besides his regular work at the university, he worked at a local welding company. As his fatigue increased, his patience decreased. More than ever, my parents argued about money, whether it was about the charge account at Temple's Meat Market, the checkbook, or money for the church. Dad was also looking to the future. He was determined that my brothers and I would go to college. One of the benefits of his working for the university was that we'd receive a significant discount on the tuition. Even with that aid, we could only continue our education if each of us earned our own money and helped Dad whenever we could.

Some nights he didn't get home from his second job until midnight. We could tell he was tired when we sat together at breakfast. Instead of lifting up from the table like he had springs in his legs, he hunched over his elbows, bracing them against the table as he pushed himself upright. If he took a short catch of breath just before standing tall, we knew his back was acting up. When he saw us studying him, we'd get some unsolicited wisdom, as if he recognized this as a teaching moment. That's when we got the short sermon about "sticking to the task at hand."

One Saturday in that hard summer, we were energetically applying ourselves to our assigned chore, painting the house. Bill and Alfie were dusty-faced from sandpapering the wood siding. I was painting the trim around the window frames, quite pleased with myself because I'd splattered very little of the Sherwin-Williams All Purpose White Primer across the glass pane. Dad was a few steps up the ladder, waterproofing the gutters with linseed oil. We'd been sanding and scraping and painting since morning, after our early breakfast. We worked right through lunch, planning to quit in early afternoon. The temperature was climbing past 90 degrees on a mid-August scorcher. Hot, sweaty, and tired, we were nearly finished for the day.

The kitchen door closed quietly behind my mother as she stepped from inside the house to the back porch. We all stopped what we were doing. Mom halted abruptly, as if surprised to find herself outside. She blinked at us, temporarily blinded by the unfriendly glare of hot sunlight. When she realized we were staring at her, she smiled back at us. Dad scrambled down from the ladder. I set my brush on the rim of the paint can. My brothers stuffed the wads of scruffy sandpaper in their pockets. We abandoned conversations. We were soldiers at attention.

Mom couldn't fasten the buttons on her winter coat, because she wore a second heavy coat underneath. The garment reflected its blue color in my mother's eyes, which were glowing in anticipation of Sunday mass.

"Damn it all, Sophie. Don't I have enough to worry about?" Dad was standing heavily on the ground, gripping the ladder with both hands. His head was bent down, as if he was about to thump it against one of the rungs. I thought he was going to cry. Then he stood up and yelled at my mother. "Do I have to tell you what to wear? It's summer, Goddamit." Then he wiped his sweaty forehead on the sleeve of his T-shirt, and lowered his voice. "And it's not even Sunday."

Mom froze in place, like a statue contemplating something in the heavens. Bill and Alfie moved quietly to the bottom steps of the porch. I slid next to my dad so I could pry his white-knuckled fingers off the rung of the ladder. But I didn't even try. He needed space more than he needed me.

Mom lowered her gaze at the three of us, blinking through her confused smile until she realized where she was and who we were. We knew to be quiet when she was like this. All we could do was wait for her to come back to us, from wherever she was.

Dad retreated to his garden and took refuge in the soil, where the obedient arrangement of carrots and lettuce and onions proved that his life had some order to it, that all was not total chaos. My brothers and I walked Mom back into the house before any neighbors could see her. We tried to hide behind our nervous humor when she did something like this, so we joked about it. The funniest comment won. But nothing felt good when Mom was in such a frightening space.

Bill and I shuffled her to the bedroom. I took off her outer coat, Bill, the inner. We hung them in her closet. Alfie tip toed in and took the bible off the rocking chair. He then took her arm, eased her down into her familiar seat. I leaned my hand over the back of the chair, pushing and pulling, until Mom trusted its rocking motion. We left her like that, swaying by the window, worrying the rosary beads in her lap. Tomorrow we'd take her to church. Tomorrow she'd be better.

It had already been a bad week for my father, who had missed three days of work at the university machine shop. His back was killing him. We could see it when he used the ladder. He always climbed left, right, left, right, one foot after the other, as if he were marching right up the air. But now it was more of a left, right, stop and catch your breath cadence.

He'd had an accident the previous month, while working at Roger's Welding four evenings a week. Dad was so exhausted that he cut his hand on a metal duct while rebuilding an air-conditioning unit. He needed stitches for the wound. My father was usually too careful to make a mistake like that. Our family was slipping and sliding again, the ground shifting beneath us.

We knew by the sound of my mother's rocking chair, that her voices were now in constant attendance. They'd returned with durable commitment, as if trained for a marathon, and they were not going away anytime soon. Mom's back and forth swaying was incessant, sometimes stopping only when she fell asleep. If I was alone with her, she told me the voices shrieked with higher pitch than before, cold and piercing as an icicle. Words came through Mom as if she were a human version of our old RCA-Victor phonograph. My brothers and I took turns being the white dog on the album cover, his attentive ear tilted at the speaker. Mom was following her instructions and we were listening for ours.

Now her visitors were back, holding on to all of us with sharp claws. My mother became especially unkind to Dad. The expression on her face was completely detached from the words she hurled against him. But he wasn't the only one losing this battle. None of us were a match for my mother's re-energized tormentors.

They emerged from the darkness, invading our family circle as we huddled around our hopeful campfire. No matter how we prayed that my mother's ears be muffled against their shrill intrusion, we were helpless.

They'd beckoned my mother to join them, as if cooing, "Sophie, we've come to play." My mother went to play.

They stole my days and nights, slithering into my thoughts with red eyes and trilling tongues, as they made fun of me. I constantly worried about tomorrow: I couldn't sleep.

My mother's voices bullied my dreams.

We were in our new home less than a year before Father Kavanaugh got his own chance to scare the demons. My father was at the stretched limit of his patience. Dad called the priest. I hoped the resonance of a different priestly voice would be harsh in the ear of Mom's tormenters. Maybe the way he carved the sign of the cross out of the air would take their breath away. *Maybe*, we hoped and prayed. *Maybe this time.*

But it was not to be. Our priest only stirred them up, as if he'd poked a stick in a hornet's nest. Mom said the voices buzzed and darted between the sacred drops of holy water that Father sprinkled at them. Like Father Gallagher's echo years before, the new *Kyrie eleisons* and *Christe eleisons* sounded their warning up and down the hallways, skimming over my father's hardwood floor. Thundering "Sed libera nos a malo," demanding that we be delivered from all evil, Father Kavanaugh shook his strong voice with deliberate intention. Once again, Mom held her hands against her ears. And just like our old priest years before, the kind man took her hands in his hands and blessed them. He could do nothing more.

I never expected it to work this time. Why should it be different? The holy water dried into hopeless spots, which I rubbed off our perfect maple floor after Father went home. Each erased watermark was an abandoned prayer. Once again, we'd been forgotten by God.

One Sunday, when I was really paying attention at mass, I heard our priest reading the gospel. Father Kavanaugh thrummed the air with his baritone promise about hope: "Ask and you shall receive; seek and you will find it; knock and it will be opened to you." I know he believed his own words.

But I knew better.

*   *   *

Much of my early religious foundation was formed when I learned to be an altar boy. I was serious about this responsibility and I wanted to be at my very best. I didn't just memorize my Latin responses, I learned what they meant: *Quia tu es Deus, fortitude mea,* for Thou, O God, art my strength; *Et introibo ad altare Dei,* I will go unto the altar of God.

I did go to the altar of God while praying for my mother, but whether I prayed in English or Latin, it didn't matter: nothing worked. Had God lost track of me? If I were not deserving of a healed mother, how could I be worthy of the kingdom of heaven? That gate would be forever closed to my timid tapping. Who among that saved population would recognize my name?

As a sixteen year-old boy, I was becoming a non-believer. The divine help promised in my tattered Baltimore Catechism was not intended for me. I still went to church and bowed my head in prayer, but I was simply going through the motions. The feelings of abandonment, loneliness, and powerlessness had overwhelmed me. I had either lost my faith, or I no longer recognized it.

The arguments between Mom and Dad were getting worse by the day. They popped up like thunderheads blooming from the afternoon humidity, spreading fear and uncertainty across the summer sky. Something was also changing in the way my mother participated in the fight, and it showed in her face. Maybe what *didn't* show in her face was what really alarmed us.

Her expression became so rigid it seemed she didn't care enough about my dad to even scowl at him. Mom would squint into a focused glare, concentrating her hostility right into my father's heart. Lowering her voice into a monotone whisper, she argued more softly, until Dad's frustration drove him to raise his voice louder than ever. Their quarrels became a seesawed duet of near-silence and desperate screaming. She sometimes fought with total silence, until she rippled her mute anger with detached pronouncements about *not casting the first stone,* or *not having false gods before you.* She pushed my father's anger right to the edge of the cliff. One more shove and he'd be free-falling.

If the fight wasn't about being a better Catholic, it was surely about money. My father said for every extra hour he worked, he felt as if we were two hours poorer. Mom was sending money to the church without his knowledge. She never paid attention to the checkbook balance because it didn't matter: *Jesus would provide.* He would keep our family in his healing light, whether we had money for ourselves or not. She pronounced that God's work is not free. The return on our offerings would be the safety of being cradled in the arms of Jesus, just as long as she kept the collection basket littered with checks for the church.

"Let's just see if Jesus sends the mortgage payment to People's National Bank. Can he put some meat and potatoes on our table, after I work my ass off all day? Goddamit Sophie, I can't live on a skinny little wafer of communion. Neither can your boys," Dad confiscated the checkbook. He couldn't understand why our priests even cashed the checks. "Don't they understand our situation? Don't they know how hard I work?"

But they didn't know everything about us. No one else did either, other than our relatives. Even they knew that Mom was getting worse. She was pulling away from her brothers and sisters, isolating herself, as well as our family. We didn't talk with anyone about what was going on in our home.

We were better at keeping secrets than sharing them. Besides, who would believe us? And even if they did, what could anyone do?

One morning Dad woke up with chest pains. At that moment, Mom was frightened and clear-headed enough to call Dr. Light, who answered the phone himself. He hadn't started his daily office hours, so he jumped in his car and came right to our house. We were all scared as we waited for him to come out from our parents' bedroom. Mom sat at the kitchen table with her prayer book. Alfie, Bill, and I sat on my bed, across the hall from the closed door. We could hear our doctor's calm voice, but we couldn't understand what he was saying.

When the door cracked open, Dr. Light motioned for me to come in. Dad asked that he explain things to me, before he talked to my mother. I sat on the edge of the bed, next to my father. Dr. Light pulled out the bench from Mom's dresser and sat at the foot of the bed. I asked if it was Dad's heart.

"Not his heart, Carl. He has pleurisy, probably from a mild case of pneumonia." Dr. Light had a way of making me a grown-up by leaning down toward me, making my eyes level with his. "Every breath he takes in hurts him right here." He spread his open hand against my chest, gripping my ribs. "Your father's been working too hard."

Dad must have been scared because he promised to take it easy for a few days. He agreed that any unfinished work on the house would still be there next week. Our doctor's kindness buoyed up Dad's spirit. He had been given permission for a few days of rest, something he'd never do for himself. "Guess I earned a little vacation. How about it boys? I think I'll start with a short nap."

After closing the door to Dad's bedroom, Bill, Alfie, and I walked down the hallway with Dr. Light. He stopped at the kitchen table to explain everything to my mother. She momentarily searched his face, as if trying to remember what was going on. Before leaving our house, Dr. Light gave me a cautious smile. "Everything will be OK, Carl. You know how to reach me if you need me." I felt better even though I wasn't the patient.

The following week was calm and Dad did get his rest, even sleeping during the day. My mom's voices were temporarily subdued. My brothers and I felt like we were on vacation for a few weeks, with only our newspapers, housework, and baseball practice to occupy us.

Soon Dad got better, but everything else got worse. Since losing control of the checkbook, my mother began to sneak some of the weekly cash, which she gave to the church. My father tried hiding his wallet, but she usually found it. The week after he was sick, Dad and I went to the A&P to buy the week's groceries. He always lined up the items for the benefit of the checkout clerk, separating produce from meat; clustering together same-priced cans; positioning heavy items to be packed in the bottom of the bag. It was not until he opened his wallet that he discovered his money was missing. His anger drowned in the embarrassment of being unable to pay for the orderly display of fruits and vegetables, canned goods, milk and meat, neatly lined up at the cash register. He could hardly speak to the cashier.

When we got home my father's anger bounced off every wall in the house. "Goddamit, will this ever end. What in the name of hell do I have to do for one day, just one day of peace?" He slammed his fist on the dining room table, knocking a dish onto the floor. Now when he got angry, we stood a little further back.

Dad went outside and sat on the porch steps. For a long time, he held his head in his hands. When he finally looked up, I went out and sat just close enough to let him know that I was there. There was nothing for either of us to say.

During the next week, Dad found unpaid bills that my mother had been hiding so we'd have more money to give to the church. Mom had also given away a pot roast that we bought at Temple's Meat Market. Earlier in the week, Dad had sent me downtown with money for our Sunday dinner. He gave me extra so we could pay something on our balance. But he didn't expect Mom to give our Sunday dinner to Uncle Tony when he stopped in for a visit. As soon as the door closed on my uncle's departure, Dad hollered at Mom. "It's bad enough that the pope gets all my money. Now we have to feed your brothers and sisters. I've had enough, Goddamit! Enough!"

Mom glared. Coldly.

We were running out of breath and running out of space. When Dad was home, he intercepted the mail before it got in my mother's hands. Otherwise, Mom would hide any requests for money from the church. Sooner or later, she'd find a way to send a contribution. Dad was mowing grass on that terrible Saturday, when the mailman cheerfully greeted him from the sidewalk. My father took the mail and carried the bundle inside the house.

That's when the explosion went off: an uncontrolled eruption of profanity, unlike anything I'd ever heard from my father. He had finally been pushed off the cliff. Dad was spinning out of control, cart-wheeling in the air, headed for a crash on the rocks below.

Alfie came charging in from his bedroom, just as Bill and I leaped up the cellar stairs, two steps at a time. Stunned for a moment, we froze in place. My father's voice was pure despair, full-throated and unrelenting. Shrieking and moaning, he yelped like a kicked dog, a wild animal screeching at my mother. I felt his thumping rage, pounding for a way out of his awful life.

Mom was a statue at one end of the table, her hands gripping the back of the chair. Her face was grim and flat, revealing not a trace of fear or feeling for my father; her vacant eyes, once again, cold on my father's heart.

Dad's arms flailed and stabbed the air. That's when I saw his right hand, fierce around the hard-rubber grip of his handmade kitchen knife. The perfectly balanced seven-inch blade was kept razor sharp, able to slice a hard crust of bread so cleanly that not one crumb would fall away.

It was something my mother hissed about *following the Word*, something about *following the righteous path*, that triggered my father's leap around the table, the knife raised high above his head. Bill and I tackled him as he lurched at my mother. We wedged him against the wall, ducking under the glittering blade as he sliced the space above. Our own screaming blared into my father's howl, as Alfie dragged my mother down the bedroom hallway. Still gripped in her hands, the chair screeched its own alarm, scraping over Dad's perfect hardwood floor, as my mother dragged it to safety.

Bill and I pushed down as hard as we could, against my father's muscled determination to get up. He'd surrendered the knife. I kicked it into the dining room, spinning it across the floor like a low-flying helicopter. Dad trembled for a few minutes under our frightened weight, both of us sprawled heavily across his rigid body. He finally softened. After a minute or two, we rolled off and released him. Dad remained on the floor for several more minutes. Then he rolled onto his back and struggled into a sitting position, wrapping his arms around his knees. He was sobbing now, shuddering with his head down. He wouldn't look at us: he couldn't look at us.

The heavy silence pushed down on all of us. We were out of breath. Dad looked sick and pale. I thought he might throw up. *Was his heart OK?* Bill pulled out a chair and we helped him off the floor. He was so quiet. When he asked for a handkerchief, I gave him mine.

My father's explosive lunge had clattered his collection of hand-made kitchen knives across the countertop. Moments before, they'd been proudly displayed in the solid oak holder which showed off his handiwork. At the other end was the disabled telephone, its frayed connection dangling to the floor. Before my brothers and I charged into the kitchen, Dad had ripped it right out of the wall, his eruption of anger leaving a jagged hole in the plaster wall.

On the table, an explanation: the opened phone bill showed over $400 in long distance charges, verifying my mother's calls to monasteries all over the country; Sisters of the Holy Cross, Brothers of St. Benedict, or anyone else who would pray for the salvation of her family.

My father sat for a long time at the table before lifting up his eyes. Quiet now, he began to shiver. None of us could speak. Any words would crash of their own sad weight, silent in their shattering against Dad's hardwood floor.

Bill and I looked back and forth between ourselves and Dad's surrendered kitchen knife, which was glinting from the living room floor. We understood more than we ever wanted to, about what had just happened, and about what could have happened. Bill sat at the table with Dad while I walked down the hall to check on Mom. Alfie placed a finger on his lips when I opened the door. He sat on the edge of her bed, keeping watch. Mom was in her chair by the window, cuddling a small crucifix in her lap. Her head rested against the back of the chair and her eyes were closed. She'd rocked herself to sleep. Alfie stretched a light sweater over Mom's shoulders. Even though it was a warm day, the bedroom felt cold. Before we left the room, my little brother went back and folded the sweater's warmth against her bare arms. He left the door open a crack.

When I returned to the kitchen, Dad was sitting up straight, no longer hunched over the table. His eyes were closed, his hands tightly clenched together. He looked thin and scared, and so suddenly, old.

"Where's Mom?" The whispered words, more of a plea than a question.

"She's in the bedroom, Dad. Alfie's watching her. She's asleep, at least for now."

After a few minutes, Dad asked me for the phone book. "I need the number of the rectory." He thumbed through the pages as if they were sharp-edged and painful to turn. "I have to talk to Father Kavanaugh."

"I don't think the phone's going to work, Dad."

He softly closed the book and put his head down again, quieting his hands against his forehead and pulsing temples.

Once again I was sitting on the sun porch of the church rectory, waiting for Father Kavanaugh. This time, I really wanted to be here. My brothers and I decided we couldn't let Dad come by himself. We worried about him crossing Atherton Street. Saturday traffic was always busy, and Dad was too distraught to look where he was going. He would surely get hit by a car. Bill and Alfie stayed home with Mom, while I walked my father to the priest.

We'd arrived unannounced. Our telephone wouldn't be reconnected for several days. Father Ream offered to talk with my father. Otherwise we'd be welcome to wait for Father Kavanaugh to return from his hospital visits. Dad thanked the young priest for his offer. He'd wait for the older man.

Dad rested his head against the top of the stuffed chair that he'd collapsed into. An easy breeze came through the screened windows, slowly drying my father's damp forehead. I started to put my own head back. Until I sat down, I didn't realize that my neck was stiff and sore. My whole body felt like it was packed in cement. My eyelids just started to droop when the priest's shiny black Oldsmobile hummed into the driveway.

"Dad. Time to wake up." I had to touch his shoulder. Lightly. "Father Kavanaugh just pulled in." My father's eyes opened. He stared at me for a moment, then jerked straight up in his chair.

We heard Father Ream's muffled conversation from the kitchen. A few minutes later, Father Kavanaugh was sitting with us on the porch. He studied my father's face; this was not the strong, proud man the priest was used to seeing. This was not the dignified gentleman who ushered and passed the collection basket during Sunday Mass. He stood up and invited my father to come into his office. I could wait here, on the porch.

"I need my boy with me, Father." Dad looked my way. "You know my oldest boy. He's a good boy, and he knows what it's been like." My father was shaking again, looking down. "I'd like Carl to be with me."

Father smiled at me. "I know your boy, Clem. He's surely a good boy." I could tell by the way the priest looked me in the eye, that he never told Dad about my earlier visit with Mom. My secret was safe with Father Kavanaugh. He would never embarrass me. I could trust him.

"Well then. Let's just sit here. It's more comfortable anyway, with the breeze out here. Let me get something cold to drink. What would you gentlemen like?"

My father said he was fine. He didn't want to impose anymore than he already had. He'd stolen enough of Father's afternoon. The priest put up his hand and gently waved my dad into silence. Then he excused himself.

A few minutes later, he appeared in the doorway with three tall glasses of iced tea, balanced on a wooden tray. He set it on a low wicker table between Dad and me. He'd also traded his Roman collar and black shirt for a blue and white Penn State Football T-shirt. He pulled his chair closer, into our circle of three. The priest had joined us and what we brought to him.

"All right, Clem. Tell me how it is for you." Before my father began speaking, he'd drained half his cold drink. He was thirsty, after all. Dad first looked at me, then the floor. Soon his gaze rested on Father Kavanaugh's shirt, slowly lifting against the bent weight of his shame, until he dared to look our priest in the eye.

"I don't think I can go on, Father. I don't think it will ever get better." Dad was staring at his shoes; the eye contact was too much for him. "And after today, my boys. What they saw today, I just can't…" He couldn't go on.

"Take your time, Clem. I'm not going away. We're in no rush, here. You just tell me what you want to tell me. I'd like to help."

He told Father Kavanaugh how hard it had been for him. Dad explained about the voices, the lost money, even about the knife, probably still warm from his hard grip. My father's voice had no muscle in it. This story was coming from a man who was beat up and beaten down, his feet still seeking solid ground beneath him. This was my father's whisper for penance. Father Kavanaugh and I were both hearing his confession.

After Dad finished his story, the priest sat in silence. He closed his eyes for a minute before looking at me. He wanted to know about my brothers. How were the three of us doing with all that was going on? Was school OK? Were we scared, did we have nice friends, and how were all of our cousins who lived in town? How were they with us, about Mom?

"We're fine, Father. We're really, really good. We're doing good in school, getting good grades, and we're all playing really good baseball, and just the other day Bill got two hits in two times at bat, and I played center field, and I threw a runner out at second, and..."

He looked at me, waiting patiently, until I had to catch my breath. As long as I kept talking, everything was fine. It was only bad when I had time to think. We sat for a while in that durable quiet. It seemed too peaceful to be ruffled with words. Father Kavanaugh was first to break into the silence.

He told my father that he'd endured more than any man he knew. My mother's situation was beyond what could be fixed. All we could do is pray. But for the sake of my dad's health and peace of mind, there was an option: my father could leave this terrible situation. The priest shifted his eyes to me and let his gaze stay with me, before returning his attention to Dad.

My father sat up on the edge of the chair when he heard those words. The priest told him that he didn't understand how he could work and take care of his boys, much less take care of himself. Maybe the answer was to put Mom back in Danville, maybe not. But if he had to, my father could leave, one way or the other. "You are a good man, Clem. You have nothing to feel ashamed of. You've done your best. God will be kind to you." Again, Father Kavanaugh found my eyes, and I knew it would be OK.

Once again we walked along Fairmount Avenue on our way home. Dad was talking out loud, partly to himself and partly to me. He was shaking his head, so absorbed in his own thoughts that he lagged behind me.

I tried to imagine our life without Mom: no more voices or scary words about sin? We would abandon the endless list of chores planned by The Blessed Mother, with the tossed words of my mother's fear, her crumbled paper prayers? And what would happen to Mom? Would we have to go back to Danville to receive her smile or hug. Or would she be somewhere else? Would she even know who we were?

"I can't do it," my father whispered. "I can't avoid my duty. I can't break my marriage vows," he said more loudly, walking faster. "I will stay and take care of things."

Father Kavanaugh knew my father and his deep sense of responsibility. My father would never leave, and the priest realized that. So he gave my father the gift of understanding. *Someone else knew how bad it was.* Dad stood a bit taller, began to walk with more purpose. He caught up with me.

We walked home together.

It was late afternoon when Dad and I got back to the house. Bill and Alfie were still in the kitchen acting like they were busy with chores, but I knew they were just waiting for us to return from our visit. I slipped down the hallway to peek in the bedroom. Mom was asleep in her chair by the bedroom window, her sweater still draped around her.

Dad called all three of us to the back porch. He sat in his folding chair. He didn't look at us for a while. We sat sideways on the steps, waiting for him to say something.

The only noise we heard was the whack and slap of the ball game, and the cheering crowd at the Community Field. I could even hear Mr. Lytle, the coach of the Jaycee Juniors, yelling at whoever was batting. Because of the wind direction, his voice carried as clearly as if he'd been standing in our driveway. "Walk's as good as a hit." The batter must have ignored the instructions. The *thwuck* of baseball into the catcher's mitt and the crowd's low groan signaled strike three. That summer fun seemed as far away as the green mountains blurring the border between farmlands and hazy sky. How could those summer sounds be so close and so far away?

"I'm sorry boys. I don't know what got into me." Lines of worry tugged against my father's mouth when he tried to smile. "It won't happen again. You are good boys. You deserve better." We didn't have to look at Dad to know he was crying. We heard the tears in the catch and quiver of his voice.

He leaned forward to get out of his chair, but he had to sit back down and rock forward to get on his feet. He stood in front of us, a bit wobbly, as if he didn't deserve to be tall. "I'm going to take a shower and a short nap. We'll have dinner after that. So you boys play catch and enjoy some of the afternoon. Just be sure you pick some lettuce and tomatoes, maybe a carrot or two. We'll have a salad and the leftover meatloaf from yesterday."

Dad went inside while we just sat together on the porch. We tried to be funny with each other, as if we could laugh it away.

"It's good Alfie didn't try to tackle Dad." Bill elbowed me in the ribs. "The old man would have run right through him for a touchdown!"

"That's 'cause your fat butt was in Dad's way. Hooeee! Probably scared him." Alfie was getting pretty good at defending himself. We laughed a bit too loudly. And a bit too long. We ran out of funny things to say. Our conversation evaporated into the humidity of that thick air. We didn't even feel like playing catch. We were tired. We were so very tired.

Bill and Alfie picked the vegetables while I went inside to set the table. I found our blue tablecloth with green and yellow flowers around the edges. The cheerful colors brightened our dining room. It hadn't been used for a long time, so I spread it over the table. Then I set out the silverware and plates. I folded a real cloth napkin for each place. My brothers brought in their pickings from the garden. I rinsed them off and left them to drain in the colander.

After his shower and nap, Dad returned to the kitchen. He wore a clean tee shirt and newly laundered work pants. He'd shaved, too. He smelled good. I helped him slice the vegetables and a loaf of crusty bread. Dad's kitchen knife was now in my hands, sliding through the bread as if it were a loaf of butter. My father placed the meatloaf in the oven and turned the temperature to 350 degrees. I placed the knife in its wooden stand, where it once again waited to do its intended work.

Soon we heard water running in the bathroom. Mom was finally awake. In a few minutes she came into the kitchen, wearing a blue bathrobe and warm slippers. She had been asleep for over four hours and it showed. She looked rested and more peaceful than any of us. Mom stood in the middle of the kitchen as if she didn't know what to do. Bill told her she could sit down because we'd be eating soon. Alfie pulled out the bench for her.

Mom just smiled at us from her place at the table, like nothing had ever happened. Her eyes stayed on me for a long time, even when I caught her smiling at me. Dad carried the hot tray of supper to the table, and placed it on a pad. A pile of roasted potatoes smothered the meatloaf. I set the big bowl of salad next to it. This time Dad said grace, just the basics, nothing extra. Then he nodded toward the table. "Dig in boys. Vegetables are good for you. Especially carrots. Good for your eyesight."

We couldn't help snickering when my father talked about vegetables. With his German accent, the word sounded like "wegetables." Even Mom smiled at that. She knew we were biting our lips to keep from laughing. When he could no longer hold his breath, Bill started laughing out loud. I tried to stare him down, but he didn't even try to stop. He just laughed harder. Then Alfie and I joined in, letting everything go, with the three of us howling until we were almost crying. We stopped and started again, laughing until the real tears came.

Dad didn't even give us a stern look.

"I forgot the drinks." Dad pushed his chair back. He got up, and went to the refrigerator. He came back with a pitcher of lemonade for us, and a cold bottle of Yuengling beer for himself. He poured a glass of lemonade for Mom and set it in front of her, then pointed to our glasses. We could pour our own.

After we finished supper, Dad went out on the back porch to sip his beer. We cleaned up the dishes and put away the leftover food. There wasn't much left. Mom just sat at the table. Sometimes she'd fall asleep in her chair when she was peaceful like this. But this time she stayed awake and just smiled at us, as if she were watching *Leave it to Beaver* on television. That was one show we could safely watch.

Outside, the early night was cooling off. The humidity was dropping along with the sun, which was sinking into a bronze fire in the western sky. High above, a rosy blush smeared the thin layer of evening as it hovered over the mountains.

"Carl. Come out here for a minute." Dad was sitting on the top step. I thought he wanted me to bring him another beer. "Look here, the wind's almost died down." He took a long sip of his beer. "Tell your brothers to come out here. And bring their jars. Good night for catching fireflies." I looked at Dad to see if he was serious. We were little kids when we last caught fireflies. My father set the empty bottle on the step. "Yes indeed. It's going to be a good night for fireflies."

"I'll tell them as soon as we finish the dishes." I opened the door to go back to the kitchen. *Why would we want to catch fireflies?*

"One more thing, Carl. See if Mom wants to come out. Fresh air would be good for her."

Straight and tall, Dad sat on the top step, hands resting on his knees. My brothers and I crowded the bottom step, elbowing each other for space. We each hugged our jars with holes punched in the lids, but I put mine down. At the age of sixteen, I was too old to be collecting fireflies. So were my brothers. But it didn't matter. Sometimes even big kids needed magic.

Mom sat in back of us, on the chair my father had unfolded for her. More perched on the edge than sitting, she remained close to the kitchen door. For now she was smiling, but unsure about staying. It was quiet. We were waiting for fireflies.

I felt the last brush of sunset on my face, as the cool evening wrapped around our family. South of town, the hills tumbled in the distance, from green to rose to purple. Soon it was dark and my mother settled back into her chair, wiggling herself away from the edge. She'd stay for a while.

"Look. Over there!" My father pointed his empty beer bottle toward our neighbor's back yard. "Look at Tom's garden."

Mr. O'Hara's tomato plants lit up like Christmas trees, as the first wave of lightning bugs dappled them with blinking light. The darkening sky smudged, then erased the silhouette of hills; points of fire flickered in the heavens, then slowly magnified into stars and constellations. The Great Hunter lifted above us while the fireflies quivered through the yard like a shower of floating confetti. From my charts and binoculars, I knew something of the night sky.

Look! Orion and his dogs, Canis Major and Canis Minor; they are chasing Taurus the Bull! Betelgeuse, that bright star on Orion's left shoulder; Algebar, the star on his shining right foot? Alnitak, Alnilan, Mintaka: The Great Hunter's belt. The heavens are littered with mysterious names. Magical names.

My father's garden is an airport. Wings of light descend and take off, skimming over runways of lettuce and carrot tops, swirling up into a holding pattern. They wink like a million golden heartbeats.

Suddenly I am lifted off my feet. I skip into the yard, and with outstretched arms, I am spinning round and round in the splash of stars and constellations. Ribbons of light wrap around me as I dance and twirl in the congregation of fireflies.

See me flying in the rushing wind of galaxies? Do you hear the hiss of whirling planets and shooting stars? I am floating in the echoes: Taygeta, Sterope. Gloria tibi Domine. Sing to me, Sirius and Aludra. Our Father, who art in heaven. Deum de Deo, hallowed be your names, Mebsula, Mekbuda. Pleni sunt coeli, et in terra Gloria tua. Heaven and earth are filled with your glory. Dear God, keep my mother safe in her distant orbit. Gemini, Sagittarius, my Father, my Brothers, be with me in a familiar universe.

Be with me.

PART TWO

Chapter 21-Contemplation

I'm sitting at my table, the blank notebook in front of me. My pen weighs a thousand pounds, too heavy to lift. I'd rather look out the window at the gray Atlantic. The shoreline north of Boston is being pounded by a winter storm. Six miles out in Nahant Bay, Egg Rock is jagged and unyielding against the frothy surge and thump of the angry ocean. In my back yard, a cluster of white-veiled Hemlocks stands tall, like a procession of elegant brides. I've seen them bow down under the heavy burden of wet snow, as if asking forgiveness for some unknown transgression. Then comes the miracle of thawing: the trees shudder and shed their unfair weight, one branch at a time until they are again tall, at attention, stately in their rightful share of the sky.

Their resilience reminds me of my father and how he could bend without breaking. Time after time he regained his proud posture after being pushed down. I think of my mother, who could not escape the relentless tide of her disturbed emotions and the chaos left in its wake. I have learned that we are all tested by time. Branches break; trees fall, uprooted. Even Egg Rock's craggy face will be softened by water.

I should be writing, adding to these pages. As I tell my story, I am re-living my childhood, even from this safe and lovely distance of time. My memory is vividly clear about the terrible day of the knife in my father's hand. But since I've put those words on the paper, I have not had one of my nightmares. I no longer wake up my wife with my muffled shout, echoing in a long corridor from which I can't escape. Instead, I remember how that frightful day ended in my dance with the fireflies.

Isn't that a glorious ending, a gift? Is my story over?

I think not. Difficult as it was, I may have written the easier part of the memoir. Now I'm forced to consider what it all means, what I've learned. Like a sentence with no period to end it, my story hangs in the air, unless I complete it.

I now understand that there are gifts to be acknowledged: my father's determination and patience; the kindness of the priests who ministered to all of us; the humor that bonded me with Bill and Alfie. I learned from a generous coach, that I could take a risk and that I did not have to be perfect. I am still holding inside the unwritten words to describe the miracles that were my brothers. Most important, if I stopped writing now, I would not tell you how I came to truly love my mother, and how I finally understood that she loved me. Today I believe my mother was a gift and a profound teacher in my life.

I drop my gaze from the view of the New England winter. My notebook's perfect pages are white as the snow outside my window. It's time to make them imperfect. I reach for my pen.

Chapter 22

I thought my father would never break. But on that day when we three brothers exploded into the dangerous space between our parents, he did break. At the very least, he was bent. In time, my dad repaired much of his spirit. But the proud man never stood quite as tall as before.

I remember my feeling of fatigue for the rest of that summer. Each day I woke up feeling like I needed two more hours of sleep. Something was drained from my parents as well, leaving only enough energy for an uneasy truce between them. My mother pulled deeper into her own shadows. When our orbits did intersect, she circled around the edges of our secret universe, as if seeking a gentler gravity between us. Maybe the voices were wearing out: her entrances and exits were cushioned by an unfamiliar softness, which no longer altered our breathing. My father sat alone on the back porch with an empty chair beside him, as if becoming acquainted with the raging stranger who had emerged from within on that unspeakable day.

My brothers and I were on our best behavior for the remainder of that unforgettable summer. We cleaned up after meals without being asked. We put dishes and silverware away, set the table, kept our rooms clean. We did whatever we could to replenish my father's strength. Most of all, we tried to be good for my mother. We would never agitate her again; no more grumbling about being altar boys at early morning mass.

One Sunday morning shortly after our unforgettable day, Father Kavanaugh gave a sermon about the Beatitudes. "Blessed are the peacemakers, for they will be the children of God." We were ripe for healing. I remember how my brothers and I were so quiet in those spoken words, which sounded safe and welcoming. From now on, we would be the peacemakers. We would be the children of God.

* * *

We plunged into our school activities and sports. Our teachers and coaches, some of whom were becoming aware of our hushed-up life at home, embraced my brothers and me. We slowly opened ourselves to the support and guidance of adults other than our own family members. Teammates and classmates became trusted friends.

Bill became an outstanding basketball player. Alfie made the Little League All-Star team. Besides my own sports activities, I discovered music through my singing and trumpet lessons. With praise and encouragement for our efforts and accomplishments, each of us began to step out of our own shadows. The encouragement surrounding us felt like warm sunlight. Once we'd basked in it, we didn't want to leave it.

I began to reach beyond my family for meaningful relationships. I learned that I could trust my classmate Eddie, who had consoled me years earlier, when our baseball team lost the big game because of my error. It lifted my confidence that I could talk safely with my best friend about my life at home. My developing faith in others allowed me to be guided by the second most influential man in my life: Wilbur Bolton was my biology teacher and my track coach. My father's lessons were about perfection, *doing* it right. Mr. Bolton taught me about *trying* to do it right.

I had started playing soccer during my freshman year of high school. My running ability and endurance often allowed me to finish a game with more strength than the other athletes. My soccer coach invited Mr. Bolton to watch me play, but more important, to watch me run. He waited until the game was over to talk with me. "Shaynabeck!" Coach Bolton had his own way of pronouncing my name, exaggerating the "A" sound of the German umlaut. With his booming voice, there was never a doubt about whom he was speaking to. And there was no confusion about his request: "I need a miler." From that day on, I was a long-distance runner. From that day on, I had a second father.

From my first race as a sophomore until my final regular competition as a senior, I never lost a race. Bill followed my footsteps, two years behind me. After I graduated, Bill was undefeated. For several years, no other runner finished the mile in front of a Schoenebeck. My brother went on to finish second in the Pennsylvania State Cross Country Championship. Our coach's influence even extended to Alfie, who became a very good half-miler.

My mother had been rather indifferent about our participation in athletics, but now that I was in my senior year of high school, she seemed a bit more involved than before. She regained some connection with my brothers and me, although the attachment felt like holding onto a frayed rope, which was never far from unraveling. Too much tension from either direction and once again we'd be floating away from each other.

Mom often came with Dad to our track meets. She sat on the bleacher seats, quietly taking in the action on the field below. While others jumped up and down with boisterous cheering or clapping, my mother remained quiet in her own peaceful meditation, no doubt praying that her sons ran the good race, with Jesus setting our pace. When she gave me a holy medal to wear, I appeased her by pinning it inside the waistband of my track shorts. It was invisible to anyone else and it added no weight to my skinny runner's body. Besides, I kept winning. Why not wear it?

Mr. Bolton trained his athletes for more than running circles around the track. The familiar concepts of discipline, perseverance, and confidence underlined the lessons we learned under his guidance. He never asked anything unreasonable from his athletes: only that we try our very best on any given day. "That effort is noble," he told us. "And you must carry that determination into your school work and your family life." It was only by giving our best that we'd improve. "The limit of your potential must be a moving target. If you don't stretch when you reach for it, you will never grow." His words sounded good, but I thought they applied to everyone else.

On one of the most meaningful days of my life, Coach Bolton asked me to reach for a new limit, a strange concept for me. I assumed I'd reached the peak of my athletic ability, but I had actually learned to stay in a familiar comfort zone. In order to escape my mother's demons, I had to outpace them. Life at home was a long distance race, in which I'd learned to save my strength for the next hour, the next day, the next year. Something had to be kept in reserve. But I was about to abandon this cautious rationing of my energy.

I will always remember that day: the bus; the booming voice; the call to attention. "Shaynabeck!" Coach Bolton's voice cannonballed from the front of the bus. I was sitting in the back row, joking with Batty and Hass. Our high school track team was on the way to Huntingdon. We were undefeated, going to our final meet of the year, and the last regular competition of my high school career. It was a big deal for me.

"Shaynabeck. Now, I want to talk to you." The way his voice muscled the word *you* got my attention. Same with my teammates. They were all staring at me, along with my coach. Alternately bracing himself against the seats on either side, he was weaving down the center aisle, swaying with the curving turns along Route 322. Blossoms of Mountain Laurel smudged the Juniata River with white and pink reflections. But no one was looking at the summer day blurring by the windows. Not now. All eyes were on me.

"Shaynabeck. Today you run your last mile for State High. What'd I say?" That was Mr. Bolton's trademark, *what'd I say?* followed by his own exaggerated repetition of what he'd just said. "Today…you…run…your…last…mile." He stopped halfway down the bus, but he never took his eyes off me. Nor did anyone else.

"You have made me proud, Shaynabeck. Won every race of your career. Last week, a new mile record for State College High School."

Applause from my teammates. The bus was congested with his words: he owned the air. He reached his hand out in an all-inclusive sweep of benevolence. "These dedicated teammates of yours, these fine young men… on this special day, they are proud of you, too." Coach then opened both arms, as if he were the grateful father welcoming home a bus full of prodigal sons. "What'd I say? Everybody?"

"We…are…proud…of…you."

Hass slapped me on my shoulder. The clapping sound triggered more noise, as my teammates cheered and stomped their feet. But the volume dropped when Mr. Bolton folded his arms across his chest. He was perfectly balanced, no longer braced against the seats, as the bus chugged and groaned toward Huntingdon. He held his posture and locked his eyes right on mine.

"Today, Shaynabeck, I am asking for something special. And I am asking this, not for me, not for your teammates…but for you." Now his voice was barely audible, as if he'd shifted from a hoomping tuba to a quivering cello. "Today, I ask you to test yourself." It was so quiet I could hear my teammates trying to hold their breath. I waited. Everyone else waited, until he bellowed, "What'd I say?"

"Today…You…Test…Your…Self." The bus rocked.

I had stepped on the track for the first time during my sophomore year. I wasn't fast enough for the sprints, but I could run all day. Coach declared me his miler, his long distance runner. Almost faster than I could run, three years zipped by. Now I was a senior and I'd won every mile I ever raced. My pal Batty was always close enough behind me that no opposing miler had ever entered that space between us. During my senior year, my brother Bill consistently finished right behind Batty. With each race my times improved. Five minutes flat in my first race, and now I had improved to four minutes and thirty-six seconds. It was a new record for my school, but I was stuck. My last four races were within two seconds of that time.

Distance running is like any other foot race; first one over the finish line wins. But a miler must run with discipline and race with patience. Go out too fast, and you will crash at the end, maybe not even finish. With too much caution you lose. And you'll never know how fast you could have run. I was not a gambler. I had learned the importance of making sure I'd finish my race.

Mr. Bolton was on to me.

I enter that day as if it were today.

Our bus pulls in behind the football stadium. Hundreds of people mill around the field, and just as many line the bleachers. Track meets don't usually draw big crowds. The loyal fans are parents, siblings bound in chains, and curious neighbors; perhaps a few classmates. This is really different because Huntingdon lost only two meets, and they want to end on a good note by ruining our perfect season. With this exuberant crowd and the sunny weather, our track meet is more like a spring carnival.

A proper warm up is important for distance runners. Our muscles must be stretched out and loose in order to run efficiently. Batty, Bill and I warm up together. Alone, I have too much time to start worrying about the race. Butterflies are part of the experience. Too heavy a dose and nervous energy will burn you out. No butterflies, you may be done in by overconfidence.

We start our routine by walking while still in our sweat suits. We lose ourselves on the infield, which is now a fluttering collage of boys in Huntingdon's red and blue, and State's maroon and gray. At one end of the field, the muscle guys flex and bulge in the shot put area, lifting up and grunting as they push the twelve pound ball into the blue sky. Others are whirling around, spinning the discus toward the Laurel Mountains, so big in the clear air they seem like a target.

"Attention. Attention please!" The megaphone blares its authority from the starting area. "First call for the one-mile run. Second call for the high hurdles. Final call for the one hundred yard dash. Repeat. Final call, hundred yard dash. All sprinters to the starting line." The spring air is buzzing.

Now we jog up and down the infield. The mile will start in twenty minutes. We pick up our pace, breaking a sweat with repeated wind sprints. *Puffing now. Heart pumping faster.* Time to get winded, so our deep breathing can catch up to what our muscles need. Getting our second wind.

POW! Across the field, the gun goes off. The sprinters pump their arms and wheel their legs along the track. The first three runners are like one blurred shadow, not a foot of space between them. Three yards from the finish line, Sacky Lee leans into the tape, wearing it across his chest as he eases back his speed. Good start for our team; first and second.

"Attention, all runners. Final call, high hurdles. Second call for the one-mile run. Hurdlers, report to the starting line." Ten minutes to go. *Butterflies flutter.*

Batty and I walk to a sunny patch of grass, where we sit down. Bill stands nearby, warming his face in the sun. Soft thump on the ground, bursts of applause echo from the shot put circle, Huntingdon's muscle guy pumps his fist above his head. Now we all stretch in the warm sun. Joking. Trying to sound confident, trying to relax. High jumpers at the other end, rising over the spectators, floating over the bar. Applause. Batty, Bill and I wait. Thinking.

Gun splits the air, starting the high hurdlers. They skim over the barriers; stride, stride, stride and glide, over and over, striding and gliding, until the last row of hurdles is cleared. Good. We got first and third. Our team is doing great.

"Last call for the mile. Last call for the one-mile run. All milers to the starting line." Now it's our show. *We are on center stage. So are the butterflies.*

I take off my sweat suit and fold it. Hass takes it from me. "Good luck. Keep loose." Coach Bolton walks with us to the starting line. He has a plan for me. He huddles with me as we review it for a final time.

"Even pace, Shaynabeck. 67 seconds for each quarter mile." *That's the pace for a 4:28 mile. I've never run that fast.* "Don't fall for a decoy. Huntingdon might send out a rabbit to trick you into going too fast. Keep the arms loose, Shaynabeck. What'd I say? Arms...loose!"

Coach Bolton stands in front of me and clamps my shoulders in his strong hands. "Remember. Last lap. Spend everything you've got. Everything. Pay attention, don't get hypnotized. I'll be on the backstretch and you listen for me." Now he tilts my head upward. "Do I have your attention, Shaynabeck? Test yourself. Leave it all on the track...what'd I say? Leave...it...all ...on...the...track."

Eight milers approach the starting line, four from each team. I try to keep warm by jogging in place. I feel a bit chilly, even in the sun. *Butterflies, just a little bit now.*

"Runners to the line." The Huntingdon coach is the official starter. He's wearing a baseball cap and a red and blue windbreaker and he's smiling. He must have been an old distance runner, the way he tries to put us at ease. He knows what we're feeling. One by one, he brings us up to the white stripe. Since I'd run the fastest time, I am given my choice of starting position. I line up fifth from the inside. I don't want to get boxed in going around the first turn. Once the lineup is complete, the starter walks thirty feet down the infield. He turns around and faces us.

"OK boys. Simple command. I will give you 'runners ready' and then the gun. False start, I will refire immediately and we start again. Any questions?"

All quiet along the row of runners, their toes to the line. I'm calm now. *Butterflies have folded their wings.*

"Good luck. Timers ready?" Several people lift stopwatches, ready to measure and appraise the next few minutes of our lives.

"Runners ready!" We hunch into starting posture.

POW!

Eight runners bolt as if released from coiled springs. We jostle into the first turn, clearing space with elbows, legs pumping erratically, waiting for enough open space to settle into a relaxed stride. *Breathing hard.* I'm trapped behind two Huntingdon runners, until we curve around the second turn, entering the backstretch.

The pack thins out. I'm gliding now, settling into a comfortable pace. I slide in behind Marean, their best miler. He's good, but I've beat him before. Space opening up a little. *Not puffing so hard now. Feeling easy now.*

"Shay-na-beck." My coach thunders at me. He's right there, where he promised he'd be, in the middle of the backstretch. "Let him go, keep your own pace." Marean is trying to pull me out too fast. My opponent glances over his right shoulder to see where I am. His glasses are steamed up; he's working harder than me.

We round the last turn into the homestretch, completing the first lap. *Breathing deep and easy.* "66…67…68," the man with the stopwatch chants as we pass the first quarter mile. *I nailed it. 67, right on pace.* Marean is fifteen yards ahead of me. He's going too fast. *Much too fast.*

Entering the backstretch of the second lap. He's coming back to me now. "Easy, Shaynabeck. Stay smooth. Steady pace." Mr. Bolton claps at me as I move up on the lead runner. Rounding the far turn, I'm now on his shoulder. *Steady with the air; inhale, four strides; exhale, four strides.* Coming down the straightaway, here's the half-mile mark.I silently say "bye bye" to Marean. "2:12…2:13…2:14," intones the timekeeper. Perfect pace.

The third lap is always hardest. Fatigue starts in. It's the beginning of a new race, the second half. Now it's the competition between the body and the mind. *Legs a bit heavy?* I stride into the third backstretch. *Losing the spring in my muscles?* Here is where the hypnosis occurs. The trance of metronomic cadence lulling me, promising *it's OK, save it for the finish. Just relax, slow down, slow…* "Shaynabeck! Stay with it. Stay loose!" I shake out my arms. *Deep breath in.* I'm wide awake, feel the soreness binding my arms and legs. *Deep breath out.* I chop my stride into pitter-patter steps to quicken the tempo. Run as if I am fresh. *Fake it, if you have to.*

I cruise into the final lap, picking up my pace. I hear "3:22." I slipped to 68 seconds for the lap, but my three-quarter mile is faster than I've ever run before.

POW! Gun lap! Go!

My teammates line the inside of the track, yelling at me. I'm wide-awake. Alert, like never before. "Batty's in second place," someone yells. I'm pulling even further ahead, outrunning my own fatigue. Pumping my arms. Coming into the backstretch, I gather momentum for my long rolling kick, trying to sustain a quicker pace over the last half lap.

"Go for it, Shaynabeck. All out, don't save anything. Go…For…It." My coach is running beside me now, almost stride for stride. His hands megaphone his voice, "Stay loose, stay loose." On the far turn, Hass windmilling his arms, as if waving me through the air. *Deep breath in, two strides; deep breath out, two strides. Puffing. Gulping air.*

Leaning into the last turn, I fly into the final straightaway. *Pump the arms, stride, stride.* Down the homestretch, the officials cluster at the finish line: some hunch over stopwatches; two of them tensing the finish tape between them. Even the Huntingdon athletes are cheering for me, joining my teammates along the final hundred yards. Some of the fans climb down from their bleacher seats to the front railing, lean out over the edge of the track. Yelling, cheering for me!

I focus on the finish line, enlarging it as if it were coming to me. "Run through the finish," Mr. Bolton always preached. I run five yards past the tape, wearing it across my bony shoulders like a fluttering ribbon as I jog down the track. I slow down and stop, then walk back along the track. It's like a movie scene, my teammates dancing toward me, cheering and slapping me on my back. People clapping from the stands. The officials huddle together with my coach. Some hold their watches in the air, others scribble on clipboards. Everything moves in slow motion.

The Huntingdon coach squeezes in between my jumping companions. "Congratulations, son. Helluva mile." He takes my hand and shakes it. "About a second off the Pennsylvania High School record. 4:28.3. Nice going." *Did I hear correctly? 4:28?*

Some of the Huntingdon parents congratulate me. Two sports reporters walk with me as they ask questions about the race, writing down my comments. Even checking their spelling of my name. Batty came in second, with Bill right behind him. We shut out the Huntingdon milers. I feel even better when Hass wins the half-mile, clinching our perfect season. I feel more special than I have ever felt in my life.

After all those years since my big race, I can easily relive that day of pride and accomplishment. But something else happened that day, and it was more significant than the minutes and seconds registered on the timer's stopwatch.

Following the race, I was jogging around the track, loosening my muscles, cooling down; thinking about the race and how Mr. Bolton planned my strategy, with each quarter mile perfectly timed for my result, faster than I ever thought I could run. He understood something about me that no one else did, about risk and unrealized possibilities. Because of my coach, I imagined that I could be more than I was, and that I could do things I thought impossible: I could dream. *But what if I crashed? What if I couldn't finish the race?*

"Shaynabeck." I was walking alone now. As my coach fell in step beside me, he placed his hand against the small of my back, gently pushing me along. We walked for a few moments, neither one of us quite ready to talk.

Mr. Bolton broke the silence. "Shaynabeck. Today you made me proud. This is why I coach." We continued striding forward, his arm still on me. "This is what I can do." Now we stopped and he took his hand away. He swept it across the infield, where my teammates were laughing and jiggling into their sweat suits for the bus ride home. "This is my work." He nodded his head up and down, as if agreeing with himself. Then my coach turned to me and placed his hands on my shoulders. "And today, you found out what you can do. Shaynabeck. I'm proud of you." I couldn't look him in the eye; my vision was blurry. Mr. Bolton turned away and started for the other side of the field. After about a dozen steps, he abruptly halted, turned around and marched back to me. Now I could look my coach in the eye.

"Shaynabeck. One more thing." Now his voice was soft, the words just for me. "It didn't matter how you did today. I would still be proud of you."

Chapter 23

As we grew older my mother became more passive, slowly gaining weight as her activity and agitation decreased. Sometimes her appetite for sweets was out of control. Dad hid any treats he brought home from the grocery store, but Mom always found what she was looking for. She was like a child sneaking her hand in the cookie jar.

Dr. Light thought Mom got some kind of relief from consuming so much sugar. He suggested medication was available that would not only allow her to feel better emotionally, but might curb her increasing weight. But any information our doctor offered about Mom's general health was simply for our education. My mother was suspicious of such discussion and there was no way she would trust anyone to give her a pill

By now her demons seemed to be losing interest in my mom, as if her decreased mobility interfered with their fun. She no longer danced to their harsh singing. Mom seemed content to sit in her rocking chair with her prayer book on her lap. My brothers and I began to trust that we no longer had to look over our shoulders as much as before.

We cautiously entered a new chapter in our lives, a period of transition in which we gradually detached from our childhood, as Bill and Alfie followed me to college and to our lives beyond. Mom and Dad were aging and so were we. Finding our ways to our respective careers and marriages, we started families and experienced fatherhood and new responsibilities. Although our roles separated us physically and emotionally from Mom and Dad, our connections were never broken. Each of us came home whenever possible, no matter what distance we had to travel.

Soon my parents were gifted with six grandchildren, whose presence energized my father, and tranquilized my mother into a state of good humor and peace. Every two or three weeks, my brothers and I called each other, checking on the news. "What's cooking with Mom and Dad? How is he holding up? Who's going to visit next, and when?"

I needed the space between Boston and State College to gain my own perspective about passing time. I was forty years old before I looked at my parents with the deserved compassion for the hard lives they'd lived. I realized that they'd both done their best in our unique circumstances. Equally important, I finally understood that I had unfinished business with both of them.

* * *

My father was over seventy years old before I told him I loved him. What took me so long? My brothers and I never doubted that he loved us, but the word *love* seemed too sentimental for this hard-working man. Not easily spoken from my own mouth, *love* was a word I offered from a distance that allowed me to retrieve it, if I perceived that it would be flung back at me like a sharp-edged boomerang. I'd mastered the art of anticipating how others felt, but I was a novice at understanding how I felt. I had formulated my own rule for communication: *be careful about what you let out.*

I remember the summer day when I risked that word with my father.

I'd driven from Massachusetts to State College for a weekend visit. Dad was going to plant some new shrubs around the house. Even though he never asked for help, I knew he wouldn't turn it down.

We dug holes and wheelbarrowed the bushes to their new locations. Together we lifted the heavy plants and eased them into the ground. At the age of seventy-two, Dad could do the work of a young man. But I noticed how he arched his cramped back after the arduous bending and shoveling. But he denied my suggestion that he let me do the heavy work. "Hell's bells, man. I'm not dead yet."

My mother sat in shade on the back porch, relaxed and content, her prayer book unopened in her lap. Now in early dementia, she seemed to be slowly going away from us, and from her voices. Dad and I stopped for a simple lunch of sandwiches and iced tea. Mom sat across from me and smiled her curiosity as I flickered in her memory, somewhere between stranger and son.

By late afternoon our labor was nearly complete. But the mixture of soil, fertilizer, and water had to be perfect. Dad tamped the ground with his shoe. He claimed the soles of his feet could feel the density of dirt packing against the roots of each plant. He finally gave me permission to spread a layer of pine mulch around each new planting. Any loose slivers of bark had to be raked up and put in their proper place. Now it was time for a refreshing shower and a well-earned nap.

Mom cleaned up the dishes after supper. She still managed some of the chores that were now routine to her. Anything different was disruptive. "I've learned to not rock the boat," Dad told me. "That's how I keep the peace."

Dad and I took his dog for a walk. Christoph was a spunky dachshund, who had to be walked several times during the day. He was a great companion, whether exercising with my dad or amusing my mother with his comic behavior. Shortly after Alfie left home, Bonnie and I brought Christoph as a Christmas gift and companion for my parents.

We walked through the neighborhood, eventually circling the Community Field, where my brothers and I played ball so many years before. We reached the empty bleachers by the deserted baseball diamond and sat down. Leaning back against the rising steps, Dad and I stretched ourselves in the soft warmth of sunset. It was quiet, except for the dog's tail sporadically thumping against the wooden seats.

My father was in a reflective mood. When we all lived at home, Dad was too busy surviving from one moment to the next to think about the past. "Why couldn't I fix her?" As if he knew there was no easy answer, my father's forceful inquiry was directed outward, more toward the Tussey Mountains than at me. Those hills were lovely this time of day, with their purple silhouette curved into the spreading copper-orange sky. We quietly listened to the quickened drumming of Christoph's tail, responding to Dad's voice. "I tried my best to provide for you boys. If I couldn't make Mom happy, at least I wanted to give you boys a good home." My father looked down at his calloused hands.

I studied him in that honest light at day's end. I saw an ordinary man of extraordinary strength. In my father's once-proud posture, there was the slump of doubt; in his walk, unfamiliar hesitation. His age was catching him.

I told him he was a wonderful father and he did his very best. I told him that his sons knew it. We'd always be grateful. He sat up straight now, and I leaned into him, resting my arm around his tense shoulders. Now I looked right into his eyes and said, "I love you, Dad. You have been a good father. You did your very best."

My hand on his shoulder felt his crying.

My work with my father was only half of what I had to do. I could no longer deny my unfinished business with my mother. Time was marching faster for her than for my dad. She became more forgetful with each visit. Bill thought she might have suffered a series of miniature strokes. It would not be a surprise, given her family medical history. All of her brothers suffered from strokes and coronary problems.

If I could tell my father that I loved him, why couldn't I do this for my mother? She deserved my love and understanding. Though weakened with time, my resentment was still there. I remembered too clearly the day she brought me and my soiled sheet to Father Kavanaugh, and how I wanted never to see her again. It was too easy to recall the Fourth of July sting of my mother's hand, hot and red on my cheek, when she heard the devil in my words. Whenever I tried to place my mother in sunshine, my resentment clouded the effort.

Throughout my marriage, Bonnie helped me with honesty about my feelings. She recognized how I'd learned to avoid looking inward. My wife encouraged me to make my long overdue amends with my mother: if not for her, for me.

By the time I was ready to tell my mother that I truly loved her, it was too late. I finally understood that she had never asked for her disease, but I had procrastinated to the point of no return. My mom was floating away on that outgoing tide of senility. I'd lost whatever hold I had on her.

I had already pardoned myself, convinced that my confused mother wouldn't even understand what my apology was all about. I told myself that my intention was sincere, and that must count for something; I just waited a little too long. End of story!

But it was not the end of the story. Making amends involves more than wishful thinking. I had yet to learn that it's never too late to ask forgiveness.

Chapter 24

My mother's worsening senility and deteriorating health took its toll on my father. By now he did all the cooking and most of the housework. He cut the grass, trimmed the shrubs, kept up the maintenance of their home. Other than driving to the market and walking Christoph, his only excursion from his house was the weekly journey to Sunday Mass. That was no easy task. Dad washed and dressed Mom. Because of her increased weight, he had to maneuver her down the sidewalk, and into the car. The return trip was even more difficult, helping her climb back up the sidewalk, coaxing and steering Mom up the steps from the yard into the kitchen. On the phone he grumbled, "What's this about Sunday being a day of rest?"

Each morning, afternoon, and evening, my father and his dog managed to escape for their walk. The weather never stopped Dad from getting his own exercise. The neighbors chuckled over the image of my father, bundled in his heavy blue parka, as he skidded Christoph over the icy sidewalk. The dog's little legs seemed permanently braced in a futile attempt at halting their hike.

One Saturday afternoon, he had to call the Alpha Fire Company for help in lifting Mom out of the bathtub. He'd hurt his back and he couldn't pull with enough strength to overcome my mother's weight. Dad said that when the firemen came on their mission of kindness, Mom just smiled at them. She was more amused than embarrassed by this visit of strangers. For my father, it was one more humiliation, one more task he could not manage by himself.

On a stormy winter evening, Dad returned to the house to find the door wide open. My mother was gone. The burners on the oven were glowing. He found her in a neighbor's yard, clothed in her nightgown and boots. Mom said she heard *me* outside in the dark, calling for help. She had a vision that I was cold and hungry, lost in the snow. My mother turned on the stove so she could cook for me, once she found me and brought me in from the cold.

Now my father had to worry about leaving to walk the dog.

＊　＊　＊

In the spring of 1983, Kristen and I took my father to Germany to celebrate his 80th birthday. It was the first opportunity for my daughter and me to meet my German relatives. Dad could visit his aging sister and his homeland. Bill and Alfie took turns caring for Mom during his absence. My father's spirit was lifted during this reunion, but his joy didn't last long.

After coming back from Germany, he injured his leg while cutting down weeds in front of our house. Dad had been standing on the side of a steep slope, swinging a large scythe, when he severely strained the calf muscle in his right leg. He complained that he had too much work to do. There was no way he could rest. "No big deal. Anyone who's used to hard work has a pulled muscle from time to time."

When Dad described the swelling in his lower leg, I insisted that he call Dr. Light, immediately. "If you don't call, I will." Once again I appreciated the thoughtfulness of our small-town doctor, who called me back as soon as he examined my dad.

"Your father's got a blood clot, Carl. It's turned into phlebitis. I'm sending him to the hospital right away." I understood the diagnosis: a small clot could break away and circulate to the lungs, causing a pulmonary embolism. It could be fatal for Dad. Before I could even worry about my mother, Dr. Light had made arrangements for her care. *Renaissance* was a nearby facility which provided assisted-living and short-term health support. It was run by two compassionate nurses, who were dedicated to allowing elderly patients to live in comfort and dignity. Because of Dr. Light's call, they made room for my mother until our future plans could be determined.

Dr. Light ended his conversation with a warning. "This is OK for right now, but I'm worried about your mother for the long term. Dad's going to be laid up for a while. The earliest we'll let him come home is about ten or twelve days."

My brothers and I faced a new challenge. Dad would need support when he came home. We arranged our work schedules so we could be with my father when he returned from the hospital. No need to worry about Mom for now; she was in capable hands. She had no idea of what had happened to Dad.

Since Renaissance could not keep Mom indefinitely, Dr. Light put her on the waiting list for full-time residential care at Centre Crest, the County Nursing Home in nearby Bellefonte. He said it was the best place for my mother. The facility was clean and safe and the staff was capable and compassionate. "You can't beat those Pennsylvania farm girls for hard work. They are cheerful when they come in and they leave in the same spirit. Mother will feel loved and fussed over."

Dr. Light gave my brothers and me an assignment: we had to convince my father to let Mom go. "It will be much better for everyone, if your father feels that he made this decision. He won't like it if it's forced on him." Dr. Light sure knew his patient.

The morning after we brought him home from the hospital, Dad sat with us by the living room window. We convinced him to do as the doctor said: take it easy, and keep the leg elevated. For the moment, my father was held captive by his three sons and his swollen leg. He had to listen to us. Bill, Alfie, and I looked at each other, took a deep breath and pulled our chairs around Dad. This would not be an easy conversation. The way he looked at each of us, he knew something was up.

"Dr. Light thinks it's time to do something about Mom." I started the conversation. The room was quiet, except for the hum of cars driving up and down Atherton Street.

Bill picked up. "You can't get better yourself, if you have to take care of Mom. In fact you might have a setback." Bill was now a talented physical therapist, practicing his profession on behalf of his father.

Alfie started in. "Yeah, the way it is now, you'll keep getting weaker, and Mom won't even know what's going on. No point in having both of you out of commission."

We told him about Dr. Light's concern. When we told my father that Mom's name was on the waiting list for the nursing home, he just looked down. "What do you think, Dad. Are you OK with that? Sending Mom to Centre Crest?"

"I can't do it." He couldn't look at us. "Can't just send her away."

Who was my dad if he couldn't carry out his responsibilities, but a diminished shadow of himself? He sobbed through his list of unfulfilled dreams for my mother, as if voicing this litany of disappointment was a plea for forgiveness that he could not make her happy. My father, who never gave up, finally had to give up. We could only sit with him in his grieving. His tears dried and he finally looked each of us in the eye. He had surrendered.

My brothers and I knew what we had to do. We took the decision away from my father. Bill, Alfie, and I told him that *we* were sending Mom to the nursing home. We had become fathers to our father.

By the end of that summer, Dad had regained most of his strength. When he questioned whether it was time "to bring Mom back," we reminded him that his health improved because he had only himself to take care of.

My father's life took on new energy. His garden thrived from his renewed attention. He picked and canned his vegetables. Now he spent time with relatives and some of his old friends from the University. He shared dinner with some of his elderly neighbors, as they took turns cooking for each other. They sometimes shared a bottle of wine and conversation about their families, Penn State football, or how our country isn't what it used to be. I can just hear my father grousing, "You can't trust the damn politicians as far as you can throw them." That line started many a conversation for my father; it ended them, too.

He frequently visited my mother, never going more than three days between trips. Aunt Regina often went along on those short journeys to Bellefonte. My brothers and I came to town as often as we could, bringing our families whenever possible. Even though Mom was often confused and distracted, she loved seeing the children. Her mood bightened in their company. When it was time to leave, her hard hug told me she'd been with us.

The nurses and helpers at Centre Crest were good-natured and loving with Mom, always attentive to her needs. Whenever we left, we knew she would be safe and warm. "Don't you boys worry now." They'd pat us on the cheek as if we were first-graders as they walked us to the door. "Sophie is on her best behavior with us." My mother always smiled as we waved goodbye.

During her third year in the nursing home, my mother deteriorated dramatically. More detached and distant than ever, she no longer participated in any meaningful conversation with me. Any words of mine floated out the open window and blew away with the summer breeze. I could do nothing more than say "hello" and tell her everyone was fine. Her smile seemed more of a reflex than recognition. My voice seemed no different than any other voice. My mother didn't know me.

Would she even know I had been with her? Would I have regrets about my unspoken apology for the angry feelings of my childhood? Would she ever know I loved her?

The last time I sat with my mother was in late September, three weeks before she died. I was on my way from Boston to see my Dad. Centre Crest was only a few minutes out of the way, so I stopped for a visit. I walked down the corridor to Mom's room. Two of the aides had just bathed her. A big woman named Nancy delicately brushed her hair, fluffing and stroking it with her meaty hands. A younger aide named Betsy propped up Mom's legs one at a time, then pulled warm slippers on her feet. Before leaving, they each patted Mom's cheek, and mine, promising they would continue fussing over her. She basked in the warmth of her freshly laundered robe and the kindness of the two women.

I pulled my chair close, so I could look directly at her. Her bath left her perfumed and glowing. "Hi, Mom." She lifted her face and narrowed her eyes as if trying to focus me into her memory. "We're all thinking about you, Mom. Bonnie and Kristen, too. Everyone sends their love." Her eyes relaxed, but no meaningful light came into them. My words, heavy in the air, no longer touched my mother. My greetings plunged of their own weight.

My mother's eyes fluttered their inquisition. The worried pinch above her eyebrows told me that I was a stranger. Our shared history was scattered and deflected into the unhealed space between us. I did the only thing I could do: I joined her silence.

I glanced at my watch. Fifteen minutes. No need to stay any longer. I stared at my shoes. They needed polish and buffing. That's where my attention was, when I said, "I love you, Mom." I looked down and I felt the silence of her reply. In my imagination, I heard the words that I wanted my mother to put into the hushed air between us.

When I looked up, her eyes flickered with new light. Something was being awakened. I leaned in. Now her eyes shined and softened and moistened: she knew me. The light in her eyes, blinking her recognition, on and off, on and off, told me she loved me.

I remembered fireflies.

*   *   *

The sun glowed October warmth through the multi-colored saints and angels on the church windows. The resonance of Pachelbel's Canon filled Our Lady of Victory Church, and me. Surrounded by his entire family, my father sat in quiet contemplation of the end of his half-century of marriage to Sophie Henrietta Droege.

Father Boggs gently reminded us that "Jesus invites all of us to follow him, and he promises to bring us home safely. It won't be easy, because His path was not easy. But the Lord's healing hand reached out to touch Sophie, and she is well again." *Again?* I wondered, *was my mother ever well? Is the kind priest preaching that *now* she is well?*

Alfie read from Corinthians. "Though I speak with the tongues of men and angels, and have not charity, I am become as sounding brass or a tinkling cymbal." *With whose tongue spoke my mother?*

For Bill, the selection was the Letter from Saint Paul, to the Romans: "If God is for us, who can be against us?" *Could my mother ever have asked if God was for her?*

My offering was the Prayer of Saint Francis, simple and poetic in its request for the exchange of love for hatred, light for darkness, and joy for sadness. *Would I ever be an instrument of peace? And I, who waited too long to pardon my mother…could I ever ask of the Divine Master, that in pardoning, I too be pardoned?*

My mother was buried in the gold light of October.

Chapter 25

Resurrection may be an overly dramatic description for my father's next years, but I believe it was the best time of his life. For the next thirteen years, until his death at age 96, my father's life was active and full. His energy now belonged to him alone.

He became more involved with his elderly neighbors. They continued sharing their evening meals, with longer conversations afterward. When Tom O'Hara decided to rotate his car tires, Dad was right there, leaning on his wrench and loosening the bolts. His old neighbor stood gratefully by his side, keeping track of the parts and which tire went where. If the widow across the alleyway complained about a loose board on her porch, no problem; Dad and his well-stocked tool box were steps away, eager and available to offer help.

In 1992, Dad celebrated his 89th birthday in a special way. Eight family members traveled with him on his final trip to Germany. He'd always dreamed of visiting his native country with his three sons. My father had the best birthday of his life, grateful that he had lived long enough to introduce his German family to his American family. We visited Dad's childhood home, where he had worked in his father's blacksmith shop. We prayed over the graves of his parents, brothers, and sisters; walked to his childhood school; sang German songs as we marched through the *Teutoberger Wald,* the forest where he hiked as a young man. Each evening we celebrated at a different cousin's home. With each new party, the food was tastier and the beer more delicious. My father told me that if his life ended then, it could not be more complete.

When my father was ninety years old, the first of his six great-grand-children was born. He lived long enough to cradle all of them in his arms. He was convinced that life would have been better for my mother, had she known these children.

Alfie's oldest boys lived with my father while they were students at Penn State. Even in his late 80's and early 90's, Dad was energized by their presence. He had fixed up his basement years earlier, providing a cool retreat for himself, from the summer heat and humidity and from my mother. He could nap on the pullout sofa or watch a Pirates baseball game on the old TV set. Dad even built and assembled a wood-burning stove that provided heat in the winter. With these accommodations, Eric and Jeffrey lived downstairs from my father. They reimbursed him with their help and jovial companionship.

Dad kept track of their class schedule so he could have dinner ready for them at the end of the day. He looked forward to the weekends, when the boys brought friends to stay with them. My father talked and laughed with his young companions, well into the night, and sometimes, well into a second bottle of wine. He shared stories of his journey to America. In their respectful listening, the young students honored the old man's life. The momentum of my father's aging was slowed by the happy years he shared with his young college students. He felt useful and needed. The boys graduated and moved on with their lives.

Shortly after the boys left, my father's physical health deteriorated noticeably. His mental state remained sharp and competent, but he could not accept his diminished strength, which was now a real part of his life. My brothers and I had become concerned about his driving. But any discussion about my father and his car was short in duration, as though he'd clicked the *off* button on his hearing aid.

One day he drove through a red light. Fortunately for Dad, the officer who stopped him was a high school classmate of mine. He gave my father a warning and no ticket. But my friend called me. "Just wanted to let you know, Carl. Running a red light could've had serious consequences, but I don't have to tell you that. I wanted you and your brothers to know what was going on. I didn't get the impression that your father was ready to leap to the phone and tell you about this." I thanked my childhood friend for being so considerate. But he wasn't quite finished. "By the way, your dad suggested that his eyes were just fine. Maybe I was the one who couldn't tell the difference between a red and green light."

My father lived in his own home until he was ninety-four years old. That changed one summer evening, when he felt dizzy while picking vegetables from his garden. Dad got as far as the porch steps, when he fell backward onto the grass and couldn't get up. Our neighbor had just come home from work. She ran into the yard when she heard Dad's call for help. Sarah was a nurse who worked with elderly patients and she had been checking on my father. Convinced that he was safe, she helped him to his feet and into the house. Dad did not argue with her when she told him she was going to call me. Once I shared this news with my brothers, we made a decision. We'd recently become more concerned about his safety and ability to manage by himself. It was time for Dad to leave his home.

A visiting nurse from the Renaissance Home had been providing outpatient help for Dad. Because of the thoughtful care they had given my mother, we continued that relationship for Dad's benefit. Their assisted living facility would be perfect for Dad. No space was immediately available, so they put his name at the top of the waiting list. It would be two months before they had an open room.

During that waiting period, Bill and Alfie shared custody of my father. I had his mail sent to me so I could pay the bills. Even though he would be leaving, we were in no hurry to sell the house. Keeping it gave us a place to stay when we came to visit; besides, Dad believed he would return home after his convalescence at Renaissance. All he had to do was rest and regain his strength. We did nothing to dispel that notion.

The day we brought my father to his new home at Renaissance, his room had already been arranged with family pictures and his own furniture. Grandchildren and great-grandchildren beamed their framed smiles from the walls, and from atop his chest of drawers. Prior to his arrival, the husband of the nursing director had loaded his pickup truck with Dad's furnishings and his bed, a huge act of kindness for which he'd accept no compensation: "No big deal. I was driving past your house, anyway."

Dad was well cared for during the last two years of his life. Whenever one of us came to State College, we brought him back home to Atherton Street. We had dinner so he could sit at his table, just like old times. When the weather was good he unfolded a chair and sat on the back porch, so he could supervise if we were trimming shrubbery or raking leaves from the yard. Before returning to Renaissance, he marched down the hallway, inspecting the rooms one more time. There was always one last trip to the bathroom. "Just want to check out all the facilities, boys. You aren't half the plumber that I am. You never know if something needs fixing before I return home." Dad didn't even realize that he was now referring to his assisted living residence as *home*. But we noticed, and we were grateful.

He kept a mental list about which projects had to be started when he got well enough to return to Atherton Street. "I'm going to need a little help, boys. Painting, sanding, refinishing the floor. Always something to do." He never returned to that home.

Five weeks before my father died, we gathered in our home to celebrate his ninety-sixth birthday. Dad sat on that familiar back porch, watching his great-granddaughters as they danced barefoot on the summer grass, spinning like dizzy daisies until they flopped with exhaustion. The three little girls brought flowers to him, freshly picked from the yard. Dad happily ate their offerings of cake and ice cream. His white shirt was smudged with chocolate evidence that the little girls loaded too much on the spoon, but it didn't matter. His penchant for *neat and clean* was surrendered for proof that he'd been caressed by little hands, sweet and sticky in their touching.

We all shared a feeling of my father being at peace with his family. Nothing remained unspoken that had to be spoken. We sang our birthday greetings with full voice and fuller hearts, with sweet harmony and uncontrolled vibrato. We knew the next time we sang together for my father, we would be singing a hymn.

Finally, day's end: the last sunset for my father, in this home. The evening sun's ruddy descent sank below the cooling hills, west of town. I steadied Dad into the good-byes of his beloved family, which circled and closed around him like a muscular hug. Alfie, Bill, and I took him home, the long way. We helped him into his pajamas; settled him into his bed. We fluffed his pillow; pulled up the light blanket. I brushed my hand through his full head of hair, white as snow, no matter the season.

A breeze luffed the curtain by the open window: a rustle, a murmur, a whisper barely heard.

* * *

On the Fourth of July weekend following Dad's birthday celebration, Bonnie and I were on vacation in New Hampshire. It was early morning when the phone rang. Tracy was calling. She was one of Dad's favorite nurses. "Carl, your father's in congestive heart failure. He's very weak. He's having trouble speaking and his breathing is labored." Dad was on his way to the hospital. Tracy was riding with him in the ambulance.

My father had been through similar episodes in the past year or two. There was nothing unexpected about this. His doctor had called me in early spring to remind me that Dad was wearing out. We reviewed our future options to be sure there would be no misunderstanding of my father's wishes. His strong heart had been working reliably for ninety-six years. I asked Tracy if we should come to State College. Did it look like this was it?

"I don't know what to tell you. He's been through this before. Once they get the fluid out, he always bounces back." She would stay with him in the hospital, long enough to get a sense of what was going on with him. "I'll keep in touch. You'll hear from me this afternoon."

I called my brothers with the news. We agreed that we would wait until we got the afternoon report from Dad's nurse. Then we would decide what to do.

We didn't have to wait long for Tracy's call. Dad was responding nicely. "His color is better and he's breathing more easily." The nurse laughed. "He's not *like* the cat; he *is* the cat with nine lives. He's sitting up. His voice is weak, but he's told me rather emphatically, as only he can, that I should go back to work and take care of someone who really needs a nurse."

I called my brothers with the good news. It looked like he would be going back to Renaissance as soon as he regained his strength. Bill hesitated. "I'm not so sure. I have a funny feeling about this." Bill decided that he would make a quick trip to State College. It would be good to check the house anyway. He could also help Dad when he came back from the hospital.

When Bill arrived at the hospital late that afternoon, Dad was asleep. He was propped up in his bed, resting comfortably. Instead of waking him up, Bill went back to the house. He showered and napped. After a light supper, he returned. Dad was awake now, happy to see Bill.

Because my father's voice was weak, Bill didn't force any conversation. After a short visit, Dad was ready to go back to sleep. My brother got up to leave. He kissed Dad on his forehead and started toward the door.

"Bill...before...you...go..." The metered hiss of the oxygen mask punctuated the space between my father's calibrated words. "Is everybody OK?"

"Yup. Everyone's fine, Dad."

"Carl? Bonnie? And their dog, what's her name, Calli?" He paced his gentle interrogation with his available breath. "Your family, OK?" He asked about each of his sons and their wives, all the children and grandchildren. He forgot no one, not even the pets. Dad needed to know how each of us was doing in school, work, or with our own families. "The girls? How are they?" He spoke their names out loud, "Alexa, Angela, Amanda," as if taking attendance of his great-granddaughters.

Bill sat by the bed. "Everything is fine, Dad. Everyone is good."

"Well then. Thank you, Bill. You get some rest, now. Gute Nacht. Alles in ordnung. *Everything is in order.*"

Alfie called at us at five o'clock the next morning. Bonnie answered the phone. I was still asleep. She came into the room when I woke up. She didn't have to tell me: I knew. My father hushed his *Gute Nacht* into the pale hours of early morning. After everything was in order.

A year after his death, I found a reminder of that final celebration. My favorite old shirt was hidden in the closet. The teal-green cotton was beyond threadbare, because of too many washings and too many wearings. I found the grocery list for Dad's last birthday, crumpled in the left pocket.

The blurred ink spelled out my father's request: hot dogs and rolls; pretzels and beer; chocolate ice cream, the dessert spelled out in capital letters and boldly underlined.

I was wearing my green cotton shirt then, grocery list in the left pocket: a prayer, softly against my heart.

*   *   *

My father was durable and strong. He stood straight and tall, could bend far and not break. He was like the plain wood he loved to work with: true to the grain. Dad asked to be buried in an unadorned wooden casket, with no embellishment or decoration. While we were making our funeral arrangements, Bonnie found his perfect, simple coffin, hidden behind the ornate models.

Thirteen years after my mother's death, my father was escorted down the same aisle, in the same church. His pallbearers were his four grandsons and two granddaughters, holding hands with three little great-granddaughters, in white dresses, white flowers in their hair. Once again, we heard the resonant chords of Pachelbel's Canon. My father received his final blessings in the church filled with sunshine.

When I last looked at my father, he lay straight and tall, enclosed in simple wood.

Chapter 26

My father's legal affairs were in perfect order. Now it was time to settle and divide his modest estate, but before we could sell our childhood home, we had some repairs and cleanup projects ahead of us. The garage door had been bruised by an encounter with the front bumper of Dad's car. We decided to brighten up the dingy kitchen with a fresh coat of paint. The most important task was right under our feet; Dad's perfectly finished floor was in need of restoration.

First we had to divide and claim the contents of the house: Dad's furniture, fireplace accessories, handmade dishes and serving trays. A dust-covered treasure of instruments and tools, each in its proper place, lay at rest in his basement workshop. Besides the good stuff, there was an accumulation of old newspapers, worn-out clothing, and stale paint; plenty of junk and near junk.

The question: what to keep, and what to pitch?

Within three weeks, we had a buyer for the house. After negotiating for enough time to get everything in order, we got busy right away. By early September everything was in good shape, with the exception of the floor, which would be the biggest project. We saved it for last. We didn't want to splatter it with the Benjamin Moore *White Dove* we'd just painted on the kitchen walls.

Bill and Alfie went downtown to Porter Brother's Paints to buy brushes, polyurethane, and an assortment of sandpaper. I studied the blemished floor in the bedrooms and hallway, planning time and strategy for our big effort. Looking at the floor, I realized we were taking on a familiar task. Like it or not, my father's ghost would be in our midst, inspecting our work.

Most of the damage was in Mom's bedroom. She'd gouged Dad's perfect floor while rocking the chair to the rhythm of her prayers. Just like my father many years before, I knelt down and rubbed my hands over the rutted floorboards. I wanted to brush away those scarred reminders of my mother's illness. I planned to repair my mother's room by myself.

I felt my mother's presence in that empty room, as if she were waiting for me. My knees hard on the floor, my hands praying through the sandpaper, stroking the wounded wood, tracing the back and forth sway of my mother's rocking chair. This room of dead voices now screeched with the raspy scrape of sandpaper, coarse, medium, fine; the pitch softening as I smoothed the splintered ruts, brushing away the remnants of my mother's creaky dance. I did not stop until the wood was renewed and unscarred; didn't stop until my hand could glide over the wood, smooth as marble.

And over my shoulder, my father's ghost whispers, "Good job. You did it right," and my mother is at peace.

* * *

Our final weekend in our boyhood home came in late September. I traveled from Boston a day before my brothers arrived. Because I was executor of my father's estate, I had reviewed the legal papers involving the sale of our house. According to the Purchase and Sale Agreement, our home, when finally empty, had to be *broom-clean.*

I sat at my father's desk, cleaning out old checkbooks and papers. He must have saved evidence of every bill he'd ever paid. That's when I found the brochure for *Matthew's Memorials.* I stared at my mother's words in the margins, her graceful penmanship like a poem, grieving for Frances. I held that pamphlet for a long time, reading it like a prayer.

I took inventory of our boyhood home, room by room. Bill and Alfie were driving to State College the next day. In our vans we'd each take back my father's special possessions. There was an empty dumpster sitting in the driveway outside the garage door, waiting to be filled up.

The kitchen was easy. I claimed the cherry-wood table and chairs for my daughter. We'd each share the aluminum trays and dishes that Dad had hammered in his downstairs workshop. The living room contained the fireplace screen and andirons he made many years ago. Some of the bedroom furniture would be taken home with us, to be claimed by our own children. I returned to my father's bedroom, now empty except for the desk that I'd just cleaned out. The sound of my footsteps carried over that hardwood floor, echoing against the bare walls. There was nothing left to absorb the sound except the contents of Dad's closet.

I rolled back the sliding door. Winter jackets bulged into the room as if they'd been holding their breath, waiting to be released from their dark confinement. Sports coats and neatly pressed trousers hung in an orderly line, as if they were waiting for an outing: a visit to church, an evening at the Elks Club. I had a strange feeling as I pawed through the lineup of sweaters. I ducked my head back into the bedroom. *Was I being watched?*

Nothing! *My imagination?* Maybe it wasn't a good idea to be alone in the middle of all this history, some of which was going to be tossed into the empty dumpster. I resumed my inspection. Now that I was completely in-side Dad's closet, my eyes began to adjust to the darkness. I squinted along the row of sweaters. I abruptly straightened up, grazing my head against the shelf of navy blue baseball hats and sweatshirts, emblazoned with the white Nittany Lion of Penn State football. Something was spooking me. *Watching me?* I narrowed my line of vision, trying to magnify the available light in this dark space. As if sighting along the barrel of a rifle, I aimed for the far end of the closet.

"Sweet Jesus!" The words burst out of my mouth---oath, prayer, and greeting, all at once. A pair of blue eyes seared through that enclosed night, scaring the hell out of me. I hadn't seen the statue since Mom was alive and he lived at the end of the hallway. So here was the Sweet Jesus of our childhood, abandoned to his own wilderness by my father. All these years he'd been forgotten, while patiently lurking in the shadowed sanctuary of Dad's closet. His right hand was still extended in blessing, minus Bill's baseball glove.

Sunshine streamed through the window, as if the statue had commanded, *Let there be light!* I wobbled him out of the closet, into the daylight. He glowed at me, as if being resurrected after all those lost years. It seemed like yesterday when my brothers and I played catch with him. I looked on the floor for the Pirates baseball hat that Alfie once placed on the sacred head, but it was nowhere to be found.

Could it really have been sixteen years ago, that Mom went to the nursing home? That's when Dad relocated Sweet Jesus from the hallway to his closet. I remembered his parting comment to our plaster companion: "If I wanted you to stare at me all day long, I'd have lived in a damn monastery." So our beloved figure was cloaked within the wool, cotton, and polyester garments of my father's wardrobe. "He's out of sight, Boys, but not out of mind." Dad reassured us. "I always ask his guidance in what to wear." My brothers and I had long ago concluded that Sweet Jesus was not a fashion expert.

Bill and Alfie would arrive the next morning. In the meantime, what should I do with him? I knew he was just a hunk of brittle plaster, adorned with a white robe and a red shawl. But what color would his eyes take on, looking into my soul, as I heaved him into the dumpster? I still carried enough Catholic guilt to know that I couldn't chest-thump enough *mea culpas* to atone for such blasphemy.

I told myself, "It's plaster and paint. What's the big deal?" I decided to sleep on it. I'd figure it out by morning, when Bill and Alfie would be here. I re-wobbled Sweet Jesus back into the cloistered darkness.

My brothers were both downstairs, straightening out Dad's workshop. They'd arrived together, bright and early, each with their own minivan. They had eaten their breakfast along the way and we were making the best of our time. The clanking and clattering of tools vibrated in the basement under my feet, which were anchored with indecision on Dad's bedroom floor. What should I do with Sweet Jesus?

I made up my mind. I started to dance the statue out of the closet, into the daylight for the last time. I was going for the dumpster and I had to act forcefully. "Let's just get this over with!" I told myself. "Out of sight, out of mind."

Footsteps! Before I could react, the bedroom door opened. "Sweet Jesus!" Alfie stopped on a dime. "Where the hell did you find him?"

"Dad's closet. He's been there since Mom went to Centre Crest." I felt like I'd been caught in a sinful act. "He's gotta go, Alfie. You know. Dumpsterland." My brother lifted an eyebrow in concern.

Just then, Bill started cursing about something downstairs, an angry response to the metallic sprinkling that preceded it. He'd knocked over a can of nails.

"I'm not so sure, Carl. It's not like junk in the attic, you know?" Alfie made a tossing motion with his arms. "I wouldn't feel right putting Jesus in the…"

"I know, I know."

The three of us stood in silent meditation, Alfie and me in shallow breathing, Sweet Jesus holding his breath. No matter how tentatively we circled the four-foot statue, he maintained eye contact with us. His vision locked right onto us, following every nervous twitch, as if he could stare into our souls.

Another clatter of bouncing nails downstairs. "Dammit all to hell!" Bill wasn't having a good morning. But the jolt of noise triggered Alfie and me out of our dilemma. Without one spoken word, we knew what we were going to do. Our muffled laughter clinched the deal. We quietly slapped each other with a high five.

We'd keep our newly resurrected Jesus in the dark until the next morning. When it was time to help Bill load his van, we'd wait until he was out of sight. Then we would find a comfortable nook for the sacred passenger, safe from the crush of a shifting load. We'd place him low on the floor, swaddled in the protective warmth of my father's threadbare blankets. He'd suffer no whiplash in the event of a sudden stop. Most of all, he'd be out of Bill's sight. How could this not be an act of brotherly love, providing him with such company? And wouldn't Mom be proud of us? We'd be saving Sweet Jesus *and* Bill.

I was too excited to sleep well that night. Our plan was to follow Alfie home the next day. After unloading my youngest brother's van and saying goodbye, Bill and I would continue on to his house. I planned to stay with him overnight before driving on to Boston. But not before the two of us unloaded Bill's van. I'd keep Sweet Jesus bundled in his warm quilt until the coast was clear. That's when I planned to hide him in Bill's garage. Surely there would be a hiding place between an old sofa and a chair, or a rolled-up carpet. Alfie and I would just sit back and wait for the phone call from Bill, acknowledging that we nailed him! If anyone deserved to be on the receiving end of a *gotcha,* it was Bill.

For the rest of our busy day, Alfie and I avoided each other's eyes. We had to be especially careful next morning at breakfast, as we spent our final hours in the house. We couldn't afford to laugh; no way we were going to give away our secret. We had to wait for the opportunity to sneak our holy traveler into Bill's vehicle; this was not a time to rush things.

We were rewarded for our patience. Bill knocked a pint of Rust-Oleum off Dad's workbench, exploding a mural of *Tranquil-Blue* on the basement floor. Bill's colorful description of what he'd just spilled was anything but tranquil, and his words were already bouncing around the nearly-empty rooms upstairs. I opened the door and called down to my brother. "Take your time, Bill. It could happen to anyone. You clean up the floor, and Alfie and I will load your car. And you don't have to thank us." I winked at my youngest brother. "After all, what are brothers for?" Bill's response was as blue as the paint by his feet.

With the choreographed efficiency of ballet dancers, Alfie and I swirled into action. I lifted Sweet Jesus from the dark tomb of the closet, shielding his eyes from the explosion of sunshine which greeted him on his emergence. My brother gently wrapped Dad's flower-patterned blanket around the statue. I waltzed the padded statue through the kitchen, past Alfie, who had placed himself protectively against the door. We hovered like angels as we floated over the yard, down the steps to the driveway, cradling Sweet Jesus between us.

In less than a minute, we had settled our traveler in Bill's minivan. He was laid to rest between my father's desk and two cartons containing jugs of his home-made wine. We cushioned the nest with flannel shirts and wool sweaters, some with a musky trace of Prince Albert, from Dad's pipe-smoking days. The scene looked a lot more appealing than a drafty manger with a few cows huddled over the holy child. The blanket slipped off the feet when I closed the door, so I found a bungee cord and cinched the loose covering around the protruding toes. No cold feet for Sweet Jesus!

By noontime we had finished our project. Our three minivans were packed with what we kept and the dumpster was filled with what we pitched. I tossed the last trash bag outside the garage, where it collapsed homelessly on a discarded mattress. I swept out the house, room by room, leaving it *broom clean* as legally specified, ready for its new owner.

My brothers and I took our final tour of our boyhood home, breathing in the musty history of each bedroom and closet. We circled through the living room, and touched the stone fireplace one last time. Standing silently in the kitchen, we remembered that one day we did not want to remember. I followed my brothers to the back porch, where, on that unforgettable summer night many years before, we had waited for the fireflies.

In my father's room, the low angle of sunlight bled the autumn afternoon against the pale green walls. An escaped cloud of dust must have shuddered and settled with the hollow echo, when for the last time, I slammed shut and latched the back door.

*   *   *

It was twilight when we arrived at Alfie's home in Leesport. We moved quickly and efficiently to empty his van. Loretta had prepared dinner for us, which we would share before Bill and I continued on to his home in Newtown. We had just finished moving the last piece of furniture from Alfie's car, when his wife called for him to come upstairs to the telephone. His oldest son was calling from Philadelphia.

Bill and I were alone in the driveway. Alfie was inside. I stared at Bill. Something was cooking. I began to gnaw my lip. I recognized a new opportunity.

"Why are you giving me such a goofy look?" Bill was right in my face. "What are you up to?"

I realized that when payback time came about, Bill would be much harder on me than my youngest brother. I moved toward Bill's minivan, waving for him to follow me. "Check this out. Quickly though, and you have to be absolutely quiet." My index finger indented my lips. "Let's open your van."

I slid the side door open. I untangled the bungee cord and steered the shrouded statue to its feet in Alfie's driveway. With grandiose flair, I flung off the flowered blanket, as if performing a magic trick. I know it was just a reflection of the setting sun, but it sure looked like Jesus glittered an approving wink at me.

"Sweet Jesus!" Bill's mouth opened so wide I could see his molars. "What the hell…where did you get him?"

There wasn't much time. I described the plan that Alfie and I had for placing the long lost statue in Bill's garage. But we decided, immediately and decisively, that Alfie needed the holy presence more than Bill did.

"Let's go." Bill nodded his head toward the open door. "We gotta move before he's off the phone."

We planted Sweet Jesus in Alfie's garage. Draped in the tulips of Dad's quilted blanket, we nestled him between an old refrigerator, and a bag of clothes destined for the Salvation Army. My brother's L.L. Bean Dome Tent formed a nice curtain in front of the statue, making the scene look like a small passion play was about to start. We could only guess when Sweet Jesus would be revealed. Later on, while driving home to Boston, I couldn't help laughing out loud, every time I conjured up the scene of his discovery. I was pretty pleased with myself. Bill and I would just sit back and wait for the call, when Alfie finally discovered our prank.

＊　＊　＊

Time is a mystery to me. The ongoing months and years seem to blur through my life, as if the hands of the clock no longer circle its circumference at a predictable pace. Even though it has been years since Bill and I played our harmless trick, I remember every detail and secretive move as if it were yesterday. I'm still waiting for the big reaction from my little brother. Instead, there has been nothing: zero, zip, nada!

I used to call Alfie every few weeks, then every couple of months. I tell him I just want to see how he is. "And by the way, have you heard anything from Bill?" After all, Alfie thinks that's where Sweet Jesus is.

But I don't stop with that. I thoughtfully inquire about the boys. Eric and Jeff are still in graduate school, Greg is floating around somewhere on a submarine. I try to detect a slight hitch in his voice, a shade in the tone, a clue that Jesus has been found in Leesport.

I do no better with Bill. He swears he's had no news of a discovery. He can't figure it out, either. I caution, "I think he's throwing a big fake at us, Bill. He's planning retribution." My brother says nothing. Even that makes me nervous. "We're gonna get Sweet Jesus in the mail, or in a UPS delivery. Something like that. Just you wait. We are going to do penance. Amen."

I don't like the way Bill laughs. "Well, Carl. If he does find him, he'll know it was you. Your fingerprints are all over this. He's our little brother, but he's no dummy." I wonder if both my brothers are planning a surprise for me?

Usually, I laugh. This is funny, a harmless bit of fun. We repeat the same conversation several times a year. Nothing changes.

For the last few Christmases, I wake up rather easily in the night. I imagine I hear the hoarse groan of a UPS truck, straining its brown hulk up Cedar Hill Terrace. Just where the road turns right, toward my home on Bay View, the sound evaporates. I drift back to sleep. A twinge of the imagination? My mind does the same dance around Easter. I wonder if Sweet Jesus will rise again, with the assistance of the U.S. Postal Service.

It is pretty funny, though. An innocent joke. After all, there is nothing mean-spirited here. Anyone can see that. Retribution is sort of outdated, anyway. And when we were kids, I was the one who insisted we call him "Sweet Jesus."

That is a good thing, a respectful thing.

Isn't it?

Chapter 27

Writing this memoir has been an exercise in introspection. Through my self-interrogation, I've learned to appreciate the good memories and meaningful lessons imbedded in my story. But I sometimes questioned my honesty. Is it a conflict of interest to chronicle my own history? Was I imagining the past, making my brothers and me heroes of our childhood? Were my family's struggles any different from others? My ability to recall details and images can be remarkable at times. I also had the help of those family albums and the stories shared by my brothers and cousins. But I encountered some uncertainty about time and sequence. Most of all I had to consider that mixed gift of deniability, which often saved me as a child. The question kept popping up: was it really so bad with my mother?

I asked for help, and I received it.

In January of 2009, I called Danville State Hospital. I spoke with a kind woman in the Medical Records Department. I had no legal or medical reason to ask for my mother's information. She was no longer alive, and her hospitalization took place almost 63 years earlier. "I'm writing about my mother," I explained. "I'm tying together some loose ends between us." Mary Hans said she'd look into my request.

A few days later, I received the paperwork required for release of my mother's records. I wrote a letter to underline my request. In an effort to personalize my application, I enclosed my Fourth of July story, which I'd blended into one of these earlier chapters.

The file of my mother's history with Danville State Hospital arrived ten days later. The contents yielded much more than fifteen pages of notes and painful information; the pages verified that I had remembered the truth. My mother's demons were identified and recognized by the social workers, nurses, and doctors who attended her. In reading those chronicles I understood that she suffered even more than I realized. And so did the rest of our family. I also recognized that my own denial had been a gift, which allowed me to experience my childhood in a way that worked for me.

My mother was 36 years old when she entered Danville State Hospital. For about ten years prior to her admission, she had been exhibiting paranoid delusions. Imbedded in those notes were descriptions of the voices and visual images that tormented her. There were reminders of the scenes I wanted to cancel from my memory: about the odors of dope; the messages buzzing through the electrical lines and the radio; instructions telling her to do bad things. Studying the notes from Danville was like reading the script of a play in which I'd once acted. I still remembered my lines because I was perfectly cast for my role.

My mother claimed that neighbors and strangers had mysterious powers over her. Sexual images were forced into her mind, a sign that the devil was disguised and hidden in her surroundings. Her caregivers wrote that my mother constantly talked about the rhythm method of birth control, which was approved by the Catholic Church. Artificial birth control was the work of Satan and his Legions. The term *birth control devils* appears throughout the notes, when my mother was asked to describe her tormentors. She told her nurses that she heard the screams of a woman tied up next door; someone was murdered in a neighbor's house. Shadows disappeared in doorways and reappeared, as if playing hide and seek with her, calling out "come on over here." Even without these documented words, I could never forget my mother's vigilant eyes and how they searched the dark corners of our home, taking attendance of each voice.

Buried in a large paragraph of admission notes is an attending physician's entry: *The patient has heard voices outside the house, and when she approached a window, the voices said "jump, jump." The patient states, after being told to jump, the electrical wires began to rattle, and odor would permeate the house, and her boys would stand on the radiator and fall off. She claimed she could not reason with them. When she opened the window, the odor went away, and the voices also blew away.*

"Jump, jump?" I am not finished with those words, nor are the words finished with me. I still think about how I blocked out the memory of my mother's leap when she obeyed that command, crashing with my unborn sister on her failed flight. This cancelled memory may be the most powerful example of denial working in my life. It could also be the time when I most needed it.

The first reading of my mother's records was difficult. I was pulled back into that living room of our Beaver Avenue home, remembering how we shivered by the open window as my mother fanned the dope fumes with winter's holy air. The notes were written with such detachment and clarity that I could feel my mother's fear, as the voices buzzed through the radio.

I studied the details listed under *Mental Status, Physical and Neurological Exam, Admission Notes, and General Observations.* I felt more grateful each time I reviewed those pages about my mother's life at Danville. The words under *Staff Discussion and Outline of Treatment* made it clear that my mother's caregivers were kind and compassionate. The writing was thoughtful and non-judgmental. The doctors and nurses documented their cautious hope for Mom's ability to return to us with predictable safety: they cared.

Six months after my mother's hospitalization, the staff granted my father's petition that she be allowed to come home. An earlier request had been refused, because of continued visual and auditory hallucinations. But later on there was improvement in my mother's behavior: *The patient is in a quiescent state in her psychosis, and while she cannot be considered cured, supervision is adequate, and she can be furloughed to the care of her husband and the guidance of the Social Services Department.*

Four months after my mother came home, a social worker came to our house. She carried a folder with many pages of notes. She sat down at the kitchen table with my mother and father. My brothers and I waited in the living room. We were dressed up for the occasion, as if we were going to church. The social worker's words are on the last page of the records: *Patient was somewhat upset and suspicious of the nature of the visit. Patient was not very congenial, although she tried to appear pleasant. When questioned about her illness, she changed the subject by asking how everything was at the hospital. She further states that she is feeling well, and has none of her former ideas. The patient indicates some dissatisfaction with present living situation, thinks a move will be good for the family. Husband states that he thinks the patient is improving, and he is thankful for her treatment at Danville State Hospital.*

Dad came to the living room for Alfie, Bill, and me. We sat at the table, answering simple questions as the woman wrote in her notebook. She sat at one end while my mother smiled at us from the other.

The social worker's commentary: *Worker then saw patient's three little sons who are quite well-mannered and well-behaved.*

My mother's medical history is summarized at the top of the first page, under *Listed Diagnosis.* Today her affliction would be labeled as Paranoid

Schizophrenia. But these words, capitalized and boldly typed 63 years ago, name my mother in a profound way: DEMENTIA PRAECOX: PARANOID TYPE. The words are not quiet on the page.

Another line in my mother's medical records stands out as if highlighted, especially for me: *Patient had significant and worsening attacks of nervousness in 1937, after the birth of her first child.*

My mother's illness defined the most profound connection between us. I am the first child.

Chapter 28

I return to the beginning of these pages, when Bonnie and I travelled to State College to visit my father; the time of my flashback of my visit with my mom in the hospital, when I was eight years old. This was when he answered my questions about my mother and Danville State Hospital; when my wife softly said to me, "I think you have work to do."

Bonnie and I returned from that visit with Dad on a Sunday afternoon. It was a tiring trip of 460 miles, nearly nine hours of driving time. Sleep did not come easily that night. I faded in and out of restless dreams about my childhood visit to the hospital. Old regrets were revived as I lamented my failure to offer my mother that pronouncement of forgiveness and love, while she could still understand my words. A shadow in my dreams chanted *too late, too late*.

I woke up exhausted and went to my work.

* * *

That Monday evening, I sit at my desk. I'm convinced the only way to deal with my sadness is to place it on the paper in front of me. I will write a poem for my mother. My notebook is open and ready, my pen uncapped on the desktop.

I close my eyes. I'm stuck in the lonely miles, riding to Danville Hospital with my father. Eight years old, trying to be brave. We drive through the spent fields of November: cornstalks and unmowed hay; the rusty earth, waiting for the white blanket of winter; the eternity of gray mist. Now the looming tower, my mother somewhere within; the dark wooden door, as Dad and I approach the entrance to my mother's cloistered life; the heavy locked latch; the timid tap for entry.

I pick up my pen and mark the blank page with careful words. I'm trying for restraint. It would be easy to let my feelings wash the truth away. I am detached, I think; viewing a forgotten movie of my mother and me.

I am crafting a poem, measuring word and meter, smoothing and polishing the edges of sound. I dovetail the line breaks and images into my young boy's fear and confusion. I'm in the poem with her, constructing a new way of being with my mother.

Late into the night, I scrawl and scribble and scratch, rewriting my forgotten fear: *visiting my mother in her purgatorial home.* There are no distractions for me on this night of my poem. No music on the radio, no forecast of tomorrow's weather from my silent TV. The 11 o'clock news will wait for another day. I continue well past my bedtime. The only words in the room are in my memory: *about my mother's frozen fear; remembered music, I once again hear.*

I put down my pen. I feel as if someone is behind me. Bonnie is sound asleep. Our black Lab is curled up in her bed. I return to my work. *My father and I, my mother rocking across the stone floor. Diminished light, windows with bars. Discordant noise , a chanting of a distant choir.*

Again, over my right shoulder. Someone's behind me. I turn and look, but nothing. It's late, almost two o'clock in the morning. My imagination is twitching, just thinking about my visit of 52 years ago. It's time for sleep. I'll go to my work in the morning and finish my poem tomorrow night.

The second night comes as if connected to the first by one long sustained breath. I continue without interruption, as if flicking on my desk lamp starts my pen right where it left off. *My mother's shadowed companions; the murmuring of sadness.* Again, I turn. Who is at my shoulder? Am I really alone in this night? I am in a sacred space now, writing the heart of the poem, the place of its strongest pulse.

I'm in front of my mother in that big room, lost in that noise. Her soul fluttering above, white with wings. Rising and falling, it lifts and falters in its agitated flapping, searching for rest. Her companions' skittish souls in similar flight, like my homing pigeons, hovering before landing.

Again, behind me! Suddenly, I know; it's my mother. She's been here for two nights. Now her hand resting on my right shoulder, the soft touch easily mistaken for a wrinkled seam of my shirt, pressing against me. But after all this work, I know my mother. She's been watching and waiting. She's stepped out of the failing afternoon light and unsettling noise of my childhood visit, when I was eight, and she was lost. She's come into this night to be with me. She looks over my shoulder and reads my poem, my apology, my acknowledgement of her love. My recognition that she never asked for the turmoil of her life.

Are we OK, Mom?

"We're good," she says.

*   *   *

Vespers

Intersecting with Interstate Eighty, the road to Danville
meanders through the farmlands of Central Pennsylvania.
My journey of fifty-two years past, repeated.
My dread, disguised as an eight-year-old boy, conceded.
Accompanied by my father, who could not go alone,
to visit my mother in her purgatorial home.

Countless trips past this turn,
my mind's compass pointed here,
that I revisit this route and learn
about my mother's frozen fear.

Columns of rigid trees stand sentry,
authorizing entry to my buried, worried history.
Dark brick buildings cluster into an edifice,
claiming an unfair share of autumn's slate sky.

Shrouded memories clear,
as the prison-like tower appears.
The imposing fortress draws near, with
remembered music I once again hear;
harmony and verse so empty, it could only
have been invented, by souls tormented.

I remember,
passing through the dark wooden door,
my mother rocking across the stone floor.
Her bent silhouette softened
by failing afternoon light, glinting off
windows, subdivided by purposefully-attached bars.

I remember,
as the early winter sun diminished,
a murmuring chorus of unrest replenished
the dark energy of my mother's residence.

Invisible soloists sing a song of sadness,
the undirected choir hums the music of madness.

I remember,
echoes of that mantra, swirling in the air
above my mother's shadowed companions,
swaying in common time, each
in their own rocking chair.

I remember,
their primitive singing, pleading
for meaningful location of their beings.
And in the twilight above, the sound of
fluttering wings, attached to lost souls,
circling, seeking, within their lost caretakers,
a familiar place of rest.

I remember,
As I rose to leave, my mother tearfully
faced me, embraced me, could not release me,
from her presence, could not erase me.
The rhythmic rocking and chanting halted.
Vespers… abruptly suspended, in heavy air.

Until she freed me, her hopes defaulted.
The singing resumed, continued as before.
Hummed vibrations timed our steps,
as my father and I walked to the door.

I remember,
I faced my mother and waved my hand.
My young boy's eye then saw
what my ear could not understand.
Hollow faces, unmoving mouths, monotoned:
We are lost, we are lost, we are not found…

I remember.
I wanted my mother to be found.

The end

Clemens Carl   Alfie   Bill

Sophie Henrietta Schoenebeck   Clemens Wilhelm Schoenebeck

Afterward

When I wrote the first words for this memoir, I believed that my story would have a beginning, a middle, and an end. That blueprint, once clearly defined, is now blurry. I don't think it will ever be finished.

First, there is my evolving relationship with words, and how to put them together to effectively bring the writer to the reader. Sometimes they fall in place with ease, as if the nouns and verbs have emerged from a group conference, where the adjectives and adverbs professed subservience to their masters---for the greater good of clarity. For every such phrase, I struggle with ten others, in which the parts of speech have rioted at a protest rally, asserting their right for stronger representation: every voice must be heard. The editing is never finished.

Second, there is the difficulty of dealing with the story itself: my mother's illness and her painful connection with us; my father's marathon test of providing continuity for our family; what it all meant for my brothers and me. I've written short stories and poems about my childhood. Because of that limited space, my words were weighted with the sadness of those times. But with a whole book to fill, it's as if I were pulling open the bellows of an accordion, sucking in a larger volume of oxygen to be released in the later telling. There is room on these pages for laughter and humor, playing catch and batting practice. One of the unexpected gifts of writing this story is that I have relived my childhood. I am reminded that it wasn't all bad.

The family pictures inspired so many of these words: my mother smiling from her first communion portrait, fervently surrendered to Jesus; a snapshot of my father's early discouragement, accentuated by his weary posture and lowered head, his right arm tentative on my mother's shoulder; Little Alfie, swinging a bat so hard that his baseball cap has swiveled sideways on his blond head; my grandparents, staring at me from their side of our history. Each picture casts its spell and inflicts its mood on my story. Between clicks of the camera, the images measure time. Without this reference, my own history can easily become a blur in which nothing is meaningfully defined.

*   *   *

After leaving home, life went well for Alfie, Bill, and me. My father's employment at the University offered a tuition benefit that made college affordable for us. Upon graduating from high school, each of us continued our education at Penn State.

Because of my distance running, I was fortunate enough to receive a track scholarship. Keenly aware of how much my father sacrificed for us, I studied diligently, not wanting to disappoint him. First to leave home, I finished my formal education at Tufts University School of Dental Medicine. I married Bonnie just before my senior year, and we now live on the North Shore of Boston. My daughter, Kristen, lives nearby, with her husband and two daughters.

I felt responsible for protecting my brothers; I tried to stand between them and my mother. I wanted my parents to recognize my dedication to "doing my best." I studied longer for my good grades. I trained harder to run faster. I lifted more so my father could carry less. But I couldn't pray enough to fix my mother. I always wondered if I could do more. I was the serious brother.

Bill followed me to Penn State. After graduate school, he was head of the Department of Physical Therapy at a hospital on the Eastern Shore of Maryland. Eventually Bill left his administrative career, and returned to his real talent of hands-on care. He's married to Peggy, and they have a son and daughter and two grandchildren of their own.

Bill hid his dependability behind laughter. He was able to make my father smile when there was nothing to be happy about. He monitored my own worry and my overdeveloped sense of responsibility, puncturing it frequently and effectively. He cajoled Alfie into self-assurance. "Here Alfie, slowest pitch in the world. You'll never hit it." And when he hit it, just to show Bill, they both howled. He could even make Mom smile. Bill was the brother who laughed.

Alfie became the Director of Blue Marsh Lake, near Reading, Pennsylvania. Responsible for flood control, a wildlife sanctuary, and a recreation area, he worked with the Army Corps of Engineers. In recognition of his accomplishments, Alfie was a recipient of the de Fleury medal, the highest honor given to a civilian employee of the Corps. He and his wife Loretta have three sons and four grandchildren.

Alfie was the last to leave home. He became cook, caretaker, and peacemaker for my parents, long after what could be expected of him. While in college, he continued to help with many of the chores at home. Because of his unselfishness, my parents had better days. Alfie was the brother of devotion.

Throughout our lives, my brothers and I have understood responsibility and commitment, whether in our work or as husbands and fathers. Perhaps the greatest gift my father passed on to us was his reliability. We could count on him, no matter what. As we were growing up, we learned that our own roles in the family would be defined by dependability. We too could be counted on; it was in our blood.

My brothers are miracles. They carry a generosity of spirit that sets them apart. As my parents aged and needed help, each of us did what we could, whether on a visit or by long distance. We never complained and we never kept score. We simply did our work.

I am gifted with them in my life.

*   *   *

I recently participated in a workshop, in which I was asked to sketch an image of my strongest childhood memory of church. When the exercise was finished, I saved my simple drawing. I donated it to the pile of notes and photographs on my desk, my resources for digging my way through this memoir.

In my childlike illustration, my family is viewed from behind, as we walk toward our church. Our place of worship is outlined with a steeple and a purple crucifix above the door. Four red dots mark the cross where three nails and a crown of thorns imbedded Jesus' blood into the wood. My mother is on the left, my father, the right; my brothers and I are in the space between. I am in a familiar place, closest to Mom, between her and my brothers. My right hand is grasped in Bill's left; Bill is similarly connected to Alfie, and he to Dad.

But there is open space between me and my mother. My left arm and my mother's right arm are only partially visible. Our hands disappear where they should be touching. We are all holding hands, except for my mother. As in my family's real life, she's with us, and she's not with us.

But now that's changed for me. If asked to sketch that space between us today, my mother's hand would be in mine. Writing this memoir has healed something between us. I know that we've been connected since the night we shared our Vespers poem; the night my shoulder was touched with forgiveness.

I have always carried my history, even though I tried to outrun it. Now I embrace my story, because it's with me in a different way. It is not on my back, like a carried burden. It's integrated in my muscle and bone, in my breathing and pulse. My history is in my DNA, and my mother was my teacher.

I was one element in the universe of my mother's schizophrenia, her swirling night of black holes and twinkling stars. I pray that she is out there now, reemerged in an orderly constellation, unfrightened, in which the heavens are constant and known to her.

May she be in light.

Special Thanks

My gratitude and sincere appreciation to Editor Travis Crane and Project Team Five of CreateSpace. Their patience and availability was invaluable. Their skill and competence displayed my writing in a presentation that made me proud.

About the Cover Art

"Cousin Joe" of my memoir is more than a beloved character from my childhood. Joseph Anthony Smith is an artist whose remarkable work reflects his gifts of imagination and vision. He is a graduate of Pratt Institute, where he won the Dean's Medal. He is Professor of Fine Art at that prestigious school, where he teaches drawing, painting, figure sculpture, anatomy, and a course he created in symbolic imagery and visual problem solving.

He has presented his art in many individual exhibitions. His work is placed in the collections of various museums in this country and overseas, including the New York Stock Exchange and the Library of Congress.

Joe has illustrated 25 children's books and authored one of his own. He has been a cover artist for Time, as well as editorial artist for Time, Harper's, and Newsweek. His sketches of the Watergate Trial are well-known, having been the courtroom illustrator for Newsweek magazine.

My cousin loved and accepted my mother and, at a very young age, understood her. His compassion for all of my family is reflected by this magical cover, in which he so creatively captured the elusive light we danced through in search of my mother.

Acknowledgements

First and foremost, to Bonnie, my wife and best friend, who generously supported my commitment to this story. When I slipped into denial about my family history, she reminded me of what was real and what was not.

Dennis Must, award-winning writer of fiction; mentor and dear friend, who always encouraged me to believe in my own voice; who, early on, gave me a blank journal with a card which gently commanded, "fill these pages." I did.

Paulette Bates Alden, whose firm but kind editing hand sometimes wrote in the margin, "Look Ma, I'm writing." Her skill and insight was invaluable.

Phyllis Karas, New York Times best-selling author, who, in giving generous portions of her own time, offered energetic and relentless encouragement; who taught me to "reject rejection."

Christopher Bursk, Pennsylvania poet, teacher, generous friend from the Juniper Writer's Conference, 2008, for his thoughtful reading and suggestions.

Frank Marean, for his skill and patience in refurbishing the old black and white pictures in the story, connecting old images with new words.

My daughter Kristen, for serious early editing and lessons about clear writing. My granddaughters, Alexa and Angela for young eyes looking at the story, and for being constant cheerleaders.

My Writer's Group: Betsy Morris, Pic Harrison, Sandra Winter, Jack Butterworth, and Jean Callahan. My thanks for reading, encouraging, and helping me pull out the weeds from my early revisions.

Tin Box Poets: Lee Freedman, Estelle Epstein, Paul Lahaie, Melissa Varnavas, Margaret Eckman, Tom Holmes, Marcia Molay; My poetry friends, whose thoughtful words and poems enhanced my prose writing.

My many cousins who shared stories, memories, and understanding.

My group of curious and interested readers, who encouraged publication.

Finally, my friend Charlotte Moore, who, after reading the manuscript, clutched it close to her and said, "I don't want to give it back; I want to keep your family close to me." It was then that I knew I had to let go of this story.

About the Author

Clemens Carl Schoenebeck has had poetry published in The Aurorean, Midwest Poetry Review, Caribbean Writer, Ibbetson Street Press, Small Brushes/Adept Press. Three of his poems have been nominated for the Pushcart Prize. His 9-11 poem, *For the Angels, Unwinged,* was published in the Aurorean's Favorites edition, celebrating their first fifteen years of poetry. Several of his short stories have won prizes in the Writers World competition, Marblehead Festival of Arts. In 2012, he won both the poetry and fiction prizes. His winning poem was also the winner of the Marcia Doehner Award. In addition, he was named the winner of the first Georgette Beck Award for his fiction writing.

He lives on the North Shore of Boston with his wife, Bonnie. His daughter's family lives nearby. His granddaughters are usually available for lunch.

43865564R00177

Made in the USA
Middletown, DE
30 April 2019